Issues in Progress

Proactive Behavior across Group Boundaries: Seeking and Maintaining Positive Interactions with Outgroup Members; Issue Editors: Birte Siem, Stefan Stürmer, and Todd Pittinsky.

Sexual and Gender Minority Health Disparities: Translating Stigma and Intergroup Relations Research; Issue Editors: Stacey L. Williams and Abbey Mann.

Journal of Social Issues, Vol. 72, No. 2, 2016, pp. 227–241
doi: 10.1111/josi.12164

Expanding on Psychological Theories of Engagement to Understand Activism in Context(s)

Nicola Curtin[*]
Clark University

Craig McGarty
Western Sydney University

Recent years have seen an increase in theoretical and empirical interest in the dynamics of social change. Missing from much of this literature, which has focused broadly on collective action, is attention to the people who seek to bring about social change, activists. Mass collective action is unlikely to occur without the involvement of people to recruit, mobilize, and organize social change campaigns. Including recent research from Australia, Europe, and North and South America, and studies of global online activists, this issue highlights multimethod approaches to studying activists and activism across a variety of different regional, issue-based, and sociopolitical contexts. In addition to contributing to ongoing theoretical and empirical discussions, the issue addresses the policy and strategic implications of this research for social change agents and organizations.

In December 2011, the U.S. publication *Time* declared "The Protester" to be the person of the year (Anderson, 2011). Indeed, 2011 was a year of large-scale visible protest and social change around the world: from the Arab Spring; to the "Occupy" (U.S.) and *Indignados* (Spain) movements; anticorruption protests in India; and protests over accusations of vote rigging in Russia and the Democratic Republic of Congo. In 2014, we saw waves of protest continue in Thailand and Ukraine, the "Umbrella movement" prodemocracy protests and occupation in Hong-Kong, The People's Climate March in New York and other cities around

––––––––––
*Correspondence concerning this article should be addressed to Nicola Curtin, Department of Psychology, Clark University, 950 Main Street, Worcester, MA 01610. Tel: 508-793-7261 [e-mail: NCurtin@clarku.edu].

We would like to thank Anna Kende, our coeditor, for her helpful feedback on earlier versions of this article.

the world, and The Black Lives Matter movement gained attention, and in 2015 has had visible impact on the discussion about race at the national level during the U.S. presidential primaries. Most recently, we have witnessed volunteers in Hungary act not only "out of generosity and solidarity, but are also sending a clear message to their government and fellow citizens." (Tirado, 2015, para 7).

When we think of sweeping social change, the images that tend to come to mind (and those most often depicted in the media) involve mass protests. Yet, prior to, and alongside, almost all mass expressions of dissent are the concerted but less visible efforts by committed supporters of the cause. We define activists, then, as people who actively work for social or political causes and especially those who work to encourage other people to support those causes. They can be "left-wing" or "right"; members of large grass-roots movements, or small nonprofit organizations. This group includes not only "protesters" (itself a contested term, see Stuart, Thomas, Donaghue, & Russell, 2013) perhaps marching at the front of a demonstration or leading chants, but also people who recruit for and mobilize social movements and sustain the organizational structures that support them. Many of these individuals have a range of paid (or unpaid) occupations, such as students, social workers, and other professionals, though some may work full-time for organizations supporting a particular cause. It will be apparent from this definition that the category of activists is a fuzzy set, defined by multiple dimensions and this complexity provides part of the scope for this issue.

In the recent upsurge of social psychological interest in collective action, there has been considerable progress in understanding the multiple integrated pathways that lead to participation in mass action (e.g., Klandermans, 2013; Stürmer & Simon, 2004; van Zomeren, Leach, & Spears, 2012). These successes include efforts to understand collective action as a collective process that rests on shared group identity, collective emotions and collective efficacy beliefs, as well as assessments of costs and benefits. The results of this theoretical and empirical resurgence, and the important special issues devoted to the topic, have focused almost exclusively on mass collective action (Becker, 2012; Klandermans & van Zomeren, 2011; van Zomeren & Iyer, 2009).

The specific role of activists in helping to bring about social change remains less well understood. Without activists to organize them, collective acts such as campaigns of protest, are unlikely to take place. The interface of social psychology and sociology (Klandermans & Oegema, 1987) provides good theoretical resources that can be deployed to explain activism such as the politicized collective identification model (Simon & Klandermans, 2001) but this model may not apply to many forms of activism. Added to this, activists are difficult to recruit in large numbers, as they comprise a relatively small percentage of the population, are busy supporting the causes they are committed to, and may not be readily accessible to traditional (e.g., social psychological) methods of participant recruitment. Partly for these reasons, empirical studies of social change tend to focus on the processes of collective action in mass protest. There are important exceptions, for example, in the work of Drury, Reicher, and Stott (2003), Duncan and Stewart (2007), Kelly and Breinlinger (1995), Klandermans and Oegema (1987), and Simon et al. (1998), all of whom focused on individuals engaged in sustained forms of social change behaviors. However, there has been a dearth of both qualitative and quantitative studies that draw on these perspectives.

These are some of the spaces that we seek to help fill in this issue. Contributions from Australia, Europe, and North and South America apply different methods, across a wide range of issues, to capture the ways that context shapes activists' engagement.

An Overview of "The Activist" in Psychological and Social Science Research

Much of the early psychological research on activism in psychology focused specifically on the attributes of activists and the predictors of activism. Psychological studies of student activists in the United States examined the effects of families and parenting styles on participation (Block, Haan, & Smith, 1969; Flacks, 1967; Newfield, 1966). Political activists tend to come from middle- or upper-class families (Block et al., 1969; Franz & McClelland, 1994; Verba, Schlozman, & Burns, 2004), be well-educated (Burns, Schlozman, & Verba, 2001; Fendrich, 1977), and more civically engaged (Beck & Jennings, 1982). Other predictors of engagement include biographical availability, or having fewer financial and social responsibilities (such as supporting a family, particularly for high-risk activism, McAdam, 1986) and the existence of community resources, such as active social networks, leadership, and infrastructure to support continued mobilization (McCarthy & Zald, 1977). Researchers have also focused on understanding the long-term effects that youth engagement in the 1960s and 1970s had on activists later in life (with follow-ups in the 1980s and 1990s). Student activists were more socially and politically engaged during later life than their nonactivist peers (Fendrich & Lovoy, 1988), were more altruistic (Franz & McClelland, 1994), and had different career trajectories and family configurations (McAdam, 1989; Sherkat & Blocker, 1997).

Although providing evidence as to which individual-level factors predict engagement, and to the long-term effects such engagement has, these findings do not help us understand activist recruitment, commitment, and retention (which, to be fair, was not their aim). Furthermore, they fail to differentiate between own-group, other-group (often called ally activism), and issue-based engagement.

Social psychological research focusing specifically on what activists do is relatively scarce, but much of it has examined how activists become engaged in a particular social movement (and contrasting them to nonparticipants), how activists make connections between their own "local" work and a broader "global" movement, or how engagement shapes both attitudes and identification. Klandermans and Oegema (1987) identified four distinct steps toward becoming engaged in a social movement: (1) having the potential to be mobilized (i.e., being sympathetic to the cause in question); (2) being recruited; (3) followed by some motivation to participate; and then (4) overcoming barriers to participation. They found that nonparticipation was the result of different processes (depending on each of these different steps). Their findings suggest that, in order to understand activists, we must think of each step as its own set of processes, with accompanying psychological and structural factors. Several of these factors were elaborated in Simon and Klandermans' (2001) politicized collective identification approach that explains the development of politicization in terms of membership to a group with a shared history of disadvantage that is locked in competition for third-party support (from the government or general public) with an opposing group that it blames for this disadvantage. This otherwise powerful model does not immediately extend to action to improve the status of another group, promote reconciliation, resist social change, or activism for the environment.

Drury and colleagues' (2003) found that activists do not always identify themselves as activists before a protest or before their participation (similarly, van Zomeren, Leach et al., 2010 experimentally demonstrated that group efficacy beliefs may be a cause rather than a consequence of politicized collective identification). Engagement itself may be a politicizing force (see also Simon & Klandermans, 2001); one that allows individuals to make connections between local concerns and global movements.

Cole and Stewart (1996), Duncan and Stewart (2007), and Kelly and Breinlinger (1995) have all focused on female activists. Cole and Stewart (1996) found that student activism, political identity, and a sense of social responsibility all predicted activism among middle-aged women. Duncan and Stewart (2007) focused on why some women develop more politicized identities, and others do not; identifying an individual difference variable, personal political salience that predicted the development of politicized identities and subsequent engagement (see also Curtin, Stewart, & Duncan, 2011). Kelly and Breinlinger (1995) found that identification as an activist was a stronger predictor of engagement than simply identifying with women (Simon et al., 1998 confirmed this finding among gay men).

These researchers have tended to situate their studies in the literature on collective action. However, their work is unusual in that they all pay attention, in some way, to the difference between activists and nonactivists. They also complement current integrated models of engagement and provide some excellent examples of how we can integrate the literatures on collective action, with a more explicit focus on activists and activism.

Current Integrated Models of Engagement: Their Limitations for Understanding Activism and New Developments in the Field

There is a growing literature integrating sociological and psychological models of engagement (Klandermans, 2013; Simon & Klandermans, 2001; Stürmer & Simon, 2004; Thomas, McGarty, & Mavor, 2009; van Zomeren, Leach et al., 2012), in order to develop generalizable models and testable hypotheses. These models have suggested multiple pathways to engagement involving a sense of collective identification, sense of injustice or shared grievance (Simon & Klandermans, 2001; van Zomeren, Leach et al., 2012), reward motivations (Klandermans, 2013; Stürmer & Simon, 2004), group-based emotion (Klandermans, 2013; Thomas et al., 2009; van Zomeren, Leach et al., 2012), and group-based efficacy (Thomas et al., 2009; van Zomeren, Leach et al., 2012). However, the models only explain collective engagement with in-group identity-based movements, as opposed to out-group members active in other-group movements (e.g., heterosexual people involved in LGBT movements), or engagement with issue-based movements. They also focus more on mass engagement in protest than on other important forms and stages of activism, such as recruiting, mobilizing, and organizing for social change (Klandermans & Oegema, 1987).

Opinions as the Basis for Shared Identification

Recognizing the first of these limitations (an assumption of shared group identification), Bliuc, McGarty, Reynolds, & Muntele (2007) and McGarty, Bliuc, Thomas, & Bongiorno (2009) argued that social identities based on shared opinions (called opinion-based groups; e.g., as profeminist) tend to be better predictors of engagement in collective action than those built around social categories (e.g., as a woman, or even as activist). Furthermore, the use of opinion-based groups allows researchers to predict both engagement in issue-based activism (such as environmentalism) that do not necessarily have a readily available social identity category for people to identify with, as well as to predict engagement in causes for which one is not a group member (i.e., profeminist men engaged in women's rights activism).

Research on opinion-based groups has found that identification with them is an excellent predictor of commitments to social change action (Musgrove & McGarty, 2008; Thomas, Mavor, & McGarty, 2012). Furthermore, work in this area has complemented and expanded on existing models by examining the mechanisms by which opinion-based groups foster such commitments via group-based emotions and perceptions of action efficacy (Thomas & McGarty, 2009). It has also provided theoretical integration in the development of dynamic models to explain the relationships between group-based identification, emotions, norms and social action (Thomas et al., 2009).

*Understanding Advantaged Group Members' Engagement with Disadvantaged
Groups*

Many of the social-identity-based models of collective action assume that
one belongs to the group one is acting on behalf of, often failing to account for
the fact that advantaged group members tend to occupy more powerful positions
in existing power structures than disadvantaged group members. However, there
is a new interest in theoretical frameworks that account for advantaged group
members' activism in alliance with marginalized groups (e.g., Subasic, Reynolds,
& Turner, 2008; van Zomeren, Postmes, Spears, & Bettache, 2011; Wiley &
Bikmen, 2012; Wright & Lubensky, 2009). The new theoretical focus has been
matched by a growing empirical literature.

Subasic et al.'s (2008) model of political solidarity argued that a sense of
affiliation, based on a common cause, could develop between advantaged and
disadvantaged group members. In order for social change commitments to develop,
advantaged group members must develop a critique of existing power relations,
and be in agreement with disadvantaged group members that social change is
needed. Empirical evidence has supported the claim that some degree of systemic
analyses may be predictive of advantaged group members' engagement on behalf
of disadvantaged groups (Curtin, Stewart, & Cole, 2015; Drury & Kaiser, 2014;
Duncan & Stewart, 2007; Iyer & Ryan, 2009; Russell, 2011). Other areas of this
literature have continued to build and expand on social-identity-based models,
but adapted them to make sense in a context where advantaged group members
cannot share a disadvantaged social location with marginalized groups. In a series
of experiments, van Zomeren, Postmes, & Spears (2012) and van Zomeren, Leach
at al. (2012) integrated their Social Identity Model of Collective Action with work
on moral convictions, finding evidence that advantaged group members' moral
convictions predicted identification with disadvantaged groups, and support for
collective action. Interestingly, and somewhat in contrast to this findings, in her
analysis of interviews with European-American allies, Greenwood (2015) found
that they focused "strategically" (p. 350) on positive aspects of their advantaged
group identity while avoiding negative emotions such as guilt and moral outrage.

In addition to the need for theoretical refinement of models to explain advantaged group members' engagement, there are a number of additional interesting
issues that have been raised. Recent theories and research have focused on the
benefits and challenges of (relative) power and privilege in advantaged group
members' efforts to bring about social change (Case & Iuzzini, 2012), the ways
in which helping can, in fact, maintain unequal relations between groups (Nadler,
2002; Nadler & Halabi, 2006), and the growing evidence that positive contact
between advantaged and disadvantaged group members can sometimes undermine collective action efforts (Saguy, Tausch, Dovidio, & Pratto, 2009; Wright
& Lubensky, 2009). These latter two points contribute to a growing discussion

in social psychology about the limitations of relying on increasing positive intergroup relations between majority and minority groups as a means of reducing prejudice and increasing equality (Dixon, Levine, Reicher, & Durrheim, 2012; see also Hammack & Pilecki, 2015, for a discussion of similar issues in the context of using intergroup dialogue to address historical power differences between groups and facilitate social change). Therefore, the intergroup dynamics of ally activism can be challenging, complicated, and raise challenges for activists themselves, the communities they engage with, and theories of social change.

Technologically Mediated Activism: The Arab Spring and its Imitators

In one sense, the study of activism has been overtaken by events. Lay, journalistic, and social scientific analyses of activism have struggled to deal with the torrent of online activity that has emerged alongside the massive upheavals throughout the Arab-speaking world and has struggled to balance the claims and counterclaims that relate to the role of that online activity in contributing to social change. Thus, we have the uprisings such as the Arab Spring that are referred to as the Facebook or Twitter Revolution, but other commentators express doubts that online activity makes any positive difference (Gladwell, 2010) or point to the demobilizing power of online technology in the hands of repressive regimes (Morozov, 2011). The use of online technologies has been derided as nothing more than clicktivism or slacktivism as typified in campaigns such as Kony2012 (see Bailyn, 2012 and Thomas et al., 2015, for different views). How, the critics ask, does liking something on Facebook or clicking a petition button contribute to changing the world (Hartley, Lala, McGarty, & Donaghue, 2016)? These campaigns are counterpointed, by the presence of online direct action (or hacktivism, exemplified in the operations of Anonymous, see Mansfield-Devine, 2011, a group that has launched attacks such as overloading servers and defacing Web sites).

We cannot possibly hope to do justice to this complex set of claims and counterclaims (most of which have not been exposed to full empirical scrutiny), but we can make a number of broad points. The first is that, as Castells (2012) has noted, the occupation of online spaces was a precursor to the occupation of physical spaces in numerous campaigns including the Tunisian and Egyptian uprisings, the *Indignados* in Spain, and the Occupy Movement (initially in North America). In each case, the formation of the network took place using online technology and then transferred to organizing to occupy and manage visible public spaces in major cities. In a number of cases, these spectacular events were preceded by years of less visible online organizing and expression of dissent (e.g., Howard & Hussain, 2011) and this is where the study of activism may need to look more closely. The second point is that the distinction between valid, meaningful street action and insincere, gratuitous online action may sometimes be a false one. A street protester carrying a placard for the benefit of television cameras may not be acting in a very different way from a Twitter user expressing the same message in 140 characters. Particular technologies will be better suited to some tasks and phases of a campaign. An anonymous blog may be useful for rehearsing ideological arguments but it may be next to useless for dividing up a roster of tasks for a protest rally (when political opponents and security agencies can view them).

Finally, some technologies have particular values for allowing broadcast of dissent and enabling (mass) gatherings in the face of fierce repression. When freedom of expression and association are limited by authoritarian regimes, technologies can allow partial access to those rights. McGarty, Thomas, Lala, Smith, and Bliuc (2014) and Smith, Thomas, & McGarty (2015) explored these mechanisms in relation to the Tunisian and Egyptian uprisings and showed that the interaction of YouTube, camera phones, and satellite television in Tunisia allowed activists to spread images of mass dissent despite government restrictions. In this case, social media technology may have been a game changer for activists who faced active repression.

The Methodological Toolkit for Studying Activism

One of the reasons for the relative neglect of the study of activism may be that activists are often working behind the scenes and that their work is not necessarily readily available to the dominant methodological tools of social psychology. Therefore, studies of activism tend to involve ethnographic observational studies, interviews, and surveys, rather than experiments. Thus, the balance of research included in this issue reflects these methods.

At first glance, it is difficult to imagine experimental manipulations that will induce or provoke activism, especially if we understand activism as a relatively enduring orientation to a social issue or problem. Ethical standards militate against interventions that produce long-term changes in people, especially where the benefits of those changes are in dispute. An experimental intervention to promote activism on climate change would be seen by some as a valuable contribution to public education and by others as (taxpayer-funded) political engineering.

Curiously though, there is a foundational tradition of experimental social psychology that underpins one of the deepest contributions of social psychology to social science, and is all about activism. We refer here to Lewin's (1958) work during World War II on group decision making and food preferences, and in particular promoting the choice of unpopular cuts of meat (offal) to support the war effort. Lewin demonstrated that it was possible to transform food purchasing decisions by encouraging women (the gate keepers of family meals) to make collective decisions to purchase offal. His experiment was the first demonstration of the unifying role of social interaction in promoting change. It can be seen as a study of activism at two levels, both in terms of the role of women in promoting change and in the role of researchers in making that possible. Lewin's work of

1947 was, of course, the inspiration for action research, an approach that has had a broad and deep impact in psychology and many other fields (e.g., Snyder, 2009; Stoudt, Fox, & Fine, 2012).

Very recently, researchers have used group-based interaction as a methodological analogue of the processes of mobilization of activism (Bongiorno, McGarty, Kurz, Haslam, & Sibley, 2016; Gee, Khalaf, & McGarty, 2007; Thomas & McGarty, 2009; Thomas, McGarty, & Louis, 2014; Thomas, McGarty, & Mavor, 2016; see also Smith & Postmes, 2011). Creating group discussion between people who want the same changes in the world, about how those changes can be achieved, can serve as a Petri dish for observing the processes by which nominal supporters develop a sense of solidarity with other supporters, and take action. If this argument is correct, then it follows that the well-known phenomenon of group polarization may be akin to the processes that produce activism outside the laboratory. The full exploration of those methodologies is an intriguing direction that several of the articles in this issue respond to.

This is an exciting time for the study of social action and social change. There is an increasing interest in sophisticated and dynamic models of engagement, as well as attempts at integration of different perspectives. Although this work has made great strides to broaden our understanding of collective action beyond identity-based motives and engagement, little research has focused specifically on activists themselves. Since much of the existing work has failed to differentiate activists (those who have ongoing commitments to a particular social movement, including building support, recruiting new members, and organizing a movement) from individuals who indicate support for a movement, or might occasionally show up to a protest or rally, we do not know how well these existing models explain the psychological processes, and social contexts, of activists.

Overview of This Issue

This issue is divided into three sections that aim to build on contemporary theorizing and research on collective action, but with a focus on understanding activists (not collective engagement) more deeply.

The first section, The Activist up Close, examines how activists differ from each other and from the larger population of people engaging in collective action. These articles explore the roles of social structure, power and privilege, and attachment to activist groups to explain who activists are and what makes them not only a special, but a diverse category of people.

Louis, Amiot, Thomas, and Blackwood (2016) draw on both cross-sectional and longitudinal studies of activism and political behavior to show how individuals' multiple identities can either reinforce each other (and facilitate activism) or conflict (and stifle it). Curtin, Kende, and Kende (2016) interviewed both political and nonpolitical actors engaged in different degrees with social movements in the

United States and Hungary. They illustrate how advantaged and disadvantaged identities within the same person can shape engagement, by providing individuals with experiences of marginalization and privilege on which to draw as they engage in activism both for their own group and in alliance with others. van Stekelenburg, Klandermans, and Akkerman (2016) use survey data from a large sample (over 14,000) of street demonstrations to argue that civic participation can serve as a means of engendering more politicized activities.

The second section, Ally Activism, focuses on this important area of growth in the literature on social action. While out-group activists act congruently with their ideologies and moral convictions, these actions may lead to questions about their own privileges, or make them an outsider both within their privileged group and within the disadvantaged group that they act in alliance with. These dynamics, as well as the role of identity in differentiating allies from in-group activists are addressed. All three articles in this section critically examine the role of power and privilege in the relationships between advantaged and disadvantaged group member activists. They add to two growing literatures: the first on the limits of prejudice reduction in fostering positive intergroup relations (Dixon et al., 2012; Wright & Lubensky, 2009); and the other on the psychological processes underlying support for, and resistance to, systems of privilege by advantaged group members (Case & Iuzzini, 2012).

Droogendyk, Wright, Lubensky, and Louis (2016) explore how misguided forms of ally activism can not only hinder potential for social change, but also undermine the personal relationships between advantaged group activists and the marginalized groups they are trying to help. They finish with specific suggestions for how advantaged group allies might work to ensure that they do not inadvertently diminish the likelihood of disadvantaged groups' collective action. Then, Russell and Bohan (2016) uses a case-study of a Protestant congregation's "reconciliation" process to show how ostensibly positive intergroup behaviors (such as collective action on behalf of LGBT people) can be influenced by negative intergroup attitudes (homonegativity), as well as to examine ally processes from an institutional perspective.

The final section, Identification Processes and Intergroup Relations, systematically puts established theories of collective action to the test, and covers a wide range of causes and forms of actions from diverse geographical locations. These articles rely on, but also refine, theories of politicized collective identity, ideology, and intergroup contact; while maintaining a consistent focus on social structure and context.

Cakal, Eller, Sirlopú, and Pérez (2016) examined collaborative activism among indigenous people in Mexico and Chile, and found that intergroup contact among marginalized group members facilitates activism by improving perceptions of group efficacy, though these effects are moderated by previous activist engagements. Hartley et al. (2016) then contribute to a growing social-psychological literature on social structure and online activism (Brunsting & Postmes, 2002), by examining the role of perceptions of social structure in predicting both online and offline participation. They highlight how social structures have important implications for the conditions under which traditional predictors of collective action will predict activism. They also show that online communities can play a role in building consensus, as well as building opposition to existing social structures.

Anna Kende (2016) closes the issue by integrating the findings from this issue in order to make suggestions for how we can improve the science of activism, as well as our own role as researchers and (possibly) social change agents.

References

Anderson, K. (2011). The protester. *Time*. Retrieved on December 1, 2015 from http://content.time.com/time/specials/packages/article/0,28804,2101745_2102132_2102373,00.html.

Bailyn, E. (2012). The difference between slacktivism and activism: How 'Kony2012' is narrowing the gap. *Huffington Post*. Retrieved on August 15, 2013 from http://www.huffingtonpost.com/evan-bailyn/kony-2012-activism_b_1361791.html

Beck, P. A., & Jennings, M. K. (1982). Pathways to participation. *American Political Science Review*, *76*, 94–108. doi: 10.2307/1960445

Becker, J. (2012). Virtual special issue on theory and research on collective action in the European Journal of Social Psychology [Special Issue]. *European Journal of Social Psychology*, *42*. doi: 10.1002/ejsp.1839

Bliuc, A. -M., McGarty, C., Reynolds, K., & Muntele, D. (2007). Opinion-based group membership as a predictor of commitment to political action. *European Journal of Social Psychology*, *37*, 19–32. doi: 10.1002/ejsp.334

Block, J. H., Haan, N., & Smith, M. B. (1969). Socialization correlates of student activism. *Journal of Social Issues*, *25*, 143–177. doi: 10.1111/j.1540-4560.1969.tb00623.x

Bongiorno, R., McGarty, C., Kurz, T., Haslam, S. A., & Sibley, C. G. (2016). Mobilizing cause supporters through group-based interaction. *Journal of Applied Social Psychology*, *46*, 203–215.

Brunsting S., & Postmes T. (2002). Social movement participation in the digital age: Predicting offline and online collective action. *Small Group Research*, *33*, 525–554. doi: 10.1177/104649602237169

Burns, N., Schlozman, K. L., & Verba, S. (2001). *The private roots of public action: Gender, equality, and political participation*. Cambridge, MA: Harvard University Press.

Çakal, H., Eller, A., Sirlopú, D., & Pérez, A. (2016). Intergroup relations in Latin America: Intergroup contact, common ingroup identity, and activism among Indigenous groups in Mexico and Chile. *Journal of Social Issues*, *72*, 355–375.

Case, K. A., & Iuzzini, J. (2012). Systems of privilege: Intersections, awareness, and applications. [Special Issue]. *Journal of Social Issues*, *68*, 1–206. doi: 10.1111/j.1540-4560.2011.01732.x

Castells, M. (2012). *Networks of outrage and hope: Social movements in the Internet age*. Cambridge, UK: Polity Press.

Cole, E. R., & Stewart, A. J. (1996). Meanings of political participation among Black and White women: Political identity and social responsibility. *Journal of Personality and Social Psychology*, *71*, 130–140. doi: 10.1037/0022-3514.71.1.130

Curtin, N., Stewart, A. J., & Duncan, L. E. (2010). What makes the political personal? Openness, personal political salience, and activism. *Journal of Personality*, *78*, 943–968. doi: 10.1111/j.1467-6494.2010.00638.x

Curtin, N., Stewart, A. J., & Cole, E. R. (2015). Challenging the status quo: The role of intersectional awareness in activism for social change and pro-social intergroup attitudes. *Psychology of Women Quarterly*, *39*, 512–529. doi: 10.1177/0361684315580439

Curtin, N., Kende, A., & Kende, J. (2016). Navigating multiple identities: The simultaneous influence of advantaged and disadvantaged identities on politicization and activism. *Journal of Social Issues*, *72*, 264–285.

Dixon, J., Levine, M., Reicher, S., & Durrheim, K. (2012). Beyond prejudice: Are negative evaluations the problem and is getting us to like one another more the solution? *Behavioral and Brain Sciences*, *35*, 411–425. doi:10.1017/S0140525×11002214

Droogendyk, L., Wright, S. C., Lubensky, M.E., & Louis, W. R. (2016). Acting in solidarity: Cross-group contact between disadvantaged group members and advantaged group allies. *Journal of Social Issues*, *72*, 315–334.

Drury, B. J., & Kaiser, C. R. (2014). Allies against sexism: The role of men in confronting sexism. *Journal of Social Issues*, *70*(4), 637–652. doi: 10.1111/josi.12083

Drury, J., Reicher, S., & Stott, C. (2003). Transforming the boundaries of collective identity: From the "local" anti-road campaign to "global" resistance? *Social Movement Studies*, *2*, 191–212. doi: 10.1080/1474283032000139779

Duncan, L. E., & Stewart, A. J. (2007). Personal political salience: The role of personality in collective identity and action. *Political Psychology*, *28*, 143–164. doi: 10.1111/j.1467-9221.2007.00560.x

Fendrich, J. M. (1977). Keeping the faith or pursuing the good life: A study of the consequences of participation in the civil rights movement. *American Sociological Review*, *42*, 144–157.

Fendrich, J. M., & Lovoy, K. L. (1988). Back to the future: Adult political behavior of former student activists. *American Sociological Review*, *53*, 780–784. doi: 10.2307/2095823

Flacks, R. (1967). The liberated generation: An exploration of the roots of student protest. *Journal of Social Issues*, *23*, 52–75. doi: 10.1111/j.1540-4560.1967.tb00586.x

Franz, C. E., & McClelland, D. C. (1994). Lives of women and men active in the social protests of the 1960s: A longitudinal study. *Journal of Personality and Social Psychology*, *66*, 196–205. doi: 10.1037/0022-3514.66.1.196

Gee, A., Khalaf, A., & McGarty, C. (2007). Using group-based interaction to change stereotypes about people with mental disorders. *Australian Psychologist*, *42*, 98–105. doi: 10.1080/00050060701280581

Gladwell, M. (2010). Small change: Why the revolution will not be tweeted. *New Yorker.* (Downloaded August 15, 2013 from http://www.newyorker.com/reporting/2010/10/04/101004 fa_fact_gladwell)

Greenwood, R. M. (2015). Remembrance, responsibility, and reparations: The use of emotions in talk about the 1921 Tulsa Race Riot. *Journal of Social Issues*, *71*(2), 338–355. doi: 10.1111/josi.12114

Hammack, P. L., & Pilecki, A. (2015). Power in history: Contrasting theoretical approaches to intergroup dialogue. *Journal of Social Issues*, *71*(2), 371–385.

Hartley, L. K., Lala, G., Donaghue, N., & McGarty, C. (2016). How activists respond to social structure in offline and online contexts. *Journal of Social Issues*, *72*(2), 376–398.

Howard, P. N., & Hussain, M. M. (2011). The role of digital media. *Journal of Democracy*, *22*, 35–48.

Iyer, A., & Ryan, M. (2009). Why do men and women challenge gender discrimination in the workplace? The role of group status and in-group identification in predicting pathways to collective action. *Journal of Social Issues*, *65*, 791–814. doi: 10.1111/j.1540-4560.2009.01625.x

Kelly, C., & Breinlinger, S. (1995). Identity and injustice: Exploring women's participation in collective action. *Journal of Community & Applied Social Psychology*, *5*, 41–57. doi: 10.1002/casp.2450050104

Kende, A. (2016). Separating social science research on activism from social science as activism. *Journal of Social Issues*, *72*(2), 399–412.

Klandermans, B. (2013). The dynamics of demand. In J. van Stekelenburg, C. Roggeband & B. Klandermans (Eds), *Dynamics, mechanism, and processes: The future of social movement research* (pp. 3–16). Minneapolis, MN: University of Minnesota Press.

Klandermans, B., & Oegema, D. (1987). Potentials, networks, motivations, and barriers: Steps towards participation in social movements. *American Sociological Review, 52,* 519–531. doi: 10.2307/2095297

Klandermans, B., & van Zomeren, M. (2011). Innovation in theory and research on collective action and social change [Special Issue]. *British Journal of Social Psychology, 50,* 573–574. doi: 10.1111/j.2044-8309.2011.02078.x

Lewin, K. (1958). Group decision and social change. In E. E. Maccoby, T. M. Newcomb & E. L. Hartley (Eds.), *Readings in social psychology* (pp. 197–211). New York, NY: Pearson.

Louis, W. R., Amiot, C. E., Thomas, E. F., & Blackwood, L. (2016). The "Activist Identity" and activism across domains: A multiple identities analysis. *Journal of Social Issues, 72*(2), 242–263.

Mansfield-Devine, S. (2011). Anonymous: Serious threat or mere annoyance? *Network Security, 1,* 4–10. doi: 10.1016/S1353-4858(11)70004-6

McAdam, D. (1986). Recruitment to high-risk activism: The case of Freedom Summer. *American Journal of Sociology,* 64–90.

McAdam, D. (1989). The biographical consequences of activism. *American Sociological Review, 54,* 744–760. doi: 10.2307/2117751

McCarthy, J. D., & Zald, M. N. (1977). Resource mobilization and social movements: A partial theory. *American Journal of Sociology, 92,* 1212–1241.

McGarty, C., Bliuc, A. M., Thomas, E. F., & Bongiorno, R. (2009). Collective action as the material expression of opinion-based group membership. *Journal of Social Issues, 65,* 839–857. doi: 10.1111/j.1540-4560.2009.01627.x

McGarty, C., Thomas, E. F, Lala, G., Smith, L. G. E., & Bliuc, A.-M. (2014). New technologies, new identities, and the growth of mass opposition in the 'Arab Spring'. *Political Psychology, 35,* 725–740. doi: 10.1111/pops.12060

Morozov, E. (2011). *The net delusion: How not to liberate the world.* London, UK: Allen Lane.

Musgrove, L., & McGarty, C. (2008). Opinion-based group membership as a predictor of collective emotional responses and support for pro- and anti-war action. *Social Psychology, 39,* 37–47. doi: 10.1027/1864-9335.39.1.37

Nadler, A. (2002). Inter-group helping relations as power relations: Maintaining or challenging social dominance between groups through helping. *Journal of Social Issues, 58,* 487–502. doi: 10.1111/1540-4560.00272

Nadler, A., & Halabi, S. (2006). Intergroup helping as status relations: Effects of status stability, identification, and type of help on receptivity to high-status group's help. *Journal of Personality and Social Psychology, 91,* 97–110. doi: 10.1037/0022-3514.91.1.97

Newfield, J. (1966). *A prophetic minority.* New York, NY: New American Library.

Russell, G. M. (2011). Motives of heterosexual allies in collective action for equality. *Journal of Social Issues, 67*(2), 376–393. doi: 10.1111/j.1540-4560.2011.01703.x

Russell, G. M., & Bohan, J. S. (2016). Institutional allyship for LGBT equality: Underlying processes and potentials for change. *Journal of Social Issues, 72*(2), 335–354.

Saguy, T., Tausch, N., Dovidio, J. F., & Pratto, F. (2009). The irony of harmony intergroup contact can produce false expectations for equality. *Psychological Science, 20,* 114–121. doi: 10.1111/j.1467-9280.2008.02261.x

Sherkat, D. E., & Blocker, T. J. (1997). Explaining the political and personal consequences of protest. *Social Forces, 75,* 1049–1070. doi: 10.2307/2580530

Simon, B., & Klandermans, B. (2001). Politicized collective identity: A social psychological analysis. *American Psychologist, 56,* 319–331. doi: 10.1037/0003-066X.56.4.319

Simon, B., Stürmer, S., Loewy, M., Weber, U., Freytag, P., Habig, C., Kampmeier, C., & Spahlinger, P. (1998). Collective identification and social movement participation. *Journal of Personality and Social Psychology, 74,* 646–658. doi: 10.1037/0022-3514.74.3.646

Smith, L. G. E., & Postmes, T., (2011). The power of talk: Developing discriminatory group norms through discussion. *British Journal of Social Psychology, 50,* 193–215. doi: 10.1002/ejsp.464

Smith, L. G. E., Thomas, E. F., & McGarty, C. (2015). "We must be the change we want to see in the world": Integrating norms and identities through social interaction. *Political Psychology, 36,* 543–557. doi: 10.1348/014466610×504805

Snyder, M. (2009). In the footsteps of Kurt Lewin: Practical theorizing, action research, and the psychology of social action. *Journal of Social Issues, 65*, 225–245. doi: 10.1111/j.1540-4560.2008.01597.x

Stoudt, B. G., Fox, M., & Fine, M. (2012). Contesting privilege with critical participatory action research. *Journal of Social Issues, 68*, 178–193. doi:10.1111/j.1540-4560.2011.01743.x

Stuart, A., Thomas, E. F., Donaghue, N., & Russell, A., (2013). "We may be pirates, but we are not protesters": Identity in the Sea Shepherd Conservation Society, *Political Psychology, 34*, 753–777. doi: 10.1111/pops.12016

Stürmer, S., & Simon, B. (2004). Collective action: Towards a dual-pathway model. *European Review of Social Psychology, 15*, 59–99. doi: 10.1080/10463280340000117

Subasic, E., Reynolds, K., & Turner, J. (2008). The political solidarity model of social change: Dynamics of self-categorization in intergroup power relations. *Personality and Social Psychology Review, 12*, 330–352. doi:10.1177/1088868308323223

Thomas, E. F., & McGarty, C. A. (2009). The role of efficacy and moral outrage norms in creating the potential for international development activism through group-based interaction. *British Journal of Social Psychology, 48*, 115–134. doi: 10.1348/014466608×313774

Thomas, E. F., McGarty, C., & Mavor, K. I. (2009). Aligning identities, emotions, and beliefs to create commitment to sustainable social and political action. *Personality and Social Psychology Review, 13*, 194–218. doi: 10.1177/1088868309341563

Thomas, E. F., Mavor, K. I., & McGarty, C. (2012). Social identities facilitate and encapsulate action-relevant constructs: A test of the social identity model of collective action. *Group Processes and Intergroup Relations, 15*, 75–88. doi: 10.1177/1368430211413619

Thomas, E. F., McGarty, C., & Louis, W. R. (2014). Social interaction and psychological pathways to political engagement and extremism. *European Journal of Social Psychology, 44*, 15–22. doi: 10.1002/ejsp.1988

Thomas, E. F., McGarty, C., Lala, G., Stuart, A., Hall, L., & Goddard, A. (2015). Whatever happened to Kony2012? Understanding a global internet phenomenon as an emergent social identity. *European Journal of Social Psychology, 45*, 356–367. doi: 10.1002/ejsp.2094

Thomas, E. F., McGarty, C., & Mavor, K. I. (2016). Group interaction as the crucible of social identity formation: A glimpse at the foundations of social identities for collective action. *Group Processes and Intergroup Relations, 19*, 137–151. doi:10.1177/1368430215612217

Tirado, S. (2015). In Hungary, everyday citizens pick up the slack left by government inaction. (Downloaded from http://www.huffingtonpost.com/sergio-tirado/in-hungary-civil-society-_b_8084782.html). Accessed at December 1, 2015.

van Stekelenburg, J., Klandermans, B., & Akkerman, A. (2016). Does civic participation stimulate political activity? *Journal of Social Issues, 72*(2), 286–314.

van Zomeren, M., & Iyer, A. (2009). Introduction to the social and psychological dynamics of collective action. *[Special Issue] Journal of Social Issues, 65*, 645–660. doi: 10.1111/j.1540-4560.2009.01618.x

van Zomeren, M., Leach, C. W., & Spears, R. (2010). Does group efficacy increase group identification? Resolving their paradoxical relationship. *Journal of Experimental Social Psychology, 46*, 1055–1060.

van Zomeren, M., Postmes, T., Spears, R., & Bettache, K. (2011). Can moral convictions motivate the advantaged to challenge social inequality? Extending the social identity model of collective action. *Group Processes & Intergroup Relations, 14*, 735–753. doi: 10.1177/1368430210395637

van Zomeren, M., Leach, C. W., & Spears, R. (2012). Protesters as "passionate economists": A dynamic dual pathway model of approach coping with collective disadvantage. *Personality and Social Psychology Review, 16*, 180–199. doi: 10.1177/1088868311430835

van Zomeren, M., Postmes, T., & Spears, R. (2012). On conviction's collective consequences: Integrating moral conviction with the social identity model of collective action. *British Journal of Social Psychology, 51*, 52–71. doi: 10.1111/j.2044-8309.2010.02000.x

Verba, S., Schlozman, K. L., & Burns, N. (2004). Family ties: Understanding the intergenerational transmission of political participation. In A. S. Zuckerman (Ed.), *The social logic of politics* (pp. 95–116). Philadelphia, PA: Temple University Press.

Wiley, S., & Bikmen, N. (2012). Building solidarity across difference: Social identity, intersectionality, and collective action for social change. In S. Wiley, G. Philogène & T. A. Revenson (Eds.), *Social categories in everyday experience* (pp. 189–204). Washington, DC: American Psychological Association. doi:10.1037/13488-010

Wright, S. C., & Lubensky, M. E. (2009). The struggle for social equality: Collective action versus prejudice reduction. In S. Demoulin, J. Leyens, & J. F. Dovidio (Eds.), *Intergroup misunderstandings: Impact of divergent social realities* (pp. 291–310). New York, NY: Psychology Press.

NICOLA CURTIN is an Assistant Professor at Clark University and a Visiting Scholar at Brandeis University's Women's Studies Research Center. Her research examines the role of life experiences, individual differences, and social identities in commitments to creating social change, with a particular emphasis on ally and coalitional activism. She explores the development of social change attitudes and behaviors across different social contexts, with a focus on U.S. identity-based rights activism.

CRAIG MCGARTY is Professor of Psychology at Western Sydney University. He was previously Director of the Centre for Social and Community Research and Director of the Social Research Institute at Murdoch University and Head of the School of Psychology at The Australian National University. His books include *Categorization in Social Psychology* and *Research Methods and Statistics in Psychology, The Message of Social Psychology,* and *Stereotypes as Explanations.*

Journal of Social Issues, Vol. 72, No. 2, 2016, pp. 242–263
doi: 10.1111/josi.12165

The "Activist Identity" and Activism across Domains: A Multiple Identities Analysis

Winnifred R. Louis[*]
University of Queensland

Catherine E. Amiot
Université du Québec à Montréal

Emma F. Thomas
Murdoch University

Leda Blackwood
University of Bath

Two correlational studies of activists examined the association between belonging to community organizations or groups and sustained activism within a particular domain. In Study 1 (N = 45) larger activist networks, controlling for activist identification and greater political knowledge, were associated with stronger activism intentions. In Study 2 (N = 155), larger Time 1 peace activism social networks were associated with more Time 2 peace activism and, via Time 2 activism, with sustained activism at Time 3. In contrast, Time 1 nationalist and party political identities were inhibiting factors of peace activism at Time 2, and indirectly at Time 3. In addition, larger peace activism networks at Time 1 were associated with greater international human rights activism and Christian activism at Time 3, but not as consistently with other forms of cross-domain activism. The possible organizing principles for these interrelationships are discussed.

The present article addresses activism across domains and social issues as an empirical reality, and as a theoretical and social challenge. Our approach considers a specific subset of activism, collective action, defining collective actions as "the

[*]Correspondence concerning this article should be addressed to Winnifred R. Louis, School of Psychology, McElwain Building, University of Queensland, Brisbane, St Lucia 4072, Queensland, Australia. Tel: +61 7 3346 9515 [e-mail: w.louis@psy.uq.edu.au].

intentional action of individuals sharing a common group membership to benefit a group" (Louis, 2009: p. 727). In the present article, we examine activists as those who undertake collective actions on behalf of groups (see Curtin & McGarty, 2016; Thomas & Louis, 2013, for a review).

Traditional approaches to collective action consider identification with each social movement as the key driver, with other identities irrelevant or perhaps even antagonistic to engagement (e.g., Stürmer & Simon, 2004; also Blackwood, Livingstone, & Leach, 2013; Blackwood, Terry, & Duck, 2015; Thomas, McGarty, & Mavor, 2009a,b; van Zomeren, Leach, & Spears, 2012; van Zomeren, Postmes, & Spears, 2008). If two activists on different sides of a political debate both identify as activists, this approach points out, a generalized activist identity does not make them likely to appear at each other's rallies. Yet there are other theoretical models whereby activism in one domain builds relationships, knowledge, and behavioral identities that facilitate activism across domains (e.g., Putnam, 1995, 2000). According to this perspective, wide and complex social networks will facilitate processes that are important to strong democracies, such as participating in activism. The present research presents two studies which test the association of general activist network size with specific peace activism (Study 1) and peace activist social network size with peace activism and cross-domain activism (Study 2).

Should Activism in One Domain be Related to Higher Activism in Another?

In principle, there are many reasons to expect that activism in one domain would be positively correlated with activism in another. For example, age, gender, income, wealth, and occupational prestige have been consistently associated with community activism (e.g., Kinder, 1998; Curtin, Kende, & Kende, 2016; Curtin & McGarty, 2016). These stable group and individual differences should produce third-factor correlations between activism intentions in one domain and activism intentions in another, because some respondents (e.g., wealthier, more educated, retired) might be expected to have higher intentions to engage in activism across the board. But is there a link between activism in one domain and activism in another, beyond such third-factor associations?

We can identify at least three reasons to expect that there should be such a causal association, as elaborated below: (1) increased social network size (membership in more groups which may mobilize members to action), (2) growing political knowledge (exposure to information about how the system works and other social issues of importance), and (3) a generalized or behavioral activist identity (an identity as one who is politically active in general, beyond one particular domain alone).

Social Activist Networks Should Promote Cross-Domain Activism

One outcome of past activism is expected to be strengthened relationships, which facilitate future collective actions (e.g., Drury, Cocking, Beale, Hanson, & Rapley, 2005; Drury & Reicher, 2005; Klandermans, van der Toorn, & Stekelenburg, 2008; Putnam, 1995, 2000). For example, church members can be tapped for a political campaign; sports teams can organize charity fund-raisers, and so on. Engagement in one organization can also increase skills, trust, and self-efficacy about the repertoire of political behaviors of the day, and these resources can be drawn on by other organizations (Blackwood & Louis, 2012). Activism also may promote group cohesion, and communicate appraisals of power structures and community relationships that inform cross-domain activism (Hartley, Lala, McGarty, & Donaghue, 2016; Thomas, McGarty, & Louis, 2014). Drawing on this literature, we propose that activist networks may *facilitate* cross-domain activism. In addition, we propose that two possible mechanisms can be identified—increased knowledge and stronger activist identification—which may mediate the impact of larger activist networks on cross-domain activism, but which also may be important in their own right.

Growing Knowledge

Previous research on political engagement has found that increasing knowledge facilitates more interest in issues, and promotes future political behaviors by highlighting individual's awareness of what is at stake and why their contribution matters (e.g., Galston, 2001; Kinder, 1998). With regard to activism, it seems intuitive that Cause 1 activism should increase Cause 2 activism via greater political knowledge (see also, Curtin & McGarty, 2016). In addition, greater knowledge may be promoted by factors beyond one's activist network, such as media consumption or education. For this reason, greater political knowledge may also be a predictor of activism in its own right. Study 1 tests these hypothesized direct and indirect effects explicitly.

Activist Identities

Previous research has shown that individuals may develop a behavioral identity as "the kind of person who engages in a particular action," which is predictive of intentions and of behavior over and above other motivational factors (e.g., Fielding, McDonald, & Louis, 2008; Turner-Zwinkels, van Zomeren, & Postmes, 2015). For example, people who identify as blood donors may give more blood, and self-identified voters may vote more consistently. We reason that an activist identity that is defined at this behavioral level might well lead to groups of "the usual suspects" (from the authorities' point of view) who engage in consistent protest behavior across a range of domains. Again, mediational and independent paths may both be hypothesized. Cause 1 activism should increase Cause 2 activism indirectly, to the extent that Cause 1 activism builds this generalized identification as an activist (e.g., Blackwood & Louis, 2012; Drury & Reicher, 2005; see also, Baray, Postmes, & Jetten, 2009). In addition, factors other than activist network size would be expected to contribute to a generalized activist identity (e.g., people may differ on perceived efficacy and anger, factors that promote activist identities; van Zomeren et al., 2008, 2012). Greater activist identification may therefore be associated with stronger intentions over and above activist social network size. Again, these associations are explicitly tested in Study 1.

Should Activism in One Domain be Related to Lower Activism in Another?

Although there are good grounds to argue that activism in one domain should facilitate activism in another domain, there is also some research that suggests the opposite may sometimes be true (i.e., an inhibitory relationship). For example, in activist groups, turnover and attrition are often high, which in turn is associated with damaged relationships, and decreased organizational knowledge (Louis, Terry, & Fielding, 2005). This presents a conundrum: if activism leads to greater social networks, ever-increasing knowledge, and stronger activist identities, and if these are linked to future activism in a virtuous cycle, how then can we understand social movements that dwindle?

One approach is to turn to theoretical models that propose more context-specific definitions of activist identities. For example, in Simon and Klandermans' (2001) influential model, politicized identity is thought to be comprised of three core aspects which may each be quite context specific: shared grievances, awareness of third parties, and adversarial attributions. Similarly, politicized collective identity may imply a shared social category identity (e.g., women) with whom activists identify, which has fostered an agentic, behavioral identity as activists for that category (e.g., feminists: Kelly & Breinlinger, 1995; see also, Stürmer & Simon, 2004). Identification with one such category (such as women) or political identity (such as feminists) need not flow on to identification with a second social category (such as immigrants) or political cause (such as refugee activism).

Similarly, in the social identity approach more broadly, contextually salient identities are proposed to shape behavior via meaningful, group-specific norms (e.g., for environmental activism, Fielding et al., 2008). Membership in activist groups is thus plausibly linked to stronger in-group identification (Drury & Reicher, 2005; Drury et al., 2005), responsiveness to in-group norms (e.g., Amiot, Sansfaçon, & Louis, 2014), and greater relevant, domain-specific activism (e.g., Blackwood et al., 2013, 2015). In the same vein, the recent scholarship of opinion group membership (e.g., McGarty, Bliuc, Thomas, & Bongiorno, 2009) shows that activists' mobilization is often on the basis of an identity defined by a single issue (e.g., opposition to battery farming), with no prima facie reason for generalized activism for other causes. Drawing on this research, it is clear that the facilitating effects of activism in one domain will not necessarily generalize to any and all other activism domains.

Furthermore, when multiple identities are salient, there is the potential for conflicting in-group norms (McDonald, Fielding, & Louis, 2014). For normatively conflicting social movements, activism in one domain might not just fail to predict, but actually inhibit the likelihood of activism in other domains. This cross-domain *inhibition hypothesis* also may be derived from resource mobilization theory (McCarthy & Zald, 1977; see also, McAdam, McCarthy, & Zald, 1996), which proposes that social movement activism arises from opportunities and resources, and that the social movements that activists are involved in compete for their time, energy, money, and other resources. If activists' time and energy is limited (Curtin & McGarty, 2016), a negative association between activist network size and future activism could surely be expected.

Study 1

Study 1 tests competing and contradictory hypotheses about the role of cross-domain activism, which have received comparatively little research attention. A cross-sectional sample of peace activists in May/June 2003 was analyzed. First, we tested the competing hypotheses that activist network size (number of groups involved in, from environmental organizations to unions) would *facilitate* future activism (Curtin & McGarty, 2016; Drury & Reicher, 2005; Drury et al., 2005; Putnam, 1995), but could also work to *undermine* or compete with it (e.g., in line with McCarthy & Zald, 1977's resource mobilization theory). Second, we tested the hypothesis that indirect positive relationships might be observed between activist network size and intentions to engage in activism, via generalized activist identification (Simon & Klandermans, 2001) and greater political knowledge (Galston, 2001; Kinder, 1998). Finally, we examined the possibility that generalized activist identification and greater political knowledge might function as independent variables in their own right: that they would be important over and above any impact of social network size.

Study 1 Method

Participants

Australian activists ($N = 45$) were recruited to complete a study about media use and political attitudes and knowledge. The participants opposed the Iraq war

(97%) and had engaged in some form of pro-peace political behavior in the previous month (93%). Ages ranged from 17 to 75 with a median of 34. Most participants were female (65%), ethnically European (96%), nonreligious (51%), and Australian (91%).

Procedure

Respondents volunteered to complete a study about "the relationship between identities, attitudes, activism and media usage" via snowball sampling, initiated by advertising in activist e-lists. Participants completed the survey online, although printed copies of the questionnaire could also be requested and returned in postal mail. The recruiting period, May 20 to June 30, 2003, followed the invasion of Iraq in February, and President Bush's "Mission Accomplished" speech on May 1 which had declared victory.

Materials

The full questionnaire is available from the authors; a subset of variables are presented here.

Participants were asked to "Please list some of the political, religious or other community organizations or groups that you are a member of, if any," in order to assess *activist network size.* Answers were coded in terms of the number of groups they belonged to, which ranged from 0 to 10. The groups listed were diverse, including 13 religious (e.g., Victorian Council of Churches, Lutheran Chaplains' Support group), 10 environmental (e.g., Greenpeace, Australian Conservation Foundation), nine peace (e.g., Just Peace, Queensland Peace Network), six student/alumni organizations, six political parties, five local community organizations, five refugee groups, five professional associations, five media groups, four feminist groups, four development or international aid groups, three unions, and several others. The 45 participants reported membership in 99 groups ($M = 2.80$; median $= 2$).

Generalized activist identification was measured with three items (e.g., "I feel similar to other people who are active in the community"; 1, *Not at all*; 7, *Very much*) which were averaged, $\alpha = .87$.

A measure of political knowledge was scored from zero to 10 with higher scores reflecting a greater proportion of correctly answered questions measuring political knowledge about Australia, the United States, the UN, and Iraq (e.g., "Who is the Prime Minister of Australia?").

General activist intentions were measured with five items measuring intentions to engage in specific actions (signing a petition, donating to a group, attending a rally, volunteering my time, and "other actions for community service not listed"), on scales from 1 (*Not at all*) to 7 (*Very much*). Items were averaged such that higher scores reflected greater activist intentions, $\alpha = .63$.

Study 1 Results

Descriptive Analyses

As expected, activist network size ($M = 2.80$; $SD = 2.56$) was correlated with greater generalized activist identification ($M = 5.50$; $SD = 1.34$), $r = .48$, $p < .001$, and in turn both were associated with higher activism intentions ($M = 4.39$; $SD = 1.39$), $r = .54$ and $.53$, respectively, $p < .001$. Although greater political knowledge ($M = 6.46$; $SD = 2.43$) was associated with stronger intentions, $r = .40$, $p < .01$, contrary to expectations it was not associated with activist network size, $r = .15$, $p = .312$, nor with generalized activist identification, $r = .24$. This null finding highlights that participants were not exclusively or even primarily active in political affairs; we return to this point below. In addition, network size was not significantly associated with any demographic variables—age, gender, religious affiliation, education, and ethnicity, $r < .294$, $p > .184$—perhaps because the sample was small and comparatively homogenous.

Predicting Intentions

Given the small sample size, direct and indirect effects of activist social network size on intentions via greater political knowledge and generalized activist identification were assessed using bootstrapping, with 1,000 resamples and bias-corrected confidence intervals (using the PROCESS macro; see Hayes, 2013; Preacher & Hayes, 2008). As expected, larger activist network size was associated with greater activist identity, $R^2 = .23$, $p = .001$, $b = .25$, $SE = .07$ (95% CI = .108 and .398), but consistent with the correlations, network size was not linked with knowledge, $R^2 = .02$, $p = .432$, $b = .11$, $SE = .14$ (95% CI = $-.168$ and .387).

Together, activist network, generalized activist identity, and political knowledge accounted for 47% of the variance in activist intentions, $F(3, 39) = 11.30$, $p < .001$. The indirect effect (IE) of social network size on intentions via identification was not significant (IE = .053; 95% CI = $-.027$ and .146), nor was the indirect effect of network size via greater political knowledge (IE = .014; 95% CI = $-.005$ and .082). However, activist social movement size, generalized activist identification, and political knowledge were each independent, positive predictors of future intentions: activist network size, $b = .20$, $SE = .07$, $p = .008$ (95% CI = .056 and .351); activist identity, $b = .29$, $SE = .14$, $p = .047$ (95% CI = .01 and .58); and greater political knowledge, $b = .18$, $SE = .07$, $p = .022$ (95% CI = .027 and .327).

Study 1 Discussion

Study 1 examined generalized activist network size, activist identity, political knowledge, and future specific peace activist intentions. The findings are consistent with a facilitative role for cross-domain activism (Drury & Reicher, 2005; Drury et al., 2005; Putnam, 1995, 2000), rather than any inhibitory competition. General activist network size (the number of activist groups participants belonged to) was positively associated with generalized activist identity, and both activist network size and generalized activist identity were independently, positively linked to future activist intentions. The role of network size is striking given that over 95 community groups and organizations were reported by participants. The activist groups participants belonged to were diverse in terms of the domains they involved and there was little evidence of concentration in these networks, let alone of concentration narrowly in peace activist groups per se. The diversity itself speaks to the prevalence of cross-domain activism, as we explore further in Study 2.

The present study makes a contribution in being among the very few to explore cross-domain activism from a collective action perspective, and in testing specific paths by which activist social networks might facilitate activism. The role of generalized activist identification in predicting future intentions is also consistent with the idea that activist identities can be "behavioral" and manifested across different domains, rather than only manifested in in specific domain (Fielding et al., 2008; also Baray et al., 2009). Although there was no significant association of activist network size with political knowledge, knowledge was also independently positively associated with intentions to engage in activism, consistent with previous research (e.g., Galston, 2001; Kinder, 1998). The independent role of each variable highlights an intriguing triad of factors that promote cross-domain activism: changes to social relationships (social network size), to the self (activist identification), and to knowledge.

Nevertheless, several limitations must be acknowledged. The low sample size is a concern in terms of statistical power. However, activists can be difficult samples to access for a number of reasons (see Curtin & McGarty, 2016). It is noteworthy that each of the three factors was a significant unique predictor, despite the small sample. A more substantive limitation to Study 1 is the operationalization of cross-domain activism using a measure of activist social network size (the number of groups each participant was active in) which did not consider the specific normative content of the groups' agendas. In the sample, the focus was on the number of activist groups participants belonged to, although participants could have differed in their specific groups (e.g., one might have a profile of professional and sporting groups and the second a profile of more overtly politicized groups). Failure to find an association between activist social network size and political knowledge highlights the diversity of groups and the fact that not all of the groups had a political agenda (see also, Curtin & McGarty, 2016; van Stekelenburg, Klandermans, & Akkerman, 2016). A more direct test of the role of cross-domain activism would be to examine the association between network size in a specific domain (e.g., peace) and activism in other domains (e.g., human rights), rather than (as in Study 1) considering general network size among peace activists in relation to future activism. We address these concerns in Study 2.

Study 2

Study 2 built on the idea that activist identities specific to particular domains might facilitate each other (e.g., environmental activist and peace activist), whereas others might be mutually inhibitory, and some might be neutral to each other (neither promoting nor inhibiting activism in each other's domains). Data from a longitudinal study of peace activists (see also, Blackwood & Louis, 2012; Louis et al., 2005) were reanalyzed to examine the degree to which sustained peace activism could be predicted in relation to specific alternative identities and past activism.

In earlier analyses of these data, Blackwood and Louis (2012) found that activist identification affected perceptions of the efficacy of these behaviors for achieving group goals, as well as perceptions of individual-level benefits (see also, Evripidou & Drury, 2013). Louis et al. (2005) also drew on the Time 1 and Time 2 data to analyze identification in relation to sustained activism in the peace movement. The present article extends the analysis to Time 3, as elaborated below, and reanalyzes the data to include activists' social network size at Time 1 and Australian identification and political identification (to test their facilitating or inhibiting roles for peace activism), Time 2 identification and activism, along with support for twelve other social movements reported at Time 3. The analysis for Australian and political identification were exploratory (Louis et al., 2005), but for example, Australian identification might be expected to be linked negatively to peace activism to the extent that then-leader Prime Minister Howard successfully communicated a representation of Australian identity as united behind the war in Iraq. Similarly, political party identity might be negatively linked to peace activism to the extent that opposition to the war from Australian political parties was muted and/or mobilized in ways that might call activists away from the peace movement.

Study 2 Method

Participants

Participants had performed at least one pro-peace political action in the last month at Time 1 ($N = 155$). The Time 1 survey was conducted in February 2003, at the height of the protests against the invasion of Iraq and in attempts to keep

Australia out of the war and the "Coalition of the Willing" (the U.S. term for the partner countries in the invasion). During the survey active fighting was ongoing, but the "Coalition of the Willing" seemed to be winning (e.g., fall of Baghdad, April 9). Participants ranged in age from 16 to 75 (with a median of 35) and were disproportionately (62%) women, highly educated (93% having some form of higher education), and affiliated with the more left-wing Green Party (63%). Most participants were affiliated with at least one organized group that was participating in the peace movement (63%) and were Australian citizens ($n = 135$, 87%).

Procedure

Activists were recruited to participate in an online survey through snowball sampling from speaking at peace group meetings and disseminating the survey through e-lists for Australian peace groups and word of mouth. Participation was voluntary, and those who had indicated willingness to participate in future research at Time 1 ($n = 71$) were e-mailed a second link to the Time 2 survey four weeks later: the response rate was 71/155, or 46% (i.e., 54% attrition). Time 2 participants who indicated willingness were e-mailed a second link to the Time 3 survey four weeks after their Time 2 participation: the response rate was 35/71, or 49% (i.e., 51% attrition from Time 2). Comparing Time 1 to Time 3, the retention rate was 35/155 or 23% (77% attrition overall).

Measures

A copy of the full questionnaire is available from the authors on request. At Time 1, participants completed a survey measuring peace activist social network size, activist identity, political party identity, national identity, and intentions to engage in future collective action. At Time 2, activist identity was again measured, in addition to self-reported activist behavior over the previous month. At Time 3, the measures of activist identification, and self-report activist behavior over the previous month were repeated. In addition two measures of cross-domain activism were included: attitudinal support for twelve specific social movements and behavioral engagement with those movements.

Peace activist network size.   Participants' network of peace activist groups was measured at Time 1 with an open-ended question focusing specifically on peace groups ("Are you a member of any peace groups? If so which ones?"). The range was from 0 to 5 ($M = 1.13$; median $= 1$; see also, Table 1).

National identity.   Participants indicated their citizenship at Time 1 (as noted above, 87% were Australian citizens) and rated the importance of their

Table 1. Selected Means, Standard Deviations, and Intercorrelations (Study 2)

	Means	SD	1	2	3	4	5	6	7	8
1. Peace Activist Network Size	1.13	1.24	–							
2. National ID	3.96	1.98	−.05	–						
3. Political ID	3.82	1.99	.11	.14	–					
4. T1 Activist ID	3.86	0.88	.16	.01	**.21**	–				
5. T1 Past Action	4.11	2.11	**.46**	−.14	.08	**.34**	–			
6. T2 Activist ID	4.01	0.81	**.24**	−.14	.12	**.71**	**.28**	–		
7. T2 Past Action	2.47	1.85	**.33**	**−.29**	−.07	.00	**.54**	**.26**	–	
8. T3 Activist ID	3.85	0.92	.01	.10	.12	**.62**	−.14	**.65**	−.22	–
9. T3 Past Action	1.46	1.60	.17	−.24	−.31	−.18	**.62**	−.07	**.66**	−.05

Note. Correlations significant at $p < .05$ are in bold. Variables were measured on the following scales: Peace activist network size (0–5), ID (1–7), past actions (0–8).

national identity with a single item, "How important is being Australian in your everyday life?" on a scale from 1, *Not at all important,* to 7, *Very important.*

Political party identity.   Participants indicated the political party that they would vote for if an election were to be held the following day, at Time 1. The majority were affiliated with left wing parties (63% supported the Green Party). Participants rated the importance of their political party to themselves with the item, "How important is being a supporter of this party in your everyday life?" on a scale from 1, *Not at all important,* to 7, *Very important.*

Time 1–3 activist identification.   A three-item scale (e.g., "I think of myself as an activist") assessed generalized activist identity at each point in time ($\alpha = .70, .73, .77$ for Times 1–3). Items were measured on Likert scales from 1, *Strongly Disagree,* to 5, *Strongly Agree* and averaged so that higher scores measured stronger activist identity.

Peace activism intentions.   At each time point, intentions to engage in each of five forms of collective action in the next four weeks was assessed on a scale from 1, *Not at all,* to 7, *Definitely intend to,* using the stem question "In the next four weeks, how much do you intend to engage in each of these behaviors?" The five actions were signing a pro-peace petition, attending a pro-peace rally, attending a meeting of a pro-peace group, donating money to a pro-peace group, and volunteering time to a pro-peace group. Ratings were averaged with higher scores reflecting stronger intentions (Time 1–3; $\alpha = .78, .76, .78$).

Time 1–3 self-report past collective action.   At each time point, participants were asked, "In the last month, have you engaged in pro-peace/antiwar behaviors? Please tick all that apply." The five behaviors listed in the intentions were included and participants were invited to list up to three others. The total number of behaviors indicated formed the score for this variable. The range was from 0 to 8 at Time 1 ($M = 4.11$, median = 4), and at Time 2 ($M = 2.47$, median = 2); at Time 3 the range was from 0 to 6 ($M = 1.46$, median = 1).

Cross-domain activism was measured by asking respondents the extent to which they supported the goals of twelve movements behaviorally, on a scale from 1 to 7 (being active in the last year) and attitudinally. Participants were asked about support for peace ($M_{att} = 6.46$, $SD = 0.69$; $M_{beh} = 5.26$, $SD = 0.90$), and also reported on 11 other movements: international human rights ($M_{att} = 6.71$, $SD = 0.60$; $M_{beh} = 3.58$, $SD = 1.60$), refugees ($M_{att} = 6.68$, $SD = 0.61$; $M_{beh} = 4.15$, $SD = 1.59$), Aboriginal rights ($M_{att} = 6.50$, $SD = 0.64$; $M_{beh} = 3.04$, $SD = 1.53$), third world poverty/debt relief ($M_{att} = 6.54$, $SD = 0.79$; $M_{beh} = 2.89$, $SD = 1.76$), the environment ($M_{att} = 6.46$, $SD = 0.64$; $M_{beh} = 3.59$, $SD = 1.58$), antiglobalization ($M_{att} = 6.15$, $SD = 1.17$; $M_{beh} = 2.62$, $SD = 1.33$), queer/LGBT rights ($M_{att} = 5.89$, $SD = 1.45$; $M_{beh} = 2.07$, $SD = 0.96$), unions ($M_{att} = 5.68$, $SD = 0.94$; $M_{beh} = 2.32$, $SD = 1.28$), the women's movement ($M_{att} = 5.68$, $SD = 1.47$; $M_{beh} = 2.26$, $SD = 1.26$), the youth/student movement ($M_{att} = 5.57$, $SD = 1.23$; $M_{beh} = 2.32$, $SD = 1.25$), and Christian values/church ($M_{att} = 3.43$, $SD = 2.01$; $M_{beh} = 2.11$, $SD = 2.01$).

Study 2 Results

Descriptive Summary

Table 1 reports selected means, standard deviations, and intercorrelations for the identity and activism variables using all available respondents (pairwise N, intercorrelations for the 24 cross-domain activism variables are available on request from the authors). As can be seen in Table 1, number of peace actions undertaken trended downward over time. Time 1 peace network size was associated with greater Time 1 and 2 self-report past actions, and with a trend toward more action at Time 3. Time 1–3 activist identity and actions were positively intercorrelated. In contrast, greater Australian identification and political party identification were associated with trends to lower Time 2 and 3 actions.

Looking at the demographic variables, gender and party affiliation showed no associations with network size ($p > .05$). Peace network size was higher for older people and those affiliated with a religion ($r = .20$ and $.27$, respectively, $p < .05$), but younger and nonreligious people reported equal activism in the peace movement at Time 3 ($p > .448$).We did not control for demographics in the analyses below, due to the low ratio of respondents to parameters in the models and concerns about power. Our samples were relatively homogeneous (e.g., highly educated), which is consistent with previous work on this topic, but could also reflect snowball sampling from particular networks. (Study 2 age and religious affiliation were associated with larger peace networks, but not with sustained activism; in Study 1 no effects were found. Further large, diverse samples are needed.)

Predicting (Same-Domain) Peace Activism

We tested the expected positive association between Time 1 peace activist network size and Time 3 peace activist behavior, along with the impacts of Time 1 Australian identity and political party identity. Time 2 peace activist identification, and Time 2 peace activist behavior were included as potential mediators. Given the small sample, analyses were conducted using bootstrapping with the PROCESS macro, with 1,000 resamples and bias-corrected confidence intervals (Hayes, 2013; Preacher & Hayes, 2008).

The model accounted for significant variance in Time 2 behavior, $R^2 = .50$, $F(3, 20) = 6.75$, $p = .003$. Larger Time 1 networks were associated with more Time 2 peace activism, $b = .44$, $SE = .17$, $p = .020$ (95% CI = .076 and .794). In contrast, Time 1 Australian identification, $b = -.31$, $SE = .13$, $p = .021$ (95% CI = $-.576$ and $-.054$), and political party identification, $b = -.32$, $SE = .14$, $p = .040$ (95% CI = $-.617$ and $-.015$), were associated with significantly lower Time 2 peace activism.

In turn, the model accounted for significant variance in Time 3 peace activist behaviors, $R^2 = .47$, $F(6, 17) = 3.15$, $p = .032$. Time 2 activism was strongly associated with Time 3 activism, $b = .70$, $SE = .24$, $p = .009$ (95% CI = .196 and 1.196). No other coefficients were significant ($p > .05$), but the positive indirect effect of Time 1 network size on Time 3 activism via sustained Time 2 activism was significant, IE = .285, CI = .040, .938. Significant negative indirect effects were also observed for Time 1 Australian identity (IE = $-.206$, CI = $-.728$ and $-.007$) and political party identity (IE = $-.221$, CI = $-.562$, $-.021$). In short, Time 1 peace activism network was a significant indirect facilitator of later (same-domain) peace activism, while Time 1 nationalist and party political identities were inhibiting factors.

Considered alongside Time 2 peace activism, the indirect effect of social network size at Time 1 on Time 3 intentions via Time 2 activist identification was not significant (IE = .054; 95% CI = $-.038$, .369) and identification was not associated with Time 3 behavior when Time 2 behavior was controlled or predicted by network size at Time 1 ($p > .05$). Our present analysis already stretched the acceptable ratio of parameters to respondents, but with larger sample size, it might be interesting to put forward a serial mediation in which Time 1 network size predicted Time 1 intentions and identity which flowed on to Time 2 activist behavior and identity, and in turn to Time 3 activist behavior and identity. Considered jointly, the more behavioral Time 2 measure was a stronger predictor at Time 3. We return to this point in the discussion.

Cross-Domain Activism

The identity and activism variables were then examined in relation to cross-domain activism for the committed peace activists sampled at Time 3. Correlational analyses linking the Time 1 variables to the eleven other activism domains at Time 3 were followed up by nonparametric analyses to address restriction of range.

Correlations. Time 1 Australian identification was correlated with significantly lower attitudinal support for the anti-Globalization movement ($r = -.61$) and more support for Christian values/churches ($r = .46$), $p < .05$. Political party identification was associated with significantly more support for the environmental movement attitudinally ($r = .40$) and behaviorally ($r = .53$), $p < .05$.

Turning to peace identities and actions, peace network size was associated with greater likelihood of having acted to support international human rights in the last year ($r = .56$) and Christian values/churches ($r = .45$), $p < .05$. Time 1 peace actions were also associated with greater behavioral support for the peace movement in the past year ($r = .42$). Time 3 peace actions were associated with greater support for the peace movement ($r = .40$), feminism ($r = .38$), reconciliation with Indigenous Australians ($r = .43$), and refugees ($r = .41$), $p < .05$.

Nonparametric analyses. These correlational analyses grossly underestimated the associations, however, in that the range was found to be severely restricted for most of the social movement variables (restriction of range depresses correlations; e.g., Louis et al., 2003). For example, 100% of the Time 3 respondents scored at or above the midpoint on attitudinal and behavioral support for the peace movement, which reflects our sample of committed peace activists. Reasoning that support for other social movements might in theory be equally likely to be low or high (i.e., 50% supporters vs. nonsupporters), we employed nonparametric tests, namely chi-squares, to test if participants significantly deviated from equal high and low support across the social movements sampled. Such an analysis reveals disproportionately high attitudinal support in the sample for the environmental/green movement (100% approved; $X^2 = 66.67, p < .001$) as well as for human rights, refugee support, and reconciliation with Indigenous Australians (each 100% approved), third world poverty/debt relief (96% approved, $X^2 = 53.68, p < .001$), anti-Globalization/anti-WTO, organized labor unions, and queer/LGBT rights (all 89% approved, $X^2 = 35.86, p < .001$), the youth/student movement (82% approved, $X^2 = 22.82, p < .001$) and feminism (79% approved,

$X^2 = 18.36, p < .001$). In comparison, lower attitudinal support for Christian values/church was observed (33% approved, $X^2 = 5.27, p < .015$).

Behavioral support in the last year for cross-domain causes was less consistently above or below the baseline, if 50% is the appropriate baseline to consider (we will return to the question of appropriate baseline in the discussion). Only international human rights were endorsed more strongly than expected (79% had undertaken activism for this cause in the last year, $X^2 = 18.36, p < .001$). Among the movements endorsed at baseline, in the environmental movement in the last year, 61% were active; 44% in the anti-Globalization/anti-WTO movement; and 39% each in third world poverty/debt relief and reconciliation ($p > .05$). Only 25% of the sample had engaged in Christian activism in the last year, or in queer/LGBT rights activism, feminism, or the youth movement; all were below the 50% baseline ($X^2 = 13.33, p < .001$), along with union participation at 29% ($X^2 = 9.227, p = .002$).

Study 2 Discussion

Study 2 supports the argument for the context-specific nature of the activist identity, as opposed to a generalized facilitating role. We observed variability in the facilitating and inhibitory associations between specific identities and activism domains, as well as in impeding relationships. For example, those who identified more strongly as Australian and as political party members at Time 1 (before the invasion of Iraq) were less likely to report having engaged in pro-peace activism at Time 2 (after Australia joined the invasion as part of the "Coalition of the Willing"; see also, Louis et al., 2005), which in turn flowed on to lower activism at Time 3 (i.e., there were significant negative indirect effects).

In contrast, peace movement social network size (affiliation with more groups involved in the peace movement) was associated with greater Time 2 activism, and through this with greater Time 3 activism. Clear patterns of disproportionate support for other domains of activism were observed among the Time 3 activists, with stronger positive associations from peace activism to international human rights activism, and weaker associations with domains such as union or LGBT activism. To us, the data highlight the importance of considering higher order patterns (ideologies, political structures) that link identities both positively and negatively; we return to this point in the general discussion.

Several limitations must be acknowledged. The results from Time 3 specifically highlight interrelationships among social movements as well as the differences in degree of mutual facilitation, and in the likelihood that attitudinal support had been translated recently into action. Ideological positioning within the Australian political context may explain some of the stronger vs weaker interrelationships, and windows of political opportunity or issue salience some of the variance in likelihood of action. Yet, whether a 50% baseline is the right standard against which to judge the significance of disproportionate attitudinal and behavioral support for cross-domain activism is open to question. Christians were a minority of peace activists (only 25% of the Time 3 peace activist sample were also active as Christians), yet more Christian activism was associated with greater peace network size at Time 1, showing facilitation effects. Similarly, if the community is disproportionately conservative or nonactivist, the threshold for the associations observed among activists would be much lower, potentially revealing even stronger roles of cross-domain activism. The list in Study 2 of cross-domain issues is also ad hoc, and neglects right-wing causes (Curtin & McGarty, 2016; see also, Louis et al., 2016; Sweetman, Leach, Spears, Pratto, & Saab, 2013). Pilot testing to establish an appropriate list including conservative causes would be informative, and would allow more accurate diagnosis of the extent to which ideological alignment moderates the association between activism in one domain and activism in a second.

Finally, it is the strength of Study 2 to examine activism across three time points and at a highly interesting moment in the peace movement. We know of very little similar work that has been published and as such the simple descriptive statistics are of great interest (see Thomas et al., 2015, for another exception). However, the low sample size at Time 3 raises concerns about statistical power, despite the use of methods such as bootstrapping that partially address them (Hayes, 2013; Preacher & Hayes, 2008). Larger sample size would allow for more complex models to be estimated reliably. In addition, the high attrition gives rise to concern: To the extent that the Time 3 sample of activists is unrepresentative, caution in generalizing from the present findings is clearly warranted, and replication in future research is needed.

General Discussion

In two studies, positive associations were found between activist social network size, generalized activist identification, and intentions to engage in future activism. In Study 1, future activism in a sample of peace activists was predicted by generalized activist identification, and independently by activist social network size and political knowledge. The sheer number of community groups with which participants were associated was linked to increased activism, even though many groups were not specifically political or peace oriented. In Study 2, peace activist social network size at Time 1 was associated with same-domain activism (greater Time 2 and 3 self-report peace actions). In addition, at Time 3, patterns of attitudinal and behavioral support for cross-domain activism were clearly observed. For example, 100% of Time 3 peace activists also supported the environmental movement, international human rights, refugee rights, and reconciliation with Indigenous Australians. Support for a number of other causes was equally disproportionate.

However, negative cross-domain relationships were also observed, such that national identification and political party identification were associated with less sustained engagement with the peace movement in Study 2. Further, some domains of activism (such as union or LGBT/queer activism) were not consistently facilitated in the same way that others were. The findings provide support for both of our competing hypotheses: activism does apparently have a facilitating role for cross-domain activism, but equally clearly there are moderating variables such that negative or null relationships can also be observed.

Facilitating Effects for Cross-Domain Activism

We highlighted four reasons in the introduction to expect that activism in one domain would be positively correlated with activism in another: third factors such as demographics (e.g., Kinder, 1998), social network size (c.f. Putnam, 1995, 2000), political knowledge (e.g., Galston, 2001), and activist identification (Fielding et al., 2008; Simon & Klandermans, 2001). We did not engage systematically with demographic factors, and that is a limitation of the studies and a direction of future research. However, support for the role of social networks and identification clearly emerged in both studies. Political knowledge also was associated with greater activist intentions in Study 1. However, we did not demonstrate mediation of social network size effects by either knowledge or identification. The findings suggest that future research must examine the interrelationships among the variables listed, and in particular, explore the underlying mechanisms that explain their effects. For example, activism could facilitate cross-domain activism by increasing activists' awareness of their privilege and power (e.g., Montgomery & Stewart, 2012), or by teaching or consolidating particular appraisals of authorities or intergroup relations as illegitimate (Drury & Reicher, 2005; Drury et al., 2005; Hartley et al., 2016; Stuart, Thomas, Donaghue, & Russell, 2013; Thomas et al., 2014). Activism in one domain could also result in a search for allies (e.g., Curtin et al., 2016; Droogendyk, Wright, Lubensky, & Louis, 2016; see also, Saab, Tausch, Spears, & Cheung, 2015; Subašić, Reynolds, & Turner, 2008) which could lead to activism in the second domain motivated by the strategic perception that the second cause's supporters would reciprocate to support one's own. Directly exploring such mechanisms in future research is theoretically interesting and important.

Inhibitory Effects for Cross-Domain Activism

Traditional approaches to collective action consider identification with each social movement as the proximal predictor, with other identities possibly functionally antagonistic (e.g., Thomas et al., 2009a,b; van Zomeren et al., 2012; van

Zomeren et al., 2008). Particularly if multiple identity salience makes salient conflicting norms from different in-groups (McDonald et al., 2014), it is possible to imagine that activism in one domain would actually inhibit activism in (some) other domains. Further, resource mobilization theory (McCarthy & Zald, 1977; see also, McAdam et al., 1996) also specifically proposes that movements compete for activists' time, energy, etc. Consistent with these perspectives, in Study 2, we found evidence of inhibition from national and political party identities to peace activism. Failure to find strong roles to union or LGBT activism from peace activism also highlights the important moderators which need to be explored in future research.

Ideological Conflict and Normative Fit

The findings in Study 2 suggest a hidden role of ideological alignment and normative fit, which can be articulated from a number of different theoretical positions. For example, social capital scholars now distinguish between bonding social capital (which promotes in-group cohesion), bridging social capital (which promotes intergroup cooperation and shared resources) and linking social capital (which promotes cooperation between a group and authorities; Putnam, 1995; see also Subašić et al., 2008). One reason why activism in Study 2 that promotes specific minority group's rights (e.g., LGBT or union activism) was not as consistently positively linked with cross-domain activism may be that these networks generate more bonding capital, and the bonding social capital does not necessarily generalize across domains. Specifically measuring the types of capital generated as moderators of the association between activism in one domain and a second seems like a fruitful direction of future research.

However, another exciting direction of future research would be in pursuing the question of higher order normative fit, or ideological alignment, which is suggested by an intergroup perspective (e.g., Baray et al., 2009; Drury & Reicher, 2005; McDonald et al., 2014; Thomas et al., 2009a,b; Turner-Zwinkles et al., 2015). From an applied perspective, it may be that social movements have greater potential for fostering cross-domain activism when they overlap in terms of their relationship to third parties, or link to more central identities, or when they invoke the same political orientations or abstract values (Kinder, 1998; Simon & Klandermans, 2001; see also, Subašić et al., 2008). At the same time, with greater ideological alignment of two movements comes a greater possibility for competition over activists' hearts and minds, as well as their time and energy (McAdam et al., 1996; McCarthy & Zald, 1977). Explicitly addressing the limits of activists' time and energy commitments in relation to movement demands and ideologies is a vital issue for leaders.

From a similar perspective, explicitly measuring norms will be important. It is possible to interpret the association between peace activism and national identity in terms of a changing normative context (with Australia's entry into the war, at Time 2 and 3, and the Prime Minister's call to unite behind the troops, all creating a negative association between national identification and peace activism which was not apparent at Time 1; Louis et al., 2005). However, without explicit measures of normative consensus, such inferences are speculative. If a greater degree of normative or ideological fit determines whether facilitating relationships are found for cross-domain activism, then framing the message of the campaign in such a way as to align with constituents' other identities emerges as a key challenge in mobilization for organizers. Similarly, authorities' attempts to frame activists' messages as peripheral to their social group's core values, or contradicting them, might then be understood as attempting to lower perceptions of alignment, creating new inhibiting relationships. Testing these hypotheses would be of great importance for decision-makers and organizers, from an applied perspective.

Conclusions

The present data invite consideration by scholars of collective action of the constellation of identities which define collective actors (Louis, Mavor, La Macchia, & Amiot, 2014). If some identities reinforce each other, while some conflict, issues of norm and identity consistency vs diversity, and empowerment versus marginalization, are of strong theoretical interest. The present data contribute to such a discussion, and are among very few studies in the social psychology of collective action that directly speak to cross-domain activism. The findings highlight the possibility of facilitating as well as inhibitory roles, suggesting that future research in this area will find much of interest to explore.

References

Amiot, C. E., Sansfaçon, S., & Louis, W. R. (2014). How normative and social identification processes predict self-determination to engage in derogatory behaviors against outgroup hockey fans. *European Journal of Social Psychology, 44*, 216–320. doi: 10.1002/ejsp.2006

Baray, G., Postmes, T., & Jetten, J. (2009). When I equals we: Exploring the relation between social and personal identity of extreme right-wing political party members. *British Journal of Social Psychology, 48*, 625–647. doi: 10.1348/014466608×389582

Blackwood, L. M., Terry, D. J., & Duck, J. M (2015). When believing in the union is (not) enough: The role of threat and pro-union norms in acting on union beliefs. *Australian Journal of Psychology, 67*, 65–74. doi: 10.1111/ajpy.12071

Blackwood, L. M., Livingstone, A. G., & Leach, C. W. (2013). Regarding societal change. *Journal of Social and Political Psychology, 1*, 105–111. doi: 10.5964/jspp.v1i1.282

Blackwood, L. M., & Louis, W. R. (2012). If it matters for the group then it matters to me. *British Journal of Social Psychology, 51*, 72–92. doi:10.1111/j.2044-8309.2010.02001

Curtin, N., & McGarty, C. (2016). Expanding on psychological theories of engagement to understand activism in context(s). *Journal of Social Issues, 72*(2), 227–241.

Curtin, N., Kende, A., & Kende, J. (2016). Navigating multiple identities: The simultaneous influence of advantaged and disadvantaged identities on politicization and activism. *Journal of Social Issues, 72*(2), 264–285.

Droogendyk, L., Wright, S. C., Lubensky, M. E., & Louis, W. R. (2016). Acting in solidarity: Cross-group contact between disadvantaged group members and advantaged group allies. *Journal of Social Issues, 72*(2), 315–334.

Drury, J., Cocking, C., Beale, J., Hanson, C., & Rapley, F. (2005). The phenomenology of empowerment in collective action. *British Journal of Social Psychology, 44*, 309–328. doi: 10.1348/014466604×18523

Drury, J., & Reicher, S. (2005). Explaining enduring empowerment: A comparative study of collective action and psychological outcomes. *European Journal of Social Psychology, 35*, 35–58. doi: 10.1002/ejsp.231

Evripidou, A., & Drury, J. (2013). This is the time of tension: Collective action and subjective power in the Greek anti-austerity movement. *Contention: Multidisciplinary Journal of Social Protest, 1*, 31–51.

Fielding, K. S., McDonald, R., & Louis, W. (2008). Theory of planned behavior, identity and intentions to engage in environmental activism. *Journal of Environmental Psychology, 28*, 318–326. doi:10.1016/j.jenvp.2008.03.003

Galston, W. A. (2001). Political knowledge, political engagement, and civic education. *Annual Review of Political Science, 4*, 217–234.

Hartley, L. K., Lala, G., Donaghue, N., & McGarty, C. (2016). How activists respond to social structure in offline and online contexts. *Journal of Social Issues, 72*(2), 376–398.

Hayes, A. F. (2013). *Introduction to mediation, moderation, and conditional process analysis: A regression-based approach.* New York, NY: Guilford Press.

Kelly, C., & Breinlinger, S. (1995). Identity and injustice: Exploring women's participation in collective action. *Journal of Community & Applied Social Psychology, 5*, 41–57. doi: 10.1002/casp.2450050104

Kinder, D. R. (1998). Opinion and action in the realm of politics'. In D. T. Gilbert, S. T. Fiske & G. Lindzey (Eds.), *The handbook of social psychology* (pp. 778–867). New York, NY: Oxford University Press.

Klandermans, B., van der Toorn, J., & van Stekelenburg, J. (2008). Embeddedness and identity: How immigrants turn grievances into action. *American Sociological Review, 73*, 992–1012. doi: 10.1177/000312240807300606

Louis, W. R. (2009). Collective action—And then what? *Journal of Social Issues, 65*, 727–748. doi: 10.1111/j.1540-4560.2009.01623.x

Louis, W. R., La Macchia, S. T., Amiot, C. E., Thomas, E. F., Blackwood, L. M., Mavor, K. I., & Saeri, A. (2016). Causality in the study of collective action and political behavior. In F. M. Moghaddam & R. Harré (Eds.), *Causes and consequences: A multidisciplinary exploration.* (pp. 277–302). Santa Barbara, CA: Praeger.

Louis, W. R., Mavor, K. I., La Macchia, S. T., & Amiot, C. E. (2014). Social justice and psychology: What is, and what should be. *Journal of Theoretical and Philosophical Psychology, 34*, 14–27. doi: 10.1037/a0033033

Louis, W. R., Mavor, K. I., & Terry, D. J. (2003). Reflections on the statistical analysis of personality and norms in war, peace, and prejudice: Are deviant minorities the problem? *Analyses of Social Issues and Public Policy, 3*, 189–198. doi:10.1111/j.1530-2415.2003.00025.x

Louis, W. R., Terry, D. J., & Fielding, K. S. (2005). Sustained versus eroding community engagement. In D. Gardiner & K. Scott (Eds.), *Proceedings of international conference on engaging communities* (pp. 1–21). Brisbane, Australia: QLD Department of Main Roads.

McAdam, D., McCarthy, J. D., & Zald, M. N. (Eds.). (1996). *Comparative perspectives on social movements: Political opportunities, mobilizing structures, and cultural framings.* Cambridge, England: Cambridge University Press.

McCarthy, J. D., & Zald, M. N. (1977). Resource mobilization and social movements: A partial theory. *American Journal of Sociology, 82*, 1212–1241.

McDonald, R. I., Fielding, K. S., & Louis, W. R. (2014). Conflicting norms highlight the need for action. *Environment and Behavior, 46*, 139–162. doi: 10.1016/j.jnc.2013.11.005

McGarty, C., Bliuc, A. M., Thomas, E. F., & Bongiorno, R. (2009). Collective action as the material expression of opinion-based group membership. *Journal of Social Issues, 65*, 839–858. doi: 10.1111/j.1540-4560.2009.01627.x

Montgomery, S. A., & Stewart, A. J. (2012). Privileged allies in lesbian and gay rights activism. *Journal of Social Issues*, *68*, 162–177. doi: 10.1111/j.1540-4560.2012.01742.x

Preacher, K. J., & Hayes, A. F. (2008). Asymptotic and resampling strategies for assessing and comparing indirect effects in multiple mediator models. *Behavior Research Methods*, *40*, 879–891. doi: 10.3758/BRM.40.3.879

Putnam, R. D. (1995). Bowling alone: America's declining social capital. *Journal of Democracy*, *6*, pp. 65–78. doi: 10.1353/jod.1995.0002

Putnam, R. D. (2000). *Bowling alone: The collapse and revival of American community*. Toronto, Canada: Simon & Schuster.

Saab, R., Tausch, N., Spears, R., & Cheung, W. Y. (2015). Acting in solidarity: Testing an extended dual pathway model of collective action by bystander group members. *British Journal of Social Psychology*, *3*, 539–560. doi: 10.1111/bjso.12095

Simon, B., & Klandermans, B. (2001). Towards a social psychological analysis of politicized collective identity. *American Psychologist*, *56*, 319–331. doi: 10.1037/0003-066X.56.4.319

Stuart, A., Thomas, E. F., Donaghue, N., & Russell, A. (2013) 'We may be pirates but we are not protesters': Identity in the Sea Shepherd Conservation Society. *Political Psychology*, *34*, 753–777. doi: 10.1111/pops.12016

Stürmer, S., & Simon, B. (2004). Collective action: Towards a dual-pathway model. *European Review of Social Psychology*, *15*, 59–99. doi: 10.1111/pops.12016

Subašić, E., Reynolds, K. J., & Turner, J. C. (2008). The political solidarity model of social change: Dynamics of self-categorization in intergroup power relations, *Personality and Social Psychology Review*, *12*, 330–352. doi: 10.1177/1088868308323223

Sweetman, J., Leach, C. W., Spears, R., Pratto, F., & Saab, R. (2013). "I Have a Dream": A typology of social change goals. *Journal of Social and Political Psychology*, *1*, 293–320. doi:10.5964/jspp.v1i1.85

Thomas, E. F., & Louis, W. R. (2013). Doing democracy: The social psychological mobilization and consequences of collective action. *Social Issues and Policy Review*, *7*, 173–200. doi: 10.1111/j.1751-2409.2012.01047.x

Thomas, E. F., McGarty, C., & Mavor, K. I (2009a). Aligning identities, emotions and beliefs to create sustained support for social and political action. *Personality and Social Psychology Review*, *13*, 194–218. doi: 10.1177/1088868309341563

Thomas, E. F., McGarty, C., & Mavor, K. I (2009b). Transforming 'apathy into movement'. *Personality and Social Psychology Review*, *13*, 310–333. doi:10.1177/1088868309343290

Thomas, E. F., McGarty, C., & Louis, W. R. (2014). Social interaction and psychological pathways to political extremism. *European Journal of Social Psychology*, *44*, 15–22. doi: 10.1002/ejsp.1988

Thomas, E. F., McGarty, C., Lala, G., Stuart, A., Hall, L. J., & Goddard, A. (2015). Whatever happened to Kony2012? Understanding a global internet phenomenon as an emergent social identity. *European Journal of Social Psychology*, *45*, 356–367. doi: 10.1002/ejsp.2094

Turner-Zwinkels, F., van Zomeren, M., & Postmes, T. (2015). Politicization during the 2012 US presidential elections: Bridging the personal and the political through an identity content approach. *Personality and Social Psychology Bulletin*, *41*, 433–455. doi: 10.1177/0146167215569494

van Stekelenburg, J., Klandermans, B., & Akkerman, A. (2016). Does civic participation stimulate political activity? *Journal of Social Issues*, *72*(2), 286–314.

Van Zomeren, M., Leach, C. W., & Spears, R. (2012). Protesters as "Passionate Economists". *Personality and Social Psychology Review*, *16*, 180–198. doi: 10.1177/1088868311430835

Van Zomeren, M., Postmes, T., & Spears, R. (2008). Toward an integrative social identity model of collective action. *Psychological Bulletin*, *134*, 504–535. doi: 10.1037/0033-2909.134.4.504

WINNIFRED R. LOUIS is an Associate Professor in the School of Psychology at The University of Queensland. She received her PhD from McGill University in 2001. Her research interests focus on the influence of identity and norms on social decision making.

CATHERINE E. AMIOT is an Associate Professor in the Department of Psychology at Université du Québec à Montréal. Her research program addresses: (1) how new identities are integrated into an individuals' self-concept, (2) how norms are internalized and adopted in a manner that is self-determined, and (3) social psychological principles and human-animal relations.

EMMA F. THOMAS is an Australian Research Council Early Career Researcher and Senior Lecturer in the School of Psychology & Exercise Science at Murdoch University. Her background is in social and political psychology and she researches the ways that people come together to resist social inequality and injustice.

LEDA BLACKWOOD is a Social Psychologist at the University of Bath whose research examines inter- and intragroup processes of leadership, politicization, and social movement participation. She is currently funded by the Leverhulme Trust to examine how the actions of government and other authorities shape intracommunity struggles over leadership and identity.

Journal of Social Issues, Vol. 72, No. 2, 2016, pp. 264–285
doi: 10.1111/josi.12166

Navigating Multiple Identities: The Simultaneous Influence of Advantaged and Disadvantaged Identities on Politicization and Activism

Nicola Curtin[*]
Clark University

Anna Kende
Eötvös Loránd University

Judit Kende
University of Leuven

Most identity-based models of activism assume that action is motivated either by a disadvantaged identity (predicting own-group activism), or a feeling of solidarity with disadvantaged groups (predicting ally activism). They do not account for advantaged and disadvantaged identifications within the same person. Yet many activists have both advantaged and disadvantaged identities. Two interview studies from Hungary and the United States (N = 47) were used to examine how both disadvantaged and advantaged identities influence politicization and activism (both own-group and ally), via both direct and indirect experiences of marginalization and privilege. We also discuss the emergence of new identities from activist engagements and how such new activist identities recursively influence activism and politicization. We conclude our analysis by arguing that identity-based organizations may be more successful emphasizing multiple and intersecting identities and the structural aspects of disadvantages rather than singular disadvantaged identities.

Every activist has a personal story about becoming an activist and what their activism means to them. These stories may capture important common themes that allow us to better understand the development of political identities, as well as

---

[*]Correspondence concerning this article should be addressed to Nicola Curtin, Clark University, 950 Main Street, Worcester, MA 01610. Tel: 508-793-7261; [e-mail: NCurtin@clarku.edu]. Order of the authorship is alphabetical.

motivations for activism. These stories also provide the opportunity to understand why people who occupy different positions in society, with strikingly different personal experiences within these positions, devote themselves to activism. The current paper used interview data collected from 47 activists across two national contexts to examine how attending to *both* advantaged and disadvantaged identities within the same person might deepen our understanding of activism. We use the terms "advantaged identity" and "disadvantaged identity" throughout the paper to refer to identities based on membership in either advantaged or disadvantaged groups. We recognize, however, that identities themselves are not necessarily "advantaged" or not, rather they form based on membership(s) in group(s) that occupy particular locations on a social hierarchy. We explored how activists understood their identities to be shaped by their activism, in order to capture the dynamic interplay of identity and activism. The main purpose of this article is to highlight areas that are currently underexamined in the literature on activism, but which may deepen our understanding of activists: (a) whether and how both disadvantaged *and* advantaged identities influence politicization (people's deliberate engagement in the intergroup power struggles to overcome their shared grievances; Simon & Klandermans, 2001) and activism and (b) whether and how activism provides opportunities for (re)politicization and the emergence of new identities that reconcile tensions among disadvantaged and advantaged identities.

Multiple and Intersecting Identities in Activism

Most research on activism focuses on specific issues or specific groups of activists (e.g., environmental activism or indigenous rights activists), and has most commonly sought to explain own-group, grievance-based action related to identity, with less attention paid to ally activism (those who are engaged in activism in alliance with a group they do not belong to). Characteristic of this research has been what Greenwood (2012) calls the *singular* identity approach. For example, in explaining women's rights activism, researchers have focused specifically on gender identity or activist identity. In focusing on singular identities, researchers tend to examine disadvantaged and advantaged identities in isolation from each other (see van Zomeren, Postmes, & Spears, 2008, for a meta-analysis of the literature on collective action on behalf of the own-group with a primary focus on disadvantaged identities, and van Zomeren, Postmes, Spears, & Bettache, 2011, for an extension of their model to ally activism, with a focus on advantaged groups).

However, as do all individuals, activists hold multiple, sometimes conflicting identities. We use the term "advantaged" and "disadvantaged" to refer to individuals belonging to groups with relative high or low status or power, respectively, in a particular social context. Individuals may possess a basic awareness that others perceive them as belonging to a group, or they may have a deeper sense of shared identification with other group members. Furthermore, people become engaged in activism for reasons other than the expression of a specific identity, or because they belong to a specific group (e.g., Cole & Stewart, 1996; Klandermans, 2003) and activism itself fosters identity development (which may, in turn, increase or broaden commitment; e.g., Drury & Reicher, 2009). We examined activists' own narratives in order to explore how holding more than one salient identity relevant to activism—and especially holding both advantaged and disadvantaged identities—shapes activist engagement. We also examined the mutually reinforcing and constitutive relationship between identities and activism.

Theoretical Approach and Framework

Social identity versus politicized identification.   Drawing largely on social identity theory (Tajfel & Turner, 1979) and self-categorization theory (Turner, 1985), decades of social psychological research has shown that collective action is predicted by identification with a relevant social group, the perception of group-based injustice, and beliefs in the group's efficacy in achieving social change (van Zomeren, 2013; van Zomeren et al., 2008). However, although the strength of in-group identity among members of low-status groups is important (Iyer & Ryan, 2009), simple identification with one's sociological group does not sufficiently explain engagement in collective action (e.g., de Weerd & Klandermans, 1999; van Stekelenburg, Klandermans, & Akkerman, 2016; for an overview see Klandermans, 2014).

There is evidence that politicized identities (Simon & Klandermans, 2001; van Zomeren et al., 2008), opinion-based identities (i.e., groups with whom an individual shares salient opinions, McGarty, Bliuc, Thomas, & Bongiorno, 2009) or identification with a specific social movement (Stürmer & Simon, 2004) are better predictors of engagement in collective action (e.g., van Zomeren et al., 2008) and activism (e.g., Stürmer & Simon, 2004) than identification with nominal sociological categories. In using the term *politicized identification* in this paper, we draw on Simon and Klandermans's (2001) notion of politicized identification as involving an awareness of system-based group inequalities and a sense of grievance. However, we also rely on McGarty et al. (2009) argument that some groups form opinion-based identities based on a sense of shared beliefs about a particular social issue, in this case we argue that members share a sense of grievance about group-based inequality. Collective action is therefore more accurately explained by a commitment to act on behalf of a group to challenge injustices (i.e., by the politicization of identity) than social group membership (Thomas, Mavor, & McGarty, 2012). Politicized identities are of particular interest, as they can override other impediments to action, such as low-efficacy beliefs (Kelly & Breinlinger,

1995; van Zomeren et al., 2008) or high personal costs (see Louis, Taylor, & Neil, 2004; Stürmer & Simon, 2004).

Politicized identification and activism.   The process of identity politicization is similar for both own-group activists and ally activists. Politicized collective identity develops through the process of understanding the structural aspects of shared grievances and injustices and the need for social change. It also involves a conscious engagement in power struggles to achieve this change. For own-group activists, this entails placing the in-group grievances in a political context by recognizing the collective disadvantages of the in-group (Simon & Klandermans, 2001; van Stekelenburg & Klandermans, 2010). For ally activists, the politicization of identities entails placing the out-group grievances and the in-group privileges (i.e., benefits that the in-group enjoys merely as a result of belonging to that particular group) in context, that is, recognizing the collective disadvantages of the out-group possibly as the result of the in-group's privileges, but so far research has largely neglected this issue. A notable exception is the study of Russell and Bohan (2016) that argues that second-order change (i.e., the recognition of the need for structural changes; see also Curtin, Stewart, & Cole, 2015) are necessary for true allyship.

We also drew on intersectionality theory (Crenshaw, 1991) that argues that social identities cannot be understood in isolation, and that people's lived experiences are informed simultaneously by multiple identities, and intersections of multiple group memberships create distinct identities. As Cole (2009) pointed out, some members of disadvantaged groups also identify with advantaged groups. Thus, we attended to the degree to which multiple—especially the intersections of advantaged and disadvantaged—identities played a role in participants' political socialization and activist commitments toward promoting social change to overcome social injustices that produce the system of privileges and inequalities (Case, Iuzzini, & Hopkins, 2012). The degree to which identities are politicized is central to predicting activism. However, we need to consider that the process of politicization is shaped by the multiplicity of available identities and their intersections, as well as experiences of marginalization and privilege connected to one's identities. Here we use the term marginalization to mean experiences of feeling considered less or different from others based on disadvantaged identities (e.g., discrimination, stigmatization, invisibility, or exclusion, see Smart Richman & Leary, 2009).

Recursive Relationship between Politicized Identification and Activism

Though typical unidirectional models of activism assume a sequential relationship wherein identity predicts activism, there is evidence that activism provides opportunities for (re)politicization and the emergence of new identities in a recursive way (Drury & Reicher, 2000). Furthermore, as we have stated, some activists become engaged for reasons other than identity concerns (in particular in issue-based activism or ally activism) and activism itself could foster identity development (which may, in turn, increase or broaden commitment). Therefore, we assumed that politicized identification and activism were dynamically related; and that while activism might follow the development of a politicized identification, it may also be the case that engagement in activism could precede the development of a politicized identity or further shape it. We paid attention to the ways in which activist narratives highlighted the recursive relationships between identity and activism, and how identifications emerged or changed over time, especially in case of ally activism, where in-group identity played an indirect role, rather than influencing activism through in-group grievances.

Overview of Current Project

Our goal was to understand activists' narratives of how experiences connected to their multiple advantaged and disadvantaged identities led to activism, as well as how activism informed (re)politicization or the emergence of new identities. The use of qualitative methods is justified by our interest in *how* multiple identities, the process of politicization and activism are connected, and by the fact that the quantification of these concepts is limited due to their heterogeneity described earlier. Finally, we wanted to use our analysis as the basis for suggestions for how theories of collective action might be served by attending to multiple identities and recursive processes.

Data were drawn from two interview studies, conducted in Hungary and the United States. The two sets of interviews were conducted separately and focused on different groups of activists. The Hungarian study recruited people engaged in many different forms of activism (own-group, ally, and issue-based), and offered a broad perspective to understanding the interplay between multiple – advantaged (e.g., Hungarian majority, heterosexual, and upper middle class) and disadvantaged (e.g., Roma, gay, and homeless) identities and forms of activism. The U.S. study targeted "ally" activists in particular (people who held advantaged group identities, such as heterosexual, cisgender, or European American, and were engaged in alliance with disadvantaged group members, such as lesbian, gay or bisexual people, transgender people, or people of color). Both studies examined participants' understandings of their identities and activism, the specific people and events that influenced their decisions to become or stay engaged, and challenges to being an activist. These two samples provided a unique opportunity to explore a broader set of questions related to the tensions and opportunities that multiple identities play within the same individual in activism.

Method

Sample 1: Hungarian Activists

Semistructured interviews (ranging in length from 48 to 215 minutes, $M = 122$ minutes) were conducted with 24 self-identified activists from the capital city, Budapest. Respondents participated voluntarily without receiving compensation for their participation. Convenience and snowball sampling were used. All participants were engaged in own group, ally, or issue-based activism. Twelve participants were involved with activism related to (or as a part of) their paid work, and all but two participants were currently engaged in some kind of unpaid activist work as well; 13 women, and 11 men were interviewed. The average participant age was 39 years (range of 23–59 years). All interviews were conducted in Hungarian by the 3rd author and trained research assistants. All excerpts included here were translated by the 2nd and 3rd authors.

Sample 2: U.S. Activists

Semistructured interviews (28–136 minutes, $M = 89$ minutes) were conducted with 19 ally activists from several cities in the Northeastern U.S. Participants were given a $20 gift certificate in compensation for their participation. Convenience and snowball sampling were used. Participants had to be over 18 years, identify as an "ally," and have participated in, or be currently active in, "community-based engagement" (paid or unpaid). All participants identified as an advantaged-group ally to at least one disadvantaged group (as opposed to being a disadvantaged ally to another disadvantaged group). A number of the participants were involved with activism related to their paid work, but almost all participants were currently engaged in some kind of unpaid activism. Thirteen women and 6 men participated, with an average age of 45 years (range of 22–78 years). Although participants were recruited as allies, most of them mentioned that they had also engaged in activism on behalf of groups to which they belonged. Therefore, although they were conceptualized as "ally activists," many were also active in own group or issue-based activism (e.g., environmentalism or antiwar). Participants self-identified the groups with whom they felt they were allied. All interviews were conducted in English, by the 1st author.

Interview Procedure

Similar procedures were used for interviews in both Hungary and the United States. Interviews took place at a location chosen by participants, usually their home, but also interviewers' offices and private rooms at public libraries. In both samples, interviewees were first asked to give general background information about themselves before answering questions related to their identity and activism. All interviews were semistructured, and interviewers followed up on specific issues raised by participants, even while adhering to a general question outline. The specific interview guides and questions are available upon request. All interviews were audio-recorded and were fully transcribed by research assistants or professional transcribers. All interviews were imported into NVivo 10.0 (QSR, 2012) for data management and analysis.

Analytic Procedure

We thematically coded all interview texts using deductive and inductive "theoretical" thematic analysis approach (Braun & Clarke, 2006, p. 84). We used an iterative coding process (Galletta, 2013), moving from a general discussion based on our readings of both sets of interviews, to coding first the Hungarian interviews, then the U.S. interviews (where we developed additional codes), and then moving back to the Hungarian interviews. The two studies used a different interview protocol, asking somewhat different questions of the participants. However, the purpose of our analysis was not to focus on specific responses to specific questions, but rather to focus on similar themes that emerged across the interviews, across the two countries. It is, therefore, not our claim that we are comparing responses, either across or within the two countries, but rather that we are examining each set of interviews using a set of themes that were developed both deductively (based on the relevant themes of the literature) and inductively (based on the interviews themselves; Braun & Clarke, 2006) in order to identify patterns of the dynamic interplay between identity and activism. An initial coding system was developed based on the readings of the Hungarian interviews, and applied to the Hungarian dataset (Phase 1). The Phase 1 codebook consisted of 16 codes. These codes were then applied to the U.S. interviews by the first author and trained research assistants. While coding the U.S. interviews, we identified five additional codes (Phase 2). These Phase 2 codes were applied to the Hungarian interviews (Phase 3). In this way, there was a layered iterative approach to data analysis. Within each set of interviews there were several rounds of discussion and coding, but the analysis of each sample also fed into the analysis of the other sample.

After all analyses were completed, all authors read through our coded data and decided on the general findings that were most relevant in addressing our research interests (Phase 4). To reiterate, our interest here was a focus on participants' narratives related to intersecting advantaged and disadvantaged identities, the politicization of their identities and their role in activism, and the influence of activism itself on identification and/or politicization. We do not present the themes and data here (the full codebook is available as supplementary material). Rather, we discuss general findings, extrapolated via discussion from the codes, as they relate to each of our areas of interest.

Results

Disadvantaged and Advantaged Identities Influence Politicization and Activism

All our participants held multiple disadvantaged and advantaged identities and the interplay among intersecting identities influenced their politicization and activism. Participants' experiences of marginalization as disadvantaged group members were central for both own-group *and* ally activism. Their experiences of marginalization were usually personal, but indirect and historical experiences of marginalization also opened the way for activism. Participants' experiences and awareness of being privileged were also crucial for ally activism. Again, they experienced privilege personally, but historical group-based awareness of privilege was also an entry point to ally activism.

Disadvantaged identities fostered not only own-group but also ally activism. Consistent with many models of own-group activism, participants indicated that their personal experiences of marginalization both "awakened" them to issues of justice, fostered a politicized identity (Cross, 1978; Gurin, Miller, & Gurin, 1980), and also informed their decisions to become engaged in own-group activism.

For some participants, personal experiences of marginalization facilitated both own group and *ally* engagement because participants saw marginalization of their own and other disadvantaged groups to be similar, or saw oppressive social practices as equally affecting their own and other disadvantaged groups. For example, a homeless woman activist described how she felt; she shared some experiences with members of other marginalized groups.

H004: I know what it's like when there's nobody saying: come here, I'll help you. (. . .) We went to the gay pride, and if needed, we would protest against evicting people.

Similarly, a cisgender woman indicated that her work as an ally to transgender people was related to her experiences of sexism.

US005: . . . as I mentioned before, the kinds of institutional oppressions that I care about, you know I am harmed by . . . So, for example, transphobia really comes down to sexism in a lot of ways. (. . .) there are really specific ways that men and women are expected to behave and very severe consequences for people who step out of them and transphobia is related to a particular manifestation of that.

Other participants talked about experiencing discrimination by members of their own social group based on their membership in another group. A gay participant of Roma ethnicity described how he was discriminated against in the gay community for being Roma and in the Roma community for being gay.

Such experiences of multiple marginalization made the similarities between the marginalization of both one's own and other minority groups more conspicuous.

H017: Roma people are prejudiced too. Sometimes they call me a fag. It's disappointing.
Interviewee: And gay people call you a Gypsy? H017: Yes, of course, they do that too. They have called me a dirty Gypsy, and then I told them to urgently seek a psychologist. And the Gypsies who called me a fag, I just told them off.

Identifying with historically marginalized groups also fostered own-group and ally activism. Participants recalled memories of marginalization that were not experienced directly by a participant, but by their family or by members of their in-group in the past. Just like personal experiences, historical experiences of marginalization also facilitated both own group and ally activism.

Some participants saw the historical marginalization of their in-group as related to their group's current conditions. For example, a Hungarian activist who worked for ethnic Hungarians living in other countries described her grandparents talking about their historical grievances as a basis for her current activism in the same cause.

H022: Maybe the times spent with my grandparents, the stories they told, the places they took me to. My grandfather who comes from Transylvania and who was an American prisoner of war took me to the forest that used to belong to us. I think things like these shaped my thinking.

Others connected their group's historical treatment to the current marginalization of other disadvantaged groups leading to an increased awareness of inequality. For example, an ally activist working with prison inmates told how her family's historical experience of being powerless sensitized her to powerless people today.

H009: There is a great sensitivity in all of us and it might come from family history. My father's family were aristocrats and they were cruelly mistreated after World War II. They were dumped from their castle, all their things were confiscated and they were deported to the countryside. And I think because of this, in the whole family and in the way my father brought us up there was a huge sensitization to be empathetic with and attentive to powerless people and those who have it worse.

Other participants also connected their group's historical marginalization to increased interest in politics and awareness of injustice.

US006: And I think the really big thing for me growing up, as I was born in 1942, for Jewish kids of my age (. . .) we all grew up in the shadow of the Holocaust. There were no immediate family members of ours who had been lost, but we just knew about it. (. . .) I mean, I was not an activist as a kid, or even as a teenager, but I was interested in what was going on in the world.

H021: My father and his father were ethnic Germans, a peasant family. They could have had a straightforward career path under communism, but partly because they were ethnic Germans, partly because they had these peasant roots, they were declared class enemies. Therefore, the family had very high expectation when the system changed (. . .) my awakening came in this period, when I saw these hardworking people who hated the previous [communist] system and who had it even worse in the new system, losing their jobs. And this is what I brought from home that something is really wrong with the world and I really wanted to understand why it is so.

Experiences and awareness of privilege fostered ally activism.   The awareness of privileges among ally activists was crucial for their ally activism. Similar to developing a critical consciousness related to one's group's marginal status, developing an awareness of one's own privilege, or one's group's privileges were described both a resource and an imperative for activism.

US006: (. . .) I'm straight, so I have a lot of unearned privilege. (. . .) if you have that unearned privilege in an unjust world, to me what do you do with it? To me, the answer is you use it. I mean it's like inheriting money. You use it to help people who don't have it.

These events, similar to experiences of discrimination, also sometimes elicited outrage. As one U.S. participant reported, her current antiracism work was based on anger.

US010: I was really pissed off that I had been allowed to walk the earth as a White person in such a state of what I now call a combined arrogant naiveté.

Awareness of privileges connected to one's advantaged in-group identity and experiences of marginalization connected to one's disadvantaged identities led to a simultaneous awareness of own-group privileges and out-group grievances and generalized to an interest in issues affecting other groups (although we note that this finding was only present in the Hungarian sample, no U.S. participant explicitly mentioned this). For example, a gay male participant who used to work for gay organizations switched to working against gender-based violence.

H013: We started working on the cases of battered women from the money we got for representing gay rights. (. . .) A gay man may be fired and therefore needs to find a new job that he doesn't like that much. But when a kindergarten age child is raped by her own father or stepfather (. . .) is an incomparably more severe situation than what happens to gay men, so I decided that this is hundred times more important and we use the money we got for supporting gay rights to protect these women and children.

In a similar fashion, awareness of current privileges was sometimes combined with historical experiences of marginalization. For some participants, this combination meant a responsibility for acting on behalf of disadvantaged outgroups that are currently in a similar position as the own-group used to be. In this example, a Jewish participant talks about working for Roma people as she sees the marginalization of the Roma to be similar to the historical marginalization of Jewish people.

H023: She [my mother] hates this country because she lives with a second generation [Holocaust] trauma (. . .) My mother is prejudiced, while she's so aroused about all things connected to being Jewish, she is much less so about the Roma, she doesn't understand why I want to deal with their issues. [Meanwhile] several Roma people were killed, families were attacked. I don't necessarily have to be Roma to understand what's happening and once I understand I am responsible and I have to act. I can't turn my back.

Emerging Activist and Ally Activist Identities Catalyze Activism and (Re)politicization

Activist and/or ally activist identities were frequently explicitly mentioned by all our participants. These identities emerged from doing activism and cross-cut existing social identities that participants held on the basis of belonging to various social groups and categories. The newly emerged activist and ally activist identities further catalyzed activism and (re)politicization.

"Doing activism" as an identity. Some participants reported that their engagement in activism positively reinforced their identity as members of a disadvantaged group. First, for in-group activists, activism was often related to coming to terms with their disadvantaged group membership after battling the negative stereotypes of the majority society. Countering the negative stereotypes and increased focus meant stronger in-group identification. Second, spending more time in these identity-based groups also meant an increased focus on the specific marginalized identity.

H004: [This homeless activist group] is also positive because it gives one back a kind of self-esteem.

H006: First, I was just a lonesome cyclist on the road, the cars were honking and they were cursing at me and I felt really alone. And suddenly I felt a huge support, that other people were going through the same and that we're stronger together. (. . .) I realized that this was exactly what I was looking for. I had been cycling for a long time but I didn't know any likeminded people: that we cycle and why this is important. I didn't know anybody like this, nobody. When they sought me out, I've realized that this group thinks exactly like me.

For many participants, being an activist in itself became an important group identity. At times, this activist identity was experienced as an oppositional identity related to nonactivists who held negative attitudes toward activism.

H018: My family says at a certain level that I'm a total idiot. They find it really weird that I work with psychiatric patients.

The community of activists became an important in-group, with whom they shared not just a sociological, but also an opinion-based group membership.

H003: That [my group] was a real community with values I accepted and with adventures that were formative for young people and important for me.

H002: I was volunteering in rescue shelters for dogs and I felt I was not as effective doing this work alone, so I've started to organize a team.

"Doing activism" catalyzes politicization. With few exceptions, both own-group and ally activism resulted in learning more about the groups' grievances. Participants linked this new knowledge to their increased politicization and further activism, helping them place grievances into a political context.

H005: I'd started going to the Budapest Pride when it was still a huge party. Then 2007 was the worst when we actually had to flee, there were stones the size of my fist flying half a meter from my face . . . I was reading the news after the Pride and despite the fact that a totally peaceful and harmless group was attacked, all the blogs, all the comments were against us . . . Extremists were hunting us down and a lot of people were attacked, girls too, people I know also. The police were unwilling to do anything.

Ally identities. Not surprisingly, the notion of an "ally identity" can be considered a subset of the broader "activist" identity, and was common throughout the U.S. interviews. Ally identities were complex. Being seen as an ally of a disadvantaged group was often perceived as unvalued or discouraged by other advantaged group members, thus, ally identities were also often presented as marginal or inferior. At the same time, an ally's advantaged group membership granted them protections that did not apply to members of the marginalized group they were working with.

US006: I don't have to worry that somebody's going to say something or do something. I've never had to worry about being fired from my job. (. . .) being an ally can sometimes bring on some of, not all of the same risks, but some of the same risks.

Another issue that came up was one of choice deriving from the privilege allies had. One could decide whether or not to keep the privileged identity, or do the activism.

US011: I think being an ally is an interesting position in these contexts because I feel faced with this choice all the time that this is where my values are and this is the work I want to be doing but that I have access to like the whole world of all the privileges. Like yeah, I'm gay, but whatever it's totally mitigated by my class and race. I could wake up tomorrow, get my MBA from [Business School], go into finance and make myself terrifically rich and have a lovely life for myself and do no work on change.

Some participants also indicated that "ally" is a kind of aspirational identity. This perspective is nicely summarized here:

Interviewer: *Do you consider yourself to be an ally?* **US014**: I do. I think some of my uneasiness comes in with how good of an ally I am at any given time or just in general. Certainly at the very least you can be an aspiring ally, work very hard to do that in a very honest and real way.

Also worth noting here is that participants were, at times, allies to several different groups of people or even different issues. The term "ally" seemed more to reflect the commitment to activism on behalf of other groups than a commitment to a particular group (again, as above, making it more similar to an opinion-based group than a sociological category).

In both these cases (activist identities and ally identities), multiple issues were often subsumed under a broader identity category. Therefore, for example, an "activist" identity could encompass multiple activist commitments, including both own-group and ally activism; or "ally" identities could include commitments to several other-group issues. As described, these identities usually emerged *from* at least some form of initial activism (and did not precede it), and were a means of encompassing both advantaged and disadvantaged identities. The emerged activist identities then further influenced politicization and strengthened the commitment to activism.

Discussion

The purpose of our study was to use activist narratives to explore the role that multiple identities, within the same individual, play in activism and thus identify some areas of inquiry currently understudied or undertheorized in the social psychological literature. We will summarize our findings by discussing the particular questions they raise for models of collective action, but at the same time these findings should be beneficial for organizers looking to better understand how activists become, and stay engaged.

Issue 1: Attending to Advantaged and Disadvantaged Identity in the Same Person

Ally activists linked their political awareness and activism on behalf of out-groups to their own identities as members of disadvantaged groups. The literature on discrimination rightly argues that advantaged and disadvantaged group members will have different responses to experiences of discrimination (e.g., Barlow, Sibley, & Hornsey, 2012). However, people may be advantaged along some dimensions and disadvantaged along others. Our findings suggest that some people draw on their experiences of marginalization along one identity dimension, to understand structural inequalities in other dimensions (even those in which they are relatively advantaged; see also Croteau, Talbot, Lance, & Evans, 2002). If we attend to both advantaged and disadvantaged identities, it may suggest more complex responses to discrimination than are currently accounted for in the social identity literature on collective action.

Our finding that participants associated experiences of own-group discrimination with *increased* awareness of other forms of discrimination and ally activism is different from recent research (e.g., Craig & Richeson, 2014). Craig and Richeson found that experiences of discrimination foster positive attitudes within a broad identity category (i.e., across different racial boundaries), but are associated with negative attitudes across identity categories (from race to sexual orientation). Given that our participants were activists, they are clearly a unique group of people. Their counter-typical response to personal experiences of marginalization may be the very reason they became activists, and allies, in the first place. Perhaps there is something about the small subset of people who become ally activists that fosters "altruism born of suffering" (Vollhardt, 2009). Recent work on inclusive and exclusive victim consciousness (Vollhardt, 2015) might be useful to understanding these findings. Taking into consideration the complications around establishing "victim status," we draw more on the conceptual distinctions of inclusive versus exclusive awareness of injustices and suffering. The theory highlights the difference between those who consider their in-group's suffering unique (exclusive victim consciousness) and those who understand the similarities between processes of victimization of own-group and other groups (inclusive victim consciousness). Perhaps even the difference between people whose experiences of marginalization result in own-group (exclusive victim consciousness) versus ally (inclusive victim consciousness) activism can be modeled by this distinction. However, we can supplement these findings by pointing out that the transition from in-group to ally activism was explained by the interplay between one's experiences based on multiple identities and understanding oppression through personal experiences of *both* disadvantage and privilege.

Issue 2: To What Degree are Activist Identities Dual (or Multiple) Identities?

Our participants' activist and ally identities developed over time as a result of increased behavioral commitment. These identities, rather than reflecting a sense of shared "social group" categorization, seem better represented as opinion-based groups. This is consistent with recent research arguing that opinion-based group membership can be sharpened or hardened by group-based interaction (e.g., Thomas & McGarty, 2009). The emergence of these identities as a result of activism is also consistent with research on the effects of mass protest participation on collective identification and empowerment (Drury & Reicher, 2000; though we note that not all activists here had participated in mass protests).

A sense of identification, based on shared beliefs allowed for shifting between mobilizing for different groups and create a system of inclusion or exclusion of different groups of people within a particular "activist" identity. We saw this most clearly among advantaged group members who were working in alliance with disadvantaged groups. Almost all reported being allies (based on their behavior) to at least two groups of disadvantaged people, and even as they recognized important differences between the groups, most subsumed these differences under a broad identification with a commitment to acting to create social change.

Although the previous research has established that activist or opinion-based identities may be better predictors of engagement than sociological group identities, there has been little exploration of the degree to which these "activist" and "ally" identities may be (or require) dual or multiple identifications (see Louis, Amiot, Thomas, & Blackwood, 2016). For disadvantaged groups, this may mean identification both with their marginalized group and a broader superordinate identity shared with advantaged group members (as Simon & Grabow, 2010, found for Russian-Germans active in Germany). For advantaged group members, it might mean that they identify both with their advantaged group (even as they feel some dismay or dissatisfaction with the advantage that this identity confers), and with the disadvantaged group. Though, we note that Subašić, Reynolds, and Turner (2008) argue that this sense of affiliation or political solidarity is less about shared identification than shared beliefs that something about the power structure needs to change.

Issue 3: When do Multiple Identities Encourage Activism and Build Coalitions?

All participants reported having multiple identities, and most participants drew connections between more than one social group identity and their commitment to activism. Tensions between identifying with multiple disadvantaged groups that are in conflict with each other, or between advantaged and disadvantaged identities (such as experiencing discrimination in some contexts and privilege in others), or (in the Hungarian sample) seeing the advantages conferred by one's privileged identity as somehow "outweighing" the disadvantages of a marginalized identity, all facilitated activism, and in particular ally activism.

To our knowledge, only one study (Croteau et al., 2002) has examined the ways that advantaged and disadvantaged identities influence each other in the development of awareness of power and oppression (though see also Case, 2012, for a discussion of this issue in the lives of European American antiracist women). However, in our samples, this was a common theme raised by participants that indicates that approaches based on singular identities to explaining activism may be missing the ways in which multiple identities influence each other. Of course, as discussed above, it may also be that these tensions eventually are subsumed under opinion-based group identities.

Considering the mounting evidence that shared identifications may inhibit collective action (Dovidio, Gaertner, & Saguy, 2009), we think it is especially important for models of collective action to begin asking questions about how some activists seem to have avoided these challenges (see Droogendyk, Wright, Lubensky, & Louis, 2016, for a more thorough discussion of these issues). Our findings suggest that the kind of critical awareness that allows allies to think carefully about how they are being perceived by disadvantaged groups may also allow those same people to hold complex multiple identifications. It is important to understand whether such awareness is central to successful activism. Attending to the identity-based *outcomes* of activism, such as emergent activist or ally identities, may be one way to understanding how activists build inclusive superordinate identities, and effective coalitions (see Cakal, Eller, Sirlopu, & Pérez, 2016, for the mobilizing effect of a common in-group identity).

Our results also pointed to the importance of both historical and personal experiences of discrimination in the development of politicized identifications and decisions to engage in activism. Some activists were deeply moved by events that they had not personally experienced. These activists' social identities were also influenced by the collective memory and representations of the group's historical and current intergroup relations (Liu & Hilton, 2005). They were more sensitive to out-group injustices and, when they compared their group's historical marginalization to their group's current position in society, they became more aware of the structural aspects of their current privileges.

Our findings are consistent with evidence that even "distant" sociopolitical events can have politicizing effects and facilitate activism (Curtin, Stewart, & Duncan, 2010; Stewart & Healy, 1989), yet these relationships are rarely tested directly. Further, little attempt has been made to distinguish between direct (personal) and indirect (historical) events, or even the degree to which they may be dependent on each other. Attending to intersectional identities, as we have tried to do here, allows for a more nuanced understanding of how different experiences politicize and catalyze individuals for social change (Stewart, Winter, Henderson-King, & Henderson-King, 2015).

We also want to highlight another finding in relation to this point. Several activists discussed their ally identity as aspirational. In some ways, this reflected a kind of humility. They understood that being an ally is difficult. They sometimes indicated that though they might want to be an ally, they may not always be perceived that way by disadvantaged groups, or live up to that desire. Yet, this aspirational mindset also reflected a desire to be a part of creating positive social change, and an underlying belief that things *should* be different and that they were responsible for creating that difference. Gee and McGarty (2013) have argued that these aspirations are necessary to creating "cooperative communities," or alliances of disparate groups create social change, which may not directly benefit all groups. Drawing on these aspirational identities may be another way to foster coalitions and increased sense of similarity among different groups of social change actors.

Issue 4: Activism as a Catalyst for (Re)politicization

Some participants reported that their activism was the source of increased attention to structural inequalities, and/or awareness of their own privilege. For example, the U.S. participant (US010) who mentioned that it was not until years of less successful (per her characterization) attempts at antiracist activism that she began to think about White privilege. She was not alone in reflecting on how previous engagements (not always unsuccessful) were the source of broader critiques of systemic inequality. For other participants, their activism was a source of pride and self-esteem and provided them with a community and a new in-group of fellow activists. Both activist and ally identities were interesting in that they seemed to sometimes be superordinate identities that allowed for inclusion of both advantaged and disadvantaged statuses. For example, many allies described a complex kind of tension being caught in between groups in a way that they were not in-group members of a marginalized group, but because of their shared sense of injustice with that disadvantaged group and interest in activism that challenged the advantaged group's power and status, their ally identity was also a marginalized identity, compared to identities of other advantaged group members. These complexities again show that participants exist at intersections of both advantaged and disadvantaged groups, and their multiple and intersecting identities simultaneously influence politicization and activism. Researchers and organizations need to find ways to address these identities in activism for better theoretical understanding and more successful mobilization.

Limitations and Strengths

Qualitative methods working with small sample sizes have well-known limitations in terms of generalizability, furthermore they do not allow the systematic testing of theories. Readers should note that participants in the two samples were not asked identical questions. However, we were not comparing *responses* to particular questions. Our approach focused on the entire narrative provided by our participants, and not on particular questions, as we were interested in the kinds of themes that consistently emerged as participants reflected on their identity and activism (which were central to both interview protocols). Even within the same sample, the same questions engendered different responses from participants. Further, our samples included participants engaged in a number of different types of activism (e.g., women's rights, LGBT rights, etc.) which, on the one hand, allowed us to gain a better understanding of the different ways the interplay between advantaged and disadvantaged identities and political activism can occur, but on the other hand, provided individual and context specific examples of activism with limited possibilities of generalization. As researchers take up some of the issues we have raised here, they may want to consider them in the context of a particular domain. Another limitation of our analysis was our inability to disaggregate the influence of different factors participants indicated were important to their engagement. For example, many of our participants who reported historical experiences of discrimination also had direct, personal experiences with discrimination. We were unable to disaggregate the two in order to test the degree to which historical experiences contribute directly to politicized identification and activism, independent of personal experiences. Questions such as these are best answered by methods that can achieve this disaggregation using longitudinal surveys with cross-lagged predictors. However, our methods also have great strengths, allowing us to explore identity and activism with a degree of depth that would be difficult to contemplate using quantitative methods, and to formulate precise questions (such as that about historical and personal experience) for future research.

Conclusions

We have drawn on activist narratives in order to explore how advantaged and disadvantaged identities simultaneously influence politicization and activism. The degree to which we can understand how people who have made sustained commitment to social action view themselves and make sense of their activism allows us to ask and test more complex questions related to social change efforts. We see the contribution of this qualitative study as identifying the complex role of multiple identities in the dynamic processes of politicization and activism, which we believe will be of interest to both researchers and those involved in the practice of building social movements and the necessary alliances that make mobilization successful. Inclusive identity-based social movements need to address the multiple and intersecting identities of their activists. The importance of ally activism cannot be underestimated in successful and sustained movements (see e.g., Russell & Bohan, 2016; Thomas, McGarty, & Mavor, 2010). Our findings highlight that the mobilization of ally activists could be based on similar identity processes as the mobilization of in-group activists, as people hold multiple and intersecting identities which can potentially help them understand intergroup relations, social inequalities that activists aim to change (or as a matter of fact sustain). Organizations can therefore attract allies to join their causes by highlighting the structural aspects of the collective disadvantages they are fighting to change, and strengthen the importance of intersectional rather than singular identities of both in-group members and allies.

Finally, we note that our findings also contribute to the debate around the potential limitations of "identity politics." Some critics of identity-based politics have argued that the pitfalls to movements based on identity include a focus on personal transformation, as opposed to structural change (what Kauffman, 2001, calls the "antipolitics of identity," p. 23), the essentializing of identity (Alexander, 1999), the potential exclusion of sympathetic allies who do not share the identity in question (e.g., Gitlin, 1994), as well as the assumption that one identity has primary importance above all others (see Hobsbawm, 1996; but also intersectionality theorists such as Crenshaw, 1991). Our findings indicate that at least some activists report both personal identity shifts and a critique of structural inequalities, are inclusive in their activist efforts despite recognizing the relevance of intergroup boundaries in activism, and draw on multiple identities, even if they are engaged in only one identity-based issue. In other words, many of the activists in our samples seemed to maintain a critical perspective on structural inequalities, even as they strategically draw on different identities.

Our analysis of activists' narratives points to the value of building a science that informs practice on a foundation of accounts of the "on-the ground" experiences associated with committed engagement in activism.

References

Alexander, J. (1999). Beyond identity: Queer values and community. *International Journal of Sexuality and Gender Studies, 4*, 293–314.

Barlow, F. K., Sibley, C. G., & Hornsey, M. J. (2012). Rejection as a call to arms: Inter-racial hostility and support for political action as outcomes of race-based rejection in majority and minority groups. *British Journal of Social Psychology, 51*, 167–177. doi: 10.1111/j.2044-8309.2011.02040.x

Braun, V., & Clarke, V. (2006). Using thematic analysis in psychology. *Qualitative Research in Psychology, 3*, 77–101. doi: 10.1191/1478088706qp063oa

Çakal, H., Eller, A., Sirlopú, D., & Pérez, A. (2016). Intergroup relations in Latin America: Intergroup contact, common ingroup identity, and activism among Indigenous groups in Mexico and Chile. *Journal of Social Issues, 72*(2), 355–375.

Case, K. A. (2012). Discovering the privilege of whiteness: White women's reflections on anti-racist identity and ally behavior. *Journal of Social Issues, 68,* 78–96. doi: 10.1111/j.1540-4560.2011.01737.x

Case, K. A., Iuzzini, J., & Hopkins, M. (2012). Systems of privilege: Intersections, awareness, and applications. *Journal of Social Issues, 68,* 1–10. doi: 10.1111/j.1540-4560.2011.01732.x

Cole, E. R. (2009). Intersectionality and research in psychology. *American Psychologist, 64,* 170–180. doi: 10.1037/a0014564

Craig, M. A., & Richeson, J. A. (2014). Discrimination divides across identity dimensions: Perceived racism reduces support for gay rights and increases anti-gay bias. *Journal of Experimental Social Psychology, 55,* 169–174. doi: 10.1016/j.jesp.2014.07.008

Cross, W. E. (1978). The Thomas and Cross models of psychological Nigrescence: A review. *Journal of Black Psychology, 5,* 13–31.

Croteau, J. M., Talbot, D. M., Lance, T. S., & Evans, N. J. (2002). A qualitative study of the interplay between privilege and oppression. *Journal of Multicultural Counseling and Development, 30,* 239–258. doi: 10.1002/j.2161-1912.2002.tb00522.x

Crenshaw, K. (1991). Mapping the margins: Intersectionality, identity politics, and violence against women of color. *Stanford Law Review, 43,* 1241–1299.

Cole, E. R., & Stewart, A. J. (1996). Meanings of political participation among black and white women: political identity and social responsibility. *Journal of Personality and Social Psychology, 71,* 130–140. doi: 10.1037/0022-3514.71.1.130

Curtin, N., Stewart, A. J., & Duncan, L. E. (2010). What makes the political personal? Openness, personal political salience, and activism. *Journal of Personality, 78,* 943–968. doi: 10.1111/j.1467-6494.2010.00638.x

Curtin, N., Stewart, A. J., & Cole, E. R. (2015). Challenging the status quo: The role of intersectional awareness in activism for social change and pro-social intergroup attitudes. *Psychology of Women Quarterly, 39,* 512–529. doi: 10.1177/0361684315580439

de Weerd, M., & Klandermans, B. (1999). Group identification and social protest: Farmer's protest in the Netherlands. *European Journal of Social Psychology, 29,* 1073–1095. doi: 10.1002/(SICI)1099-0992(199912)29:8<1073::AID-EJSP986>3.0.

Dovidio, J. F., Gaertner, S. L., & Saguy, T. (2009). Commonality and the complexity of "we": Social attitudes and social change. *Personality and Social Psychology Review, 13,* 3–20. doi:10.1177/1088868308326751

Droogendyk, L., Wright, S. C., Lubensky, M. E., & Louis, W. R. (2016) Acting in solidarity: The pitfalls and promise of cross-group contact for majority group activists. *Journal of Social Issues, 72*(2), 315–334.

Drury, J., & Reicher, S. (2000). Collective action and psychological change: The emergence of new social identities. *British Journal of Social Psychology, 39,* 579–604. doi: 10.1348/014466600164642

Drury, J., & Reicher, S. (2009). Collective psychological empowerment as a model of social change: Researching crowds and power. *Journal of Social Issues, 65,* 707–725. doi: 10.1111/j.1540-4560.2009.01622.x

Galletta, A. (2013). *Mastering the semi-structured interview and beyond: From research design to analysis and publication.* New York, NY: New York University Press.

Gee, A., & McGarty, C. (2013). Developing cooperative communities to reduce stigma about mental disorders. *Analyses of Social Issues and Public Policy, 13,* 137–164. doi: 10.1111/j.1530-2415.2012.01296.x

Gitlin, T. (1994). From universality to difference: Notes on the fragmentation of the idea of the Left. In C. Calhoun (Ed.), *Social theory and the politics of identity* (pp. 150–174). Cambridge, MA: Blackwell Publishers.

Greenwood, R. M. (2012) Standing at the crossroads: An intersectional approach to women's social identities and political consciousness. In S. Wiley, & T. A. Revenson (Eds.), *Social categories in everyday experience* (pp. 103–129). Washington, DC: American Psychological Association.

Gurin, P., Miller, A. H., & Gurin, G. (1980). Stratum identification and consciousness. *Social Psychology Quarterly, 43,* 30–47.

Hobsbawm, E. (1996). Identity politics and the left. *New Left Review, 217,* 38–47.

Iyer, A., & Ryan, M. K. (2009). Why do men and women challenge gender discrimination in the workplace? The role of group status and in-group identification in predicting pathways to collective action. *Journal of Social Issues*, *65*, 791–814. doi: 10.1111/j.1540-4560.2009.01625.x

Kauffman, L. A. (2001). The anti-politics of identity. In B. Ryan (Ed.), *Identity Politics in the Women's Movement* (pp. 23–34). New York, NY: New York University Press.

Kelly, C., & Breinlinger, S. (1995). Identity and injustice: Exploring women's participation in collective action. *Journal of Community & Applied Social Psychology*, *5*, 41–57. doi: 10.1002/casp.2450050104

Klandermans, B. (2003). Collective political action. In D. O. Sears, L. Huddy, & R. Jervis (Eds.), *Oxford handbook of political psychology* (pp. 670–709). Oxford, UK: Oxford University Press.

Klandermans, P. G. (2014). Identity politics and politicized identities: Identity processes and the dynamics of protest. *Political Psychology*, *35*, 1–22. doi: 10.1111/pops.12167

Liu, J. H., & Hilton, D. J. (2005). How the past weighs on the present: Social representations of history and their role in identity politics. *British Journal of Social Psychology*, *44*, 537–556. doi: 10.1348/014466605x27162

Louis, W. R., Amiot, C. E., Thomas, E. F., & Blackwood, L. (2016). The "Activist Identity" and activism across domains: A multiple identities analysis. *Journal of Social Issues*, *72*(2), 242–263.

Louis, W. R., Taylor, D. M., & Neil, T. (2004). Cost-benefit analyses for your group and yourself: The rationality of decision-making in conflict. *International Journal of Conflict Management*, *15*, 110–143. doi: 10.1108/eb022909

McGarty, C., Bliuc, A. M., Thomas, E. F., & Bongiorno, R. (2009). Collective action as the material expression of opinion-based group membership. *Journal of Social Issues*, *65*, 839–857. doi: 10.1111/j.1540-4560.2009.01627.x

QSR International Pty Ltd. (2012). *NVivo: Version 10*. Doncaster Victoria, Australia: Author.

Russell, G. M., & Bohan, J. S. (2016). Institutional allyship for LGBT equality: Underlying processes and potentials for change. *Journal of Social Issues*, *72*(2), 335–354.

Simon, B., & Grabow, O. (2010). The politicization of migrants: Further evidence that politicized collective identity is a dual identity. *Political Psychology*, *31*, 717–738. doi: 10.1111/j.1467-9221.2010.00782.x

Simon, B., & Klandermans, B. (2001). Politicized collective identity: A social psychological analysis. *American Psychologist*, *56*, 319–331. doi: 10.1037/0003-066x.56.4.319

Smart Richman, L., & Leary, M. R. (2009). Reactions to discrimination, stigmatization, ostracism, and other forms of interpersonal rejection: A multimotive model. *Psychological Review*, *116*, 365–383. doi: 10.1037/a0015250

Stewart, A. J., & Healy, J. M. (1989). Linking individual development and social changes. *American Psychologist*, *44*, 30–42. doi: 10.1037/0003-066X.44.1.30

Stewart, A. J., Winter, D. G., Henderson-King, D., & Henderson-King, E. (2015). How politics become personal: Socio-historical events and their meanings in people's lives. *Journal of Social Issues*, *71*, 294–308. doi: 10.1111/josi.12111

Stürmer, S., & Simon, B. (2004). The role of collective identification in social movement participation: A panel study in the context of the German gay movement. *Personality and Social Psychology Bulletin*, *30*, 263–277. doi: 10.1177/0146167203256690

Subašić, E., Reynolds, K. J., & Turner, J. C. (2008). The political solidarity model of social change: Dynamics of self-categorization in intergroup power relations. *Personality and Social Psychology Review*, *12*, 330–352. doi: 10.1177/1088868308323223

Tajfel, H., & Turner, J. C. (1979). An integrative theory of intergroup conflict. In W. G. Austin & S. Worchel (Eds.), *Psychology of intergroup relations* (pp. 33–47). Monterey, CA: Brooks/Cole. doi: 10.1146/annurev.ps.33.020182.000245

Thomas, E. F., & McGarty, C. A. (2009). The role of efficacy and moral outrage norms in creating the potential for international development activism through group-based interaction. *British Journal of Social Psychology*, *48*, 115–134. doi: 10.1348/014466608x313774

Thomas, E. F., McGarty, C., & Mavor, K. (2010). Social psychology of making poverty history: Motivating anti-poverty action in Australia. *Australian Psychologist*, *45*, 4–15.

Thomas, E. F., Mavor, K. I., & McGarty, C. (2012). Social identities facilitate and encapsulate action-relevant constructs: A test of the social identity model of collective action. *Group Processes & Intergroup Relations*, *15*, 75–88. doi: 10.1177/1368430211413619

Turner, J. C. (1985). Social categorization and the self-concept: A social cognitive theory of group behavior. *Advances in Group Processes, 2*, 77–122.

van Stekelenburg, J., & Klandermans, B. (2010). Individuals in movements. In B. Klandermans & C. Roggeband (Eds.), *Handbook of social movements across disciplines* (pp. 157–204). New York, NY: Springer

van Stekelenburg, J., Klandermans, B., & Akkerman, A. (2016). Does civic participation stimulate political activity? *Journal of Social Issues, 72*(2), 286–314.

van Zomeren, M. (2013). Four core social-psychological motivations to undertake collective action. *Social and Personality Psychology Compass, 7*, 378–388. doi: 10.1111/spc3.12031

van Zomeren, M., Postmes, T., & Spears, R. (2008). Toward an integrative social identity model of collective action: A quantitative research synthesis of three socio-psychological perspectives. *Psychological Bulletin, 134*, 504–535. doi: 10.1037/0033-2909.134.4.504

van Zomeren, M., Postmes, T., Spears, R., & Bettache, K. (2011). Can moral convictions motivate the advantaged to challenge social inequality? Extending the social identity model of collective action. *Group Processes & Intergroup Relations, 14*, 735–753. doi: 10.1177/1368430210395637

Vollhardt, J. R. (2009). Altruism born of suffering and prosocial behavior following adverse life events: A review and conceptualization. *Social Justice Research, 22*, 53–97. doi: 10.1007/s11211-009-0088-1

Vollhardt, J. R. (2015). Inclusive victim consciousness in advocacy, social movements, and intergroup relations: Promises and pitfalls. *Social Issues and Policy Review, 9*, 89–120. doi: 10.1111/sipr.12011

NICOLA CURTIN is an Assistant Professor at Clark University and a Visiting Scholar at Brandeis University's Women's Studies Research Center. Her research examines the role of life experiences, individual differences, and social identities in commitments to creating social change. She explores the development of social change attitudes and behaviors across different social contexts, with a focus on United States identity-based rights activism.

ANNA KENDE is an Associate Professor at Eötvös Loránd University, Budapest. Her research focuses on prejudice, intergroup relations, identity formation and political activism from a social psychological perspective. She has carried out several policy research projects about early selection in schools and worked as a policy advisor on educational integration of Roma people in Hungary.

JUDIT KENDE is a PhD student at the University of Leuven. She is interested in intergroup processes and how they are embedded in their wider climate, working on out-group activism in the Hungarian context of low political participation, intergroup contact from a cross-cultural perspective and on the effects of discrimination on minority youth in Belgium.

Journal of Social Issues, Vol. 72, No. 2, 2016, pp. 286–314
doi: 10.1111/josi.12167

Does Civic Participation Stimulate Political Activity?

Jacquelien van Stekelenburg[*]**, Bert Klandermans, and Agnes Akkerman**
Vrije Universiteit Amsterdam

Activists are the engines of social movements. What spurs their activism? This article scrutinizes the role of civic participation in stimulating political action. We examine how the type of voluntary organization, scope of involvement and intensity of activity relate to political activity. Contrary to existing studies that collapse noninstitutional political activities into a single measure, we differentiate collective activities from individualized activities, enabling us to investigate how the type, intensity and scope of civic participation differentially stimulate political activities. Our sample included 14,787 participants in 71 street demonstrations. We show that membership and interest in activist organizations stimulates political activity, especially for those actively involved and especially for collective non-institutionalized activities, while membership in leisure organizations only stimulates individualized political activities, but not collective activities. We therefore conclude that civic participation is a multifaceted phenomenon associated with various political activities in different ways.

Introduction

Activists–people who play an active role in civic organizations–are the engine of civil society. They pursue causes, set out to improve living conditions, and spark our conscience. Dalton (2008) calls them "supercitizens," people who demonstrate political knowledge, an understanding and interest in political matters and an understanding of the how the political system functions. They watch debates during an election, attend a town hall for public discussions, and attend political rallies and demonstrations. What spurs the political activism of supercitizens? This article examines the relation between civic participation and political activities.

Civic organizations are assumed to fulfill a pivotal role in stimulating political activities, as they are seen as "workplaces" where "apprentice" citizens learn

---

[*]Correspondence concerning this article should be addressed to Jacquelien van Stekelenburg, Department of Sociology, Vrije Universiteit Amsterdam, Boelelaan 1081c, 1081HV, Amsterdam, the Netherlands. Tel: +31 205986749 [e-mail: j.van.stekelenburg@vu.nl].

the virtues and skills of democratic citizenship (Norris, 2003; Putnam, 1993). According to Lichterman (2005) civic involvement stimulates political activity via a so-called "social spiral": citizens obtain the civic virtues and skills necessary for participation in a democracy, and build a broader and more varied social network. In the end, members of civic organizations are more likely to be politically active as they have obtained the skills, the mindset and the network to be so. Theoretically, leisure organizations, are considered a major stepping stone to political activities (Putnam, 1993), as they are heterogeneous and built around face-to-face relationships (van der Meer & van Ingen, 2009). Especially active members should benefit, as face-to-face contact is considered to be more effective in creating social capital.

However, recent empirical research on political activity shows inconclusive findings. Although van der Meer and van Ingen (2009) found a strong, positive, correlation between civic participation and political activities, they found no support for the effect of leisure organizations. Moreover, while passive (or "checkbook") members showed much higher levels of political activities than noninvolved members, the hypothesized additional effects of active participation were only marginal. More importantly, the correlation between civic participation and political activities was not explained by the proposed mechanisms of obtaining civic skills and civic mindedness. Hence, we know that civic participation is positively associated with political activity, but we do not know *how* or *why*.

In this article we argue that civic participation is a multidimensional phenomenon, with such dimensions being differentially associated to various political activities. Accordingly, this article contributes to the literature in at least two ways. First, we treat civic participation as a multidimensional phenomenon rather than a simple count of memberships. Inspired by Wollebæk and Selle (2002, see also Alexander, Barraket, Lewis, & Considine, 2012), we examine three dimensions and assess how each is associated with political activities: the *type* of voluntary organization (leisure, interest and activist organizations); the *scope* of involvement (few versus many affiliations); and the *intensity* of activity (active versus passive). Second, following van der Meer and van Ingen (2009), we distinguish institutional activities (i.e., voting) from noninstitutional activities (see also van Deth, 2014). Yet, contrary to existing studies that collapsed noninstitutional activities into a single measure, we differentiate between *collective* activities (e.g., demonstrations, strikes) and *individualized* activities (e.g., political consumerism, signing petitions). This enables us to investigate how the type, intensity and scope of civic participation stimulate different political activities. We find that different dimensions of civic participation are associated with different political activities.

This study examines how the type, intensity and scope of civic participation influence political action through civic mindedness and skills. The effect of civic participation is tested in three steps. First we analyze how the type, intensity and scope of civic participation affect civic mindedness and skills. Then we examine how civic mindedness and skills affect all political activity. In the third step we test the effect of the type, intensity and scope of civic participation on political activity. Finally, we test the direct and indirect effects of type and intensity of civic participation on political activity through civic mindedness and civic skills.

Political Activities: Individualized versus Collective Activities

To date, political activity has typically been operationalized as a simple summation of various activities (Alexander et al., 2012), a dichotomy of institutional versus noninstitutional political activities (e.g., Schussman & Soule, 2005; van der Meer & van Ingen, 2009), or some restricted set of choices (Corrigall-Brown, 2012; van Deth, Montero, & Westholm, 2007), ruling out the opportunity to examine whether different activities are driven by different mechanisms. In the current article, we distinguish between institutionalized, individualized and collective noninstitutionalized activities following van Deth's (2014, p. 315) conceptual map of political participation. Van Deth focuses in his conceptual map on the locus (or arena) of participation; that is, voluntary activities located in the sphere of government/state are specimen of *institutional modes of political participation*, whereas those activities located outside the sphere of government/state are specimen of *noninstitutional modes of political participation*. Noninstitutionalized activities are distinguished from individualized and collective activities, in that no organizational aspect is involved. Van Deth defines them as *individualized collective action* whereas those activities where an organization is involved are defined as *collective noninstitutionalized action*.

We include voting as an institutionalized activity. Voting is an institutionalized activity, because elections are held at regular intervals, at predefined local, national or supranational levels, and operate according to preset rules. Noninstitutionalized activities (i.e., protest events), on the other hand, are more episodic and less predictable. These noninstitutionalized activities can always take place as there is no institutionalized rhythm prescribing when and how protest events should occur (van der Meer & van Ingen, 2009). In people's attempts to influence politics, voting may be substituted or supplemented by noninstitutionalized activities. Therefore, it is important to investigate if the type, intensity and scope of civic involvement affect the choice for institutionalized (i.e., voting) and/or noninstitutionalized activities.

Regarding noninstitutionalized activities, we distinguish between individualized and collective activities. We assume it is essential to treat these political activities separately, as they are differentially affected by the type, intensity and scope of civic participation. Individualized noninstitutionalized activities such as contacting a politician, signing a petition, or buying or boycotting a product can be deployed individually at any given moment. This is in contrast to collective activities such as strikes and demonstrations, that have to be coordinated, organized and need the mobilization of participants. Hence, collective activities require more coordination, organization, and mobilization of resources, and thus, essential organizational networks rather than individualized noninstitutionalized activities. We argue that as coordination, organization, and mobilization take place in civic organizations, and especially in interest and activist organizations (van der Meer & van Ingen, 2009), it is important to examine how different forms of civic participation affect different political activities. In what follows we will theorize how the type, intensity and scope of civic participation influence these different political activities by affecting civic mindedness and skills.

Civic Participation: Civic Mindedness and Civic Skills

Scholars have paid great attention to the positive effects of civic participation on political activity (e.g., Almond & Verba, 1963; Howard & Gilbert, 2008; Putnam, 1993). Civic participation is a stepping stone to political activity, in terms of quality and quantity (Paxton, 1999). Civic participation is said to create an informed, reasoned, and rational-critical informed public opinion. Civic participants develop civic mindedness, which nurtures trust and respect for opposing viewpoints, raises political interest, and reduces political cynicism (Paxton, 1999), thus enhancing the quality of political activity. Regarding quantity, civic participation creates feelings of duty and develops political efficacy. These civic skills in turn produce more proficient and politically engaged citizens (e.g., Barnes & Kaase, 1979). Thus, civic participation is expected to influence political activity by affecting civic mindedness and skills. This reasoning brings us to our first set of hypotheses:

Hypothesis I: Participation in civic organizations will be associated with higher levels of civic mindedness and civic skills.
Hypothesis II: Higher levels of civic mindedness and civic skills will be associated with higher levels of all types of political activity.

Three Dimensions of Civic Participation: Type, Intensity, and Scope

The literature is inconclusive as to precisely which factors hamper or facilitate which political activities. Scholars disagree on the impact of the *type* of organization, or whether it matters if people participate in interest or activist organizations or leisure clubs (Van der Meer & Van Ingen, 2009; Wollebæk & Selle, 2002). Scholars also disagree about the *intensity* of civic participation. That is, they disagree about whether face-to-face contact–which active members have and passive members do not–is necessary for political activity (Wollebæk & Selle, 2002). On the one hand, one might argue that checkbook activism requires fewer resources like time, and energy, so people can engage in *more* political activities (Stolle,

Hooghe, & Micheletti, 2005), yet one might argue that checkbook activism crowds out other political activities, leading to *fewer* political activities. Finally, also inconclusive is the role that the *scope* of civic participation plays; scholars wonder if the number of affiliations with civic organizations affects levels of political activity (Wollebæk & Selle, 2002).

Type of Civic Participation and Social Capital

Following van der Meer and van Ingen (2009), we distinguished between three types of organizations based on their primary purpose: leisure organizations (church, sport or neighborhood); interest organizations (trade union/professional organization); and activist organizations (women's, LGBT, environmental and humanitarian/peace organizations). Wollebæk and Selle (2002) examined whether the association between civic participation and the formation of social capital was affected by the scope, type and intensity of civic participation. They showed that civic participation indeed led to the formation of social capital (i.e., trust, social networks and political interest), especially for those with multiple affiliations, and when nonpolitical affiliations were accompanied by political ones. Intensity of activity, unexpectedly, did not matter. Note that their dependent variable was social capital; they did not consider political activity. Van der Meer and Van Ingen (2009) on the other hand, *did* take political activity as their dependent variable, and distinguished between institutional and noninstitutional political activity (see also Howard & Gilbert, 2008). They showed that the *types* of civic organizations matter. Individuals involved in interest and activist organizations are politically more active than those in leisure organizations. As van der Meer and van Ingen argued, people join interest and activist organizations with the objective of influencing politics or to express their view. In these organizations, "people come into contact with political processes and with a network of people who have the skills and mindset to participate politically" (p. 291). Consequently, members of interest and activist organizations are more likely to obtain civic mindedness and skills. Moreover, as we argue, staging collective action is the *raison d'être* of these organizations; members are more "at risk" to be mobilized for political activities than nonmembers. So, we expect members of interest and activist organizations to be more politically active than those in leisure organizations, especially for collective activities as these organizations accrue resources and the necessary social capital for collective action.

Hypothesis III: Members of interest and activist organization will be more involved in collective noninstitutionalized activities than members of leisure organizations.

Intensity of Civic Participation and Political Socialization

Van der Meer and van Ingen (2009) distinguished between active members–those who invest time and energy in the organization, e.g., being a board member–and passive members, those who only financially support the organization, the so-called checkbook members. They hypothesized that the *intensity* of civic participation was positively related to political activity. Because active members, contrary to passive ones, are more involved in face-to-face interactions, they acquire democratic skills and values via socialization and network effects. However, they found no empirical support for their hypothesis. Although passive members showed higher levels of political activities than noninvolved, the additional effects of active participation were only marginal and not significant. Note that Wollebæk and Selle (2002) also failed to find an effect of intensity of participation on the formation of social capital. Thus, the intensity of civic participation has neither been shown to affect the social capital required for collective political action, nor to affect political activity directly.

However, van der Meer and van Ingen (2009) did not distinguish between collective and individualized noninstitutionalized political activities. Therefore, it might well be that their null results were driven by the aggregation of all modes of noninstitutional political activities. We therefore retest the hypothesis that intensity of civic participation affects political activity, but distinguish between collective and individual forms of noninstitutionalized political activities. Members of interest and activist organizations are more "at risk" to be mobilized for political activities than members of leisure organizations, and these organizations can accrue the resources required for collective noninstitutionalized activities. Consequently, active members of interest and activist organizations encounter more mobilization efforts and experience more social pressure (Klandermans, 1984) to participate in collective noninstitutionalized activities than passive members.

Hypothesis IV: Active members of interest and activist organization are more involved in collective noninstitutionalized political activities than passive members.

Scope of Civic Participation and Political Competence

Van der Meer and van Ingen (2009) did not take the amount of affiliations–that is, the *scope*–into consideration. Consequently, we know that multiple affiliations affect the formation of social capital, a stepping stone to political activity, but we do not know whether the frequency and variety of political activities increase with increasing affiliations. Yet, Wollebæk and Selle (2002) considered the "consistent cumulative effect of multiple affiliations [. . .] as one of the principle findings of their study" (p. 54). They referred to Almond and Verba (1963), who found

Table 1. Overview of Hypotheses

Hypothesis	Independent variable	Dependent variable	Direction of effect
I	Civic participation	Civic mindedness Civic skills	+
II	Civic mindedness & civic skills	All types of political activities	+
III	*Type*: Participation in interest and activist rather than leisure organization	Collective political activities	+
IV	*Intensity*: Active rather than passive membership in civic organizations	Collective political activities	+

V	*Scope*:
	Of participation in interest and
	   activist rather than leisure
	   organizations
		Collective political activities	+

Notes. Bold indicates factorloadings above .20.

that number of memberships affect civic competence cumulatively: "Membership in one organization increases an individual's sense of political competence, and membership in more than one organization leads to even greater competence" (p. 264). Thus, they proposed that being affiliated with more organizations, leads to an accumulation of political competence, which strengthens political activity. We therefore expect that the more civic organizations people are involved in, the more political activities they will undertake. However, political competence also involves coordination, organization and mobilization skills. These skills are *acquired* more in interest and activist organizations than leisure organizations, and are *required* more for collective than individualized noninstitutionalized activities. Political activism is therefore expected to increase with increasing affiliations, especially with interest and activist organizations, and for collective rather than individualized activities.

Hypothesis V: Increased scope of civic participation will be associated with increased participation in political activities, especially for interest and activist organizations, and for collective rather than individualized noninstitutionalized activities.

Method

To test our hypotheses (see Table 1 for an overview), we use a new dataset of 14,787 participants in 71 street demonstrations, the "Caught in the Act of Protest: Contextualizing Contestation" (CCC) (Klandermans et al., 2011; Van

Stekelenburg, Walgrave, Klandermans, & Verhulst, 2012). This dataset comprises data on 14,787 participants in 71 street demonstrations in eight European countries (Belgium, Italy, the Netherlands, Spain, Sweden, Switzerland, the United Kingdom, and Czech Republic) collected between November 2009 and May 2012. This CCC dataset contains rich information regarding civic participation (with measures on the scope, intensity and type of activism) and political activity (with a full battery of political activities). This dataset allows us to empirically test Putnam's (1983) proposition that civic participation positively affects political activity at the individual level, an empirical strategy that has been impeded by a shortage of good quality detailed datasets (van der Meer & van Ingen, 2009). Moreover, and important in the context of this article, 85% of the respondents of the CCC dataset were involved in at least one civic organization. Given the strong positive relation between civic participation and political activities (van der Meer & van Ingen, 2009), this is what we would expect. Hence, despite the fact that activists are a rare species, our selective sample of demonstrators comprises a sufficient share of active citizens. The relatively large share of passive and active members in a large variety of organizations, combined with detailed measures on civic participation and political activity, make this dataset highly suitable to answer our research question.

Sampling Participants and Collecting Data

The respondents completed surveys distributed during the demonstration (500–1,000) to be returned to the university. Overall 32% of the participants turned in their questionnaire, fluctuating between 13% and 52%. Identical questions and procedures were employed for each demonstration.

In order to control for response biases we also conducted short (2–3 minutes) interviews with a subsample of the respondents (100–200) at the demonstrations based on questions identical to those in the printed questionnaire. The refusal rate for these short interviews was low (10%). By comparing the answers in the interviews with those in the returned questionnaires and by comparing the interviews of those who returned their questionnaire with the interviews of those who did not, we can estimate the response bias. Comparison of those who did and did not return the questionnaire revealed that those who returned the questionnaire were on average somewhat older and more highly educated than those who did not. The analyses we conducted to assess if the nonresponse could have resulted in biased findings and conclusions did not reveal any deviating outcomes.

We applied a sampling strategy in which each participant had an equal probability to be selected. Although circumstances inevitably necessitate variation, we aimed to keep sampling procedures as identical as possible for the various demonstrations. A demonstration was covered by a team consisting of a fieldwork coordinator, 3–4 so-called pointers, and 12–15 interviewers. Each pointer had a team of four to five interviewers. The pointers selected the interviewees,

Table 2. Factor Loadings for Political Activities and Percentage of Respondents Participating in Political Activities in Previous 12 Months

	Noninstitutionalized activities		Institutionalized activities
	Individualized activities	Collective activities	Voting
Contacted a politician	**.56**	.19	−.15
Signed a petition	**.62**	.04	−.01
Donated money	**.68**	.01	−.06
Consumerism	**.63**	−.05	.27
Strike	−.23	**.72**	−.05
Direct action	.18	**.68**	−.04
Demonstration	.06	**.76**	.15
Voted last elections	−.14	−.05	**.92**

Notes. Bold indicates factorloadings above .20.

while interviewers conducted the interviews and handed out the questionnaires. Separating these two roles appeared to be crucial in preventing sampling biases. As interviewers tended to select people they believed to be willing to cooperate, they ended up producing biased samples. The fieldwork coordinator oversaw the employment of the pointer-interviewer teams. At the start of the event s/he made an estimate of the number of participants. This defined the ratio at which participants were approached for interviews and given questionnaires. In "moving" demonstrations, the teams started at different points of the march and worked toward each other approaching every nth person in every nth row. At "static" demonstrations, the space was divided into smaller areas; in each area a pointer selected interviewees, taking the density of the crowd in that area into account. We argue that resulting samples are representative (or closest to being representative) for the demonstrators present at the demonstration.

Measures

Dependent variables: political activities. We asked our respondents if they undertook any of the following political activities during the past 12 months: contacted a politician; signed a petition; donated money; buycotted or boycotted products with political motive; took part in a strike, direct action, demonstration, and voting.

The activities loaded on three factors, explaining 54.29% of the variance (see Table 2). The factors respectively represented noninstitutional activities divided into *individualized activities* (contacted a politician, signed a petition, donated money, and buycotted or boycotted products, eigenvalue 1.86, explained variance 23.28%), *collective activities* (strike, direct action and demonstration, eigenvalue

1.47, explained variance 18.37%), and *institutional politics* (voting, eigenvalue 1.01, explained variance 12.64%). The various political activities were thus conceptually and empirically distinguishable. We created an individualized, collective and institutional politics scale by aggregating the different activities.

Independent variables.
Civic mindedness.   Civic mindedness comprises high political trust, low political cynicism, and high political interest. To assess this we posed the following questions:

Political trust. "How much would you say that you trust national government/national parliament/political parties/EU?" (1 *not at all* to 5 *very much*; α = 0.78);
Political cynicism. A scale constructed of the following two items: "Most politicians make a lot of promises but do not actually do anything" and "I don't see the use of voting, parties do whatever they want anyway." (1 *strongly disagree* to 5 *strongly agree*, $\rho = 0.38$);
Talking politics. "When you get together with your friends, relatives or fellow workers, how often do you discuss politics?" (1 *never* to 5 *very often*);
Political interest. "How interested are you in politics?" (1 *not at all* to 5 *very much*).

The four measures loaded on two factors (explained variance 64%), representing political trust (being trustful and not cynical, explained variance 40% eigenvalue 2.81), and political interest (being interested in and talking politics, explained variance 24% eigenvalue 1.66). Thus, we collapsed them into two indicators of civic mindedness: political interest and political trust.
Civic skills.   Civic participation is characterized by feelings of efficacy. To assess this we posed the following questions and collapsed them into a single indicator of efficacy:

Individual political efficacy. "My participation can have an impact on public policy in this country." (1 *strongly disagree* to 5 *strongly agree*).
Collective political efficacy. "Organized groups of citizens can have a lot of impact on public policies in this country." (1 *strongly disagree* to 5 *strongly agree*).

Civic Participation: Type, Intensity, and Scope.   We asked our respondents if they had been involved in the following types of organization during the past 12 months: church, sport/cultural, community organization, trade unions or interest organizations, environmental, charity/welfare, third world/global justice/peace, human rights/civil rights/antiracist/migrant/ women's organization and lesbian, gay male, bisexual and transgender (LGBT) organizations. They could check as many boxes as applicable and could indicate whether they were a passive or an active member, in the case of multiple memberships of the same type, they were asked to tick the highest or most "active" category.

Type. Following van der Meer and van Ingen (2009), we distinguished between three types of organizations based on their primary purpose: leisure organizations (church, sport or neighborhood), interest organizations (trade union/ professional organization), and activist organizations (women's, LGBT, environmental and humanitarian/peace organizations).

Intensity. Intensity ranged from noninvolvement, to passive and active involvement in at least one of the above described types of organizations. Respondents were allocated to the "active" category in the organization they were most active in, resulting in six intensity groups, namely, passive/active leisure, passive/active interest, and passive/active activist organizations.

Scope. A simple count per type determined scope. Scope in leisure organizations ranged from 0 to 3, interest organizations (only 1) thus from 0 to 1, and activist organizations from 0 to 6, overall scope scores ranged from 0 to 11 organizations.

Results

This study examined how the type, intensity and scope of civic participation influenced political action by affecting civic mindedness and skills. The effect of civic participation was tested in four steps. First we analyzed how the type, intensity and scope of civic participation affected civic mindedness and skills (Hypothesis I). Then we examined how civic mindedness and skills affected all political activity (Hypothesis II). In the third step, we tested the direct effect of the type, intensity and scope of civic participation on political activity (Hypotheses III–VI). Finally, we tested the civic participation as stepping-stone-reasoning by testing the direct and indirect effects of type and intensity of civic participation on political activity through civic mindedness and civic skills. For the first three steps we conducted three MANOVAs: (a) type and intensity of civic involvement on civic mindedness and skills, (b) civic mindedness and skills on political activities, and (c) type and intensity of civic involvement on political activity. For the indirect effects tests we employed Structural Equation Modeling (SEM). We controlled for gender, age, and educational level, and standardized our measures. Despite the use of MANOVA and SEM, we make no claims regarding the direction of causation, as correlational data do not enable this.

Demographics and descriptive analyses

Table 3 provides an overview of the frequency of the different types of political activities, which varied widely. Nearly 80% of all respondents signed

Table 3. Percentage of Respondents Participating in Political Activities in Previous 12 Months

Item	Percentage
Individualized activities	
1. Contacted a politician	35.0
2. Donated money	43.1
3. Boycotted certain products	56.1
4. "Buycotted" certain products	68.1
5. Signed a petition	79.4
Collective activities	
6. Used violence against property or persons	1.4
7. Took part in direct action	15.4
8. Participated in strike	23.2
9. Took part in demonstration	75.0
Voting	
10. Voting	84.9

a petition, compared to just 35% who contacted a politician. The collective activities differed even more. More than 79% of our demonstrators signed a petition. These percentages are higher than the average percentage at the EU level, which are 34% for signing a petition and 24% and 10% for contacting a local/regional and national politician, respectively (Flash Eurobarometer, 2013); 75% took part in at least one other demonstration.

Affiliations also varied widely, with 12,529 respondents (85%) being passive or active members in at least one organization (Table 4). The respondents in the CCC dataset were most involved in activist and interest organizations. The majority of the general population, in contrast, is involved in sport and recreational groups (26% European Values Studies wave 2008) while involvement in interest and activist groups is much rarer (8% and 15%, respectively). Thus the respondents in the CCC dataset are involved in varied levels of political activities and involved in a broad variety of types, differing in levels of intensity and scope of civic participation.

Table 5 shows the sociodemographics per type and intensity of civic involvement. Noninvolved participants were, on average, younger than those actively and passively involved. While the differences in age and in gender are small for most of the categories presented in Table 6, the composition of those actively involved in interest organizations shows that this category is, on average older, and consists of more males than females. Concerning the educational level, in the group of active members of interest organizations, the percentage of medium level educated is relatively high, compared to its prevalence in the other groups.

Table 4. Percentage of Respondents per Type and Intensity of Involvement

Organization type	Nonmember	Passive member	Active member
Leisure	59	14	28
Church	85	8	7
Sport/cultural	75	8	17
Community organization	87	6	8
Interest			
Trade union/professional/business	58	23	20
Activist	43	30	27
Environmental	72	19	9
Charity/welfare	73	19	8
Third world/global justice/peace	75	17	7
Human/civil rights	82	14	5
Antiracist/migrant	89	6	4
Women's organizations	92	4	4
LGTB organizations	93	4	3

Table 6 provides an overview of the means, and SDs of the dependent and independent variables per group. With one-way ANOVA contrast analyses (unequal variances assumed) we tested whether the means differed significantly for the respective levels of civic involvement. Regarding civic mindedness, those actively involved in interest and activist organizations were more interested in politics than the non- or less involved (active interest and activist versus noninvolved, leisure organization, passive interest and activist: $M = 3.60$ and 3.63 vs. 3.51, 3.50, 3.47, 3.51, and 3.49, respectively: $t(939) = -17.79, p < .001; F(6, 14{,}410) = 159{,}11, p < .001, \eta^2 = .06$). Hence, neither passive nor active involvement in leisure organizations increased political interest ($t(407) = -8.53, p < .001$). We observed a similar pattern for civic skills: the non- or less involved felt politically less efficacious than those actively involved in interest and especially activist organizations (active interest and activist versus noninvolved, leisure organizations, passive interest and activist respectively: $M = 3.99$ and 4.03 vs. 3.95, 3.97, 3.96, 3.95, and 3.96, $t(955) = -11.20, p < .001; F(6, 14{,}412) = 59.73, p < .001, \eta^2 = .02$). Unexpectedly, however, active members of interest and activist organizations trusted politics *less* than noninvolved and passive members of interest and activist organizations respectively ($M = 2.77$ and 2.84 vs. 2.91, 2, 86, 2.87, 2.91, and 2.95, $t(645) = -1{,}98, p = . 049; F(6, 7437) = 18{,}85, p < .001, \eta^2 = .02$).

The groups also differed in political activities. Concerning individualized activities, the non- and less involved are the least active (noninvolved, and leisure respectively: $M = 2.37$, 2.36, and 2.44), and members of interest organizations

Table 5. Sociodemographics per Type and Intensity of Involvement

		Noninvolved (N = 2,258)
Year born (mean)		1970
Gender (% male)		50.9%
Highest education	Primary	1.7%
	Secondary	34.0%
	Tertiary	64.3%

		Leisure passive (N = 2,018)	Leisure active (N = 4,102)
Year born		1965	1965
Gender (% male)		51.7%	53.6%
Highest education	Primary	1.1%	0.9%
	Secondary	32.3%	32.0%
	Tertiary	66.6%	67.1%
		Interest passive (N = 3,394)	Interest active (N = 28,80)
Year born		1964	1962
Gender (% male)		49.3%	62.6%
Highest education	Primary	1.0%	1.7%
	Secondary	32.1%	47.8%
	Tertiary	66.9%	50.5%
		Activist passive (N = 4,436)	Activist active (N = 3,962)
Year born		1966	1966
Gender (% male)		47%	47.8
Highest education	Primary	0.9%	1.0%
	Secondary	30.7%	28.7%
	Tertiary	68.4%	70.3%

were also relatively inactive (passive $M = 2.37$, active 2.36). A one-way ANOVA with contrast analysis (unequal variances assumed, F (6, 14.780) $= 366.22$, $p < .001$, $\eta^2 = .13$) revealed that members of activist organizations were significantly the most engaged in individualized activities, both passive ($M = 2.50$) and active ($M = 2.78$, $t(1,629) = -10.91$, $p < .001$). The less and noninvolved were, as expected, less active in collective activities than those actively involved (noninvolved, leisure, passive interest and activist versus active interest and activist respectively $M = 2.22$, 2.23, 2.28, 2.22, and 2.13 vs. 2.87 and 2.57, $t(1,568) = -25.56$, $p < .001$, $F(6, 13715) = 210.68$, $p < .001$, $\eta^2 = .08$). The

Table 6. Means and *SD*s of the (In)Dependent Variables per Type and Intensity of Involvement

Noninvolved	*M* (*SD*)
1. Political trust	2.91 (0.73)
2. Political interest	3.51 (0.69)
3. Civic skills	3.95 (0.68)
4. Individualized activities	2.37 (1.19)
5. Collective activities	2.22 (1.02)
6. Voting (% yes)	74.9%

Leisure passive	*M* (*SD*)	Leisure active	*M* (*SD*)
1. Political trust	2.86 (0.74)	1. Political trust	2.87 (0.75)
2. Political interest	3.50 (0.68)	2. Political interest	3.47 (0.68)
3. Civic skills	3.97 (0.67)	3. Civic skills	3.96 (0.69)
4. Individualized activities	2.36 (1.17)	4. Individualized activities	2.44 (1.16)
5. Collective activities	2.23 (1.05)	5. Collective activities	2.28 (1.11)
6. Voting (% yes)	91.1%	6. Voting (% yes)	89.9%

Interest passive	*M* (*SD*)	Interest active	*M* (*SD*)
1. Political trust	2.91 (0.73)	1. Political trust	2.77 (0.77)
2. Political interest	3.51 (0.69)	2. Political interest	3.60 (0.67)
3. Civic skills	3.95 (0.68)	3. Civic skills	3.99 (0.70)
4. Individualized activities	2.37 (1.19)	4. Individualized activities	2.36 (1.21)
5. Collective activities	2.22 (1.02)	5. Collective activities	2.87 (1.27)
6. Voting (% yes)	91.1%	6. Voting (% yes)	89.9%

Activist passive	*M* (*SD*)	Activist active	*M* (*SD*)
1. Political trust	2.95 (0.72)	1. Political trust	2.84 (0.75)
2. Political interest	3.49 (0.66)	2. Political interest	3.63 (0.66)
3. Civic skills	3.96 (0.66)	3. Civic skills	4.03 (0.69)
4. Individualized activities	2.50 (1.04)	4. Individualized activities	2.78 (1.07)
5. Collective activities	2.13 (1.01)	5. Collective activities	2.57 (1.20)
6. Voting (% yes)	89.1%	6. Voting (% yes)	85.6%

noninvolved voted, as expected, significantly the least (74.9 %), followed by active members of activist organizations (85.6%); the other groups hover around 90% $(t(347.05) = -7.43, p < .001; F(6, 14285) = 51.50, p < .001, \eta^2 = .02)$.

Thus the groups differed systematically in terms of civic mindedness, civic skills and political activities. Taken together, this is a first indication that type of organization, and intensity of involvement affect civic mindedness, skills and

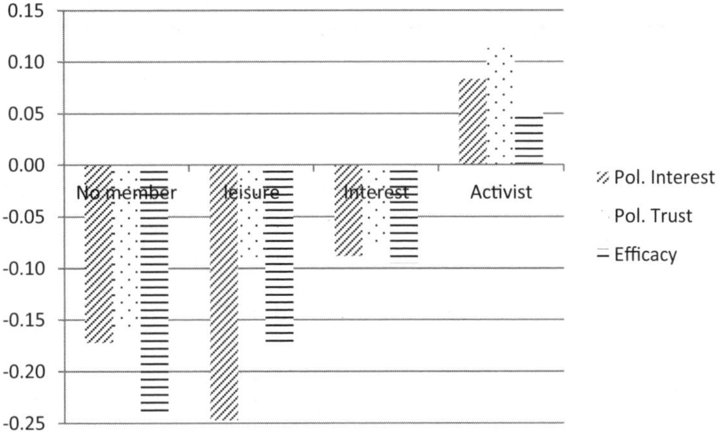

Fig. 1. Civic mindedness and skills per type of involvement.

political activities. In what follows we test this in multivariate analyses controlled for age, gender and educational level.

Does Civic Participation Nurture Civic Mindedness and Civic Skills?.
We expected civic participation to nurture civic mindedness and civic skills. Figure 1 provides an overview of the MANOVA results. Those involved in civic organizations were, as expected, more civic minded (political interest $F(3, 6820)$ $= 33.79, p < .001, \eta^2 = .02$ and political trust $F(3,6820) = 29.71, p < .001, \eta^2 = .013$) and they possessed more civic skills (political efficacy $F(3, 6820) = 29.31, p < .001, \eta^2 = .013$). However, this was only the case for those involved in interest and activist organizations. Hence, those involved in leisure organizations were only more trusting than the noninvolved, $M = -0.11$ and $-0.21, t(3,656) = -2.00, p = .04$, but did not differ from the noninvolved in terms of political interest, $M = -0.18$ and $-0.23, t(3,656) = 1.26, ns$, and efficacy, $M = -0.17$ and $-0.17, t(3,686) = -0.14, ns$. Thus, Hypothesis 1 was partly confirmed. Civic participation nurtured civic mindedness and skills, but only for those involved in interest and activist organizations. Those involved in leisure organizations trusted politics more than the noninvolved, but were no more interested in politics nor more efficacious than the noninvolved.

Do Civic Mindedness and Civic Skills Affect Political Activity?

We expected that higher levels of civic mindedness and civic skills would be associated with higher levels of political activity. Table 7 provides an overview

Table 7. Correlations of Civic Mindedness and Skills per Type of Political Activity

	Political interest	Political trust	Civic skills
Individualized activities	.37**	.17**	.25**
Collective activities	.23**	−.25**	.08**
Voting	.08**	.18**	.05**

Note. **significant at $p < .01$ level.

of the correlations between civic mindedness and skills and the different political activities. Political interest, trust and efficacy were positively and significantly related to voting, and individualized and collective noninstitutionalized activities (ranging from $r = .05$, $p < .001$ for efficacy and voting to $r = .37$, $p < .001$ for political interest and individualized activities). Thus, the more civic minded people were, and the more civic skills they possessed, the more likely they were to vote, and embark on individualized and collective noninstitutionalized activities. With one notable exception, that is, higher levels of collective noninstitutionalized activities were associated with *lower* levels of trust. Note that the associational pattern varied for the different political activities. Correlations between civic mindedness and skills and voting were relatively low, while they were stronger for noninstitutionalized activities, and particularly individualized activities. This seems to indicate that the less ritualized, organized and mobilized an activity was, the more civic mindedness and civic skills it required. In sum, Hypothesis II was partly confirmed, higher levels of civic mindedness and civic skills were associated with higher levels of voting and individualized and collective noninstitutionalized political activities, except for collective activities, which were related to lower levels of trust.

Do Type, Intensity, and Scope of Civic Participation Affect Political Activity?

The previous section addressed the question of whether civic organizations are indeed the "workplaces" where "apprentice" citizens learn the virtues and skills of democratic citizenship. In this section we examine if the type, intensity and scope of civic involvement stimulate political activities.

Type of civic involvement. We expected and found that members of interest and activist organizations were more politically active than members of leisure organizations (see Figure 2), both institutional (voting, $F(3, 13512) = 44.94$, $p < .001$, $\eta^2 = .011$, and noninstitutional activities (individualized: $F(3, 13837) = 520.30$, $p < .001$, $\eta^2 = .11$, collective $F(3, 12924) = 90.41$, $p < .001$, $\eta^2 = .021$). This confirmed Hypothesis III. Note that members of interest organizations

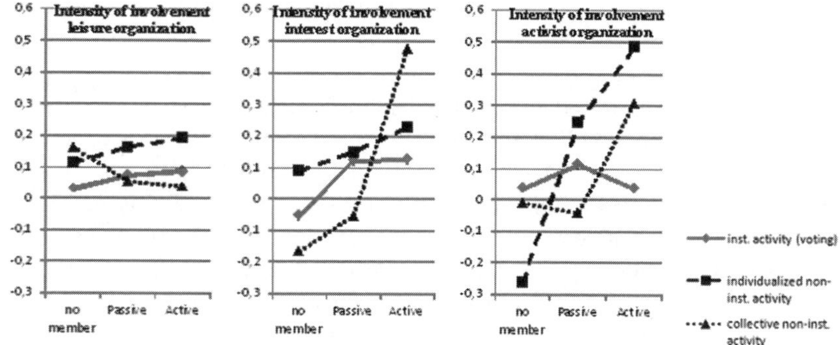

Fig. 2. Type of political activity by type and intensity of civic involvement.

embarked more on collective activities, while members of activist organizations were significantly more involved in individualized activities.

Intensity of civic involvement.   Contrary to previous null findings, we hypothesized and found that intensity of civic participation affected political activity. That is, active members of interest and activist organizations were more involved in collective noninstitutionalized activities than passive members, activist: $M = -0.18$ and 0.04, $t(4,353) = -8.40$, $p < .001$; interest: $M = -0.30$ and 0.40, $t(5,907) = -23.60$, $p < .001$. Hence, distinguishing individualized from collective activities revealed that, contrary to previous null-findings, intensity of involvement did matter. That is, active members *were* more involved in collective activities, especially those actively involved in interest organizations. This confirmed Hypothesis IV.

Scope of civic involvement.   We hypothesized and found that political activism increased with increasing affiliations, especially for interest and activist organizations, and for collective rather than individualized activities. Political activity did, as expected, not increase with increasing leisure organizations affiliations, voting: $F(3, 13837) = 0.93$, $p = .43$, individualized: $F(3, 13837) = 0.43$, $p = .73$, collective $F(3, 12924) = 2.06$, $p = .10$. However, as expected, collective activities increased with increasing interest and activist affiliations, collective interest: $F(1, 13837) = 4.85$, $p = .03$, $\eta^2 = .00$, collective activist $F(7, 12924) = 3.73$, $p < .001$, $\eta^2 = .002$. Individualized activities did not increase with increasing interest affiliations $F(1, 13837) = 1.85$, $p = .17$. However, they did unexpectedly increase with increasing activist affiliations $F(7, 12924) = 31.60$, $p < .001$, $\eta^2 = .02$. Thus, Hypothesis V was partly confirmed, that is, increasing scope of interest and activist organizations increased–as expected–collective activities, but increasing activist affiliations–unexpectedly–also increased individualized activities.

Does Civic Involvement Affect Political Activity through Civic Mindedness and Skills?

In this section we tested the direct and indirect effects of the type and intensity of civic participation on political activity through civic mindedness and civic skills. Employing AMOS, we conducted six SEM analyses in which we examined the direct and indirect effects for the noninvolved with those passively or actively involved in leisure, interest and activist organizations. If civic mindedness and skills indeed function as stepping stones to political activity, we expected to observe that civic involvement affected political activity through civic mindedness and skills. In fact, civic involvement was expected to increase political activity, especially for active involvement in interest and activist organization and for collective rather than individualized activities. Our analyses regarding the relative impact of political interest, trust and efficacy are more exploratory. The path models are presented in Figures 3–5, nonsignificant paths are represented by dashed lines, all other paths are significant at $p < .001$; total effects are reported between brackets. Table 8 provides an overview of the total, direct and indirect effects of political trust, interest and efficacy separated (Total and direct effects in Figures 3–5 may slightly differ from those in Table 6 due to the fact that bootstrapping does not allow missing values).

Figure 3 presents the models for passive (left) and active (right) members involved in leisure organizations, passive: $\chi^2(7, 2527) = 6.21$, $p = .52$, CFI $= 1.00$, NFI $= .99$ and RMSEA $< .001$; active $\chi^2(6, 3643) = 7.92$, $p = .24$, CFI $= 1.00$, NFI $= .99$ and RMSEA $= .009$. Passive involvement in leisure organization does not increase civic mindedness nor skills (–.06, –.07 and .01 respectively, *ns*). Its direct effect on individual activities is marginal (.14, $p < .001$), on voting 0, and on collective activities even negative (–.09, $p < .001$). The effect of passive involvement on individual activities was not significant via civic mindedness or skills affected (total .15, $p < .001$ and direct .14, $p < .001$). Active involvement in leisure organizations, however, was positively related to individual activities through civic skills, total .39, direct .35, indirect effect $= .05$, $p < .001$. And although active involvement in leisure organizations was positively related to voting, this was not affected by civic mindedness or by skills (total .30 direct .30, *ns*). Active involvement in leisure organizations was not related to collective activities and is neither affected by civic mindedness nor skills (total .02, ns, direct .03, *ns*).

Figure 4 presents the models for those passive (left) and active (right) involved in interest organizations, passive: $\chi^2(1, 11907) = 5.68$, $p = .02$, CFI $= 1.00$, NFI $= .99$ and RMSEA $= .02$; active: $\chi^2(2, 10351) = 3.66$, $p = .16$, CFI $= 1.00$, NFI $= .99$ and RMSEA $= .009$. Most notable was that contrary to the result in leisure organizations, civic mindedness and skills were significantly affected by involvement in interest organizations. With trust as a notable exception, passive

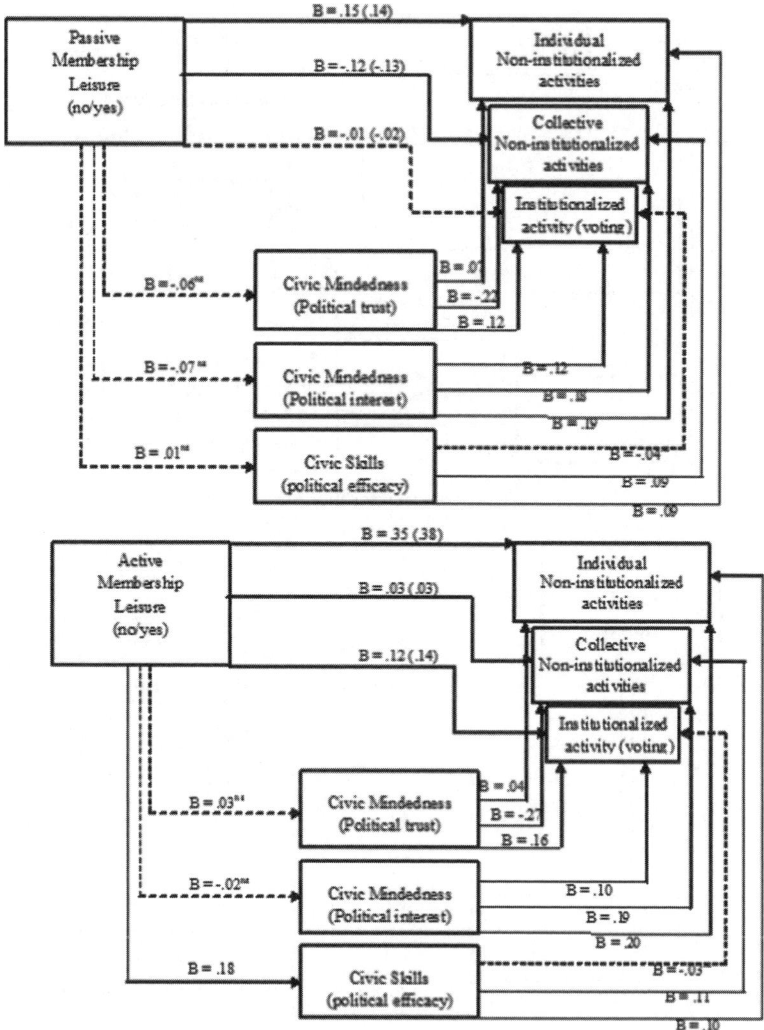

Fig. 3. Mediation models passive/active involvement in leisure organizations.

involvement in interest organizations was positively related to trust in politics (.35, p <.001), while active involvement was not (–.01, *ns*). Yet, for both groups, the less they trusted politics, the more they embarked on collective activities. Passive involvement in interest organizations stimulated individual activities through political trust and efficacy (total .15, p < .001, direct .10, p < .001, indirect trust .01 and efficacy .09, p <.001). These indirect effects were not observed for collective

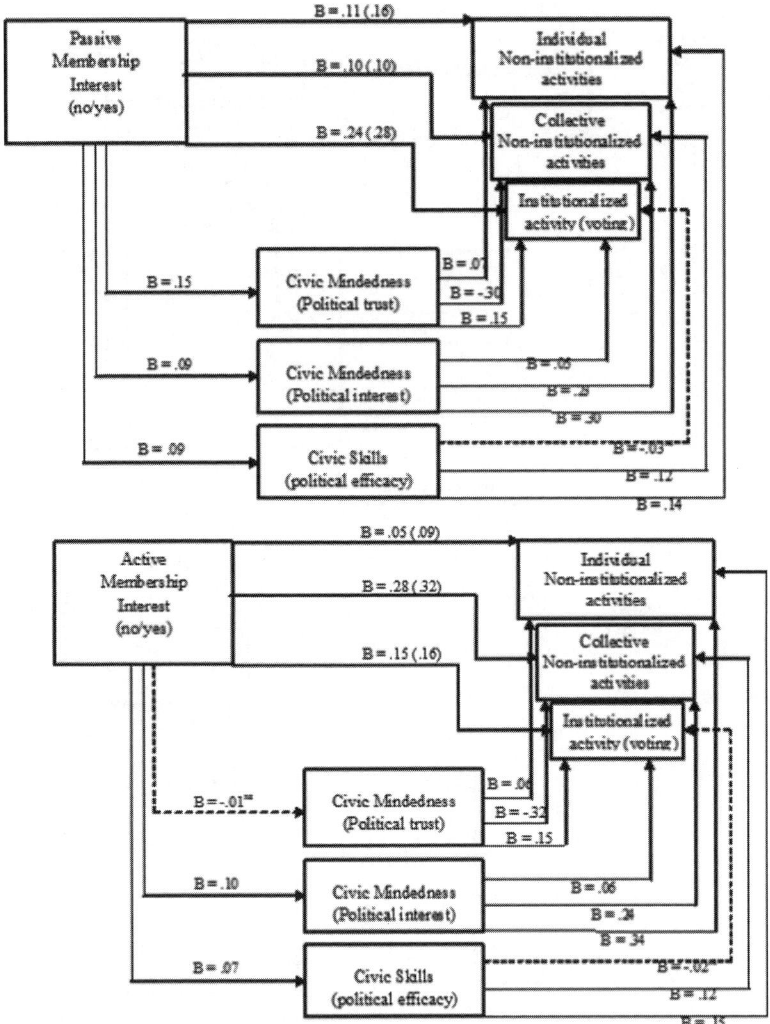

Fig. 4. Mediation models passive/active involvement in interest organizations.

activities and voting. Their significant total effects are largely due to direct rather than indirect effects (total/direct collective .10, $p < .001$ and .11, $p < .001$; voting .25, $p < .001$ and .23, $p < .001$).

Active involvement in interest organizations, on the other hand, showed a different pattern. Those active in interest organizations undertook the most collective activities, stimulated through civic mindedness and skills (total .33,

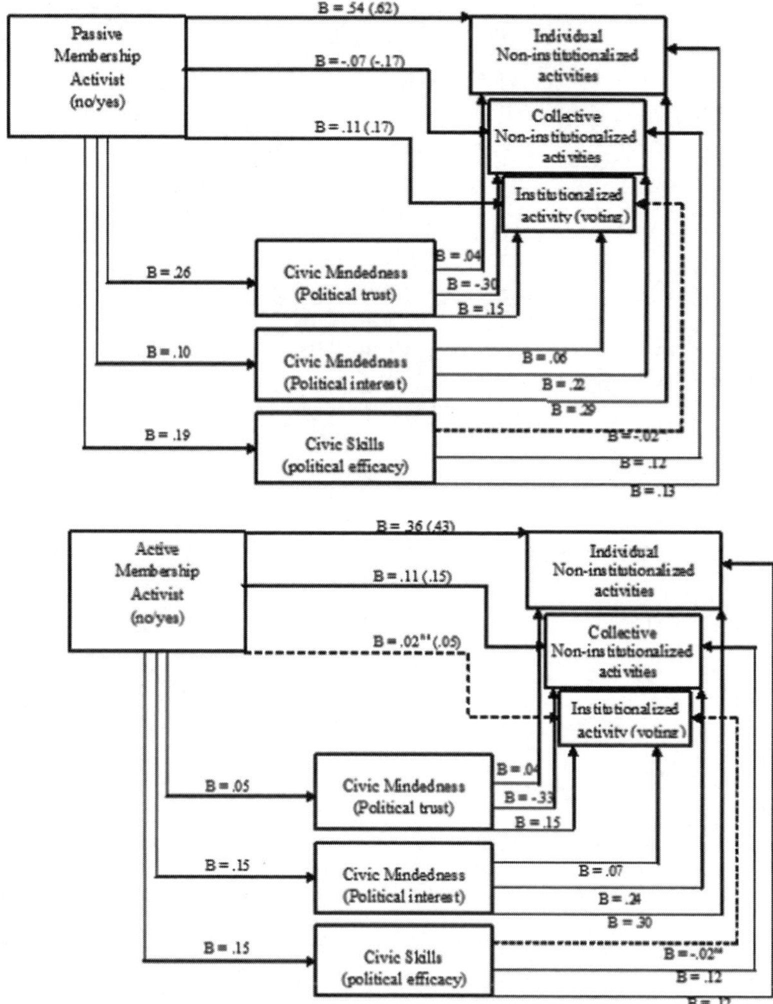

Fig. 5. Mediation models passive/active involvement in activist organizations.

direct .28 and indirect .01 via trust, .04 via political interest, and −.05 via political efficacy, p, .001). Interestingly, the indirect effect of efficacy is negative (−.05, p < .001), indicating that the strong positive effect of active involvement in interest organizations on collective activities is dampened when respondents deem such actions inefficacious. And, although much weaker, it also affected their individual activities through civic mindedness and skills (total .05, direct .01 and indirectly

Table 8. Total, Direct, and Indirect Effects of the Mediated Relationships between Civic Involvement and Political Activity

| | Total effect | Direct effect | Indirect effects | | Civic skills | Mediation |
| | | | Civic mindedness | | | |
	β (95% CI)	β (95% CI)	Trust	Political interest	Efficacy	
Passive membership leisure on:						
Individualized activities	.15 (.11−.23)	.14 (.08−.19)	.02 (.01−.03)	.00[ns]	.10 (.09−.11)	No mediation
Collective activities	−.10 (−.15−.03)	−.09 (−.12−.01)	.02 (.01−.02)	.00[ns]	−.04 (−.06−.03)	No mediation
Voting	.03 (.01−.04)	.00 (00.00)[ns]	.01 (.00−.02)	.00[ns]	.09 (.08−.11)	No mediation
Active membership leisure on:						
Individualized activities	.39 (.24−.45)	.34 (.23−.42)	.00[ns]	.00[ns]	.05 (.03−.06)	Via skills
Collective activities	.02(−.11−.14)[ns]	.03 (−.08−.15)[ns]	.00[ns]	.00[ns]	−.06 (−.08−.03)	No mediation
Voting	.30 (.15−.44)	.29 (.14−.42)	.00[ns]	.00[ns]	.09 (.07−.11)	No mediation
Passive membership interest on:						
Individualized activities	.15 (.09 −.20)	.10 (.04 −.15)	.01 (.01−.02)	.00[ns]	.09 (.08−.10)	Via trust, skills
Collective activities	.10 (.04 −.16)	.11 (.07 −.17)	.01 (.01−.02)	.00[ns]	−.05 (−.06−.03)	No mediation
Voting	.25 (.19−.30)	.23 (.16 −.27)	.01 (.01−.02)	.00[ns]	.08 (.06−.09)	No mediation
Active membership interest on:						
Individualized activities	.05 (.02 −.08)	.01 (−.02.04)[ns]	.02 (.01−.03)	.00[ns]	.10 (.08−.11)	Via trust, skills
Collective activities	.33 (.30 −.36)	.28 (.26−.32)	.01 (.01−.02)	.04 (.00−.07)	−.05 (−.07−.04)	Via trust, political interest, skills
Voting	.13 (.10−.16)	.13 (.10−.16)	.00 (.00−.01)	.00[ns]	.08 (.07−.10)	No mediation
Passive membership activist on:						
Individualized activities	.55 (.50−.61)	.47 (.42−.52)	.02 (.01−.03)	.00[ns]	.08 (.07−.09)	Via trust, skills
Collective activities	−.12 (−.18− −.07)	−.06 (−.11−.00)	.00[ns]	.00[ns]	−.10(−.12−.09)	No mediation
Voting	.16 (.13−.24)	.12 (.09−.17)	.00[ns]	.00[ns]	.07 (.05−.08)	No mediation
Active membership activist on:						
Individualized activities	.41 (.38−.44)	.33 (.31−.36)	.02 (.01−.03)	.00[ns]	.09 (.08−.10)	Via trust, skills
Collective activities	.14 (.11−.17)	.11 (.08−.14)	.01 (.01−.02)	.03 (.01−.06)	−.05 (−.06−.03)	Via trust, political interest, skills
Voting	.05 (.03−.08)	.02 (.00−.04)	.00[ns]	.00[ns]	.08 (.07−.09)	No mediation

Notes. ns = non significant.

via trust .02 and skills .10, $p < .001$). Active involvement in interest organizations, finally, is positively related to voting, yet this is neither through civic mindedness nor skills (total .13, direct .13, *ns*).

Figure 5 depicts the models for those passive (left) and active (right) involved in activist organizations, passive: $\chi^2(1, 10825) = 1.98$, $p = .16$, CFI $= 1.00$, NFI $= 1.00$ and RMSEA $= .01$; active: $\chi^2 (2, 10351) = 5.74$, $p = .06$, CFI $= 1.00$, NFI $= .99$ and RMSEA $= .01$. In line with interest organizations, involvement in activist organizations affects civic mindedness and skills, both for passive and active involvement. And, again, active members trust politics much less than passive members, and for both, the less they trust politics, the more collective activities they do. Yet, individual activities stand out. Active but especially passive activist members engage in individual activities, affected by civic mindedness and skills (passive total .55, direct .47 and indirect .02 via trust and .08 via efficacy; active total .41, direct .33 and indirect .02 via trust and .09 via efficacy, all significant at $p < .001$ level). Active members do undertake collective activities–although less than active interest members–affected by their civic mindedness and skills (total .14, direct .11 and indirect .01 via trust and .03 via political interest, all significant at $p < .001$). Note that efficacy has again a negative indirect effect on collective activities. Passive members, on the other hand, undertake the least collective activities of all (total $-.12$, $p < .001$), indirectly caused by feelings of inefficaciousness $(-.10, p < .001)$. In line with interest organizations, finally, passive members more often cast a vote than active members (total passive .16 vs. total active .05, $p < .001$), yet this is not significantly affected by civic mindedness nor skills.

Discussion

Does civic participation stimulate political action through civic mindedness and skills? This study shows that it depends on the combined effect of type and intensity on political activities. In a nutshell, leisure organizations do function as democratic workshops but only marginally so, passive membership only directly affects individualized activities yet not indirectly through civic mindedness or civic skills. Active membership of leisure organizations does stimulate individualized political activities through civic skills, but not collective activities. Moreover, active leisure membership is directly associated with the highest level of voting, yet this is not indirectly stimulated through civic mindedness or civic skills. Hence, we know that individuals active in leisure organizations are the ones who cast their votes, but civic skills and civic mindedness as assessed in this study does not explain why this is the case.

Involvement in interest and activist organizations does however stimulate political activity, especially for those actively involved and especially for collective noninstitutionalized activities. Interest and activist organizations coordinate, organize, and mobilize for collective action; as such active involvement directly stimulates collective activities, but also indirectly through nurturing political interest and political trust (see also Louis, Amiot, Thomas, & Blackwood, 2016). Taken together these results replicate the findings of van der Meer and van Ingen (2009) that interest and activist organizations nurture civic skills and civic mindedness more than leisure organizations.

Are these findings restricted to this specific sample of demonstrators, or can they be generalized to citizens in general? Our "supercitizens" may not be very representative of citizens in general. As for the observed direct effects of type and intensity of involvement on political activities, these may be stronger but not unique for this sample, but the indirect effects might be more specific for demonstrators. In fact, van der Meer and van Ingen (2009) did not find this mediation. They therefore conclude that civic organizations are "pools" rather than "schools" of democracy. In other words, they pool together the more civic minded and skilled citizens rather than providing a space where people acquire these virtues and skills. Obviously, correlational designs cannot confirm this idea, but we *did* find indirect effects. Perhaps we found those indirect effects due to the high power of our design, given the overrepresentation of hyperaffiliated citizens who are regular participants in uncommon political activities, or because we distinguished individualized from collective activities. Moreover, the indirect effects leave much variation unexplained, especially for individualized activities. Be this as it may, type and intensity of involvement do affect various political activities via civic mindedness and skills, but more research is needed.

We discuss the theoretical and practical implications of these findings, as well as the limitations of the current studies, below. First and foremost, they show that it is essential to treat individual and collective noninstitutionalized political activities separately, as they are differentially affected by the type, and intensity of civic participation. This was conceived of theoretically and corroborated empirically–we argued that the one political activity requires more coordination, organization, and mobilization of resources than the other. Take intensity, both Wollebæk and Selle (2002) and van der Meer and van Ingen (2009) found that passive members showed much higher levels of social capital (Wollebæk & Selle, 2002) and political action (van der Meer and van Ingen, 2009) than noninvolved, whereas the additional effects of active participation were marginal. Our passive members showed also higher levels of social capital/political action than noninvolved, but, contrary to their findings, the additional effects of active participation were significant. While Wollebæk and Selle treated interest and activist organizations as one category (i.e., political organizations), we, building on van der Meer and van Ingen, differentiated between interest and activist organizations. Yet, van der Meer and van Ingen collapsed noninstitutional political activities into one measure, while we distinguished between individualized and collective activities. Had we neglected the variation in interest and activist organizations and collapsed the political activities into a single measure, we would not have discerned the diverging patterns of political activity spurred by differences in type, and intensity. Yet, it is precisely in this interaction of type and intensity on various activities where we find the most interesting results.

It is worth comparing for instance the political repertoire of those passively and actively involved in interest and activist organizations. Passive members of interest organizations are the least active in movement politics, but they vote the most. Passive members of activist organizations prefer individualized activities, but are the least active in collective activities. Active members of interest organizations prefer collective activities, while active members of activist organizations employ both individualized and collective activities, but vote the least. Interest organizations, for example, labor unions, still specialize in staging collective action and accrue the necessary resources to do so, while new social movement organizations professionalize and reduce the role of members and supporters to "checkbook activism" (Stolle et al., 2005). As a result, their passive and active members' political actions do not only differ quantitatively, they also embark on qualitatively different political activities.

Two limitations of this study should be noted. Civic organizations might be pools or schools of democracy, or citizens' civic virtues and political activities might come about by a combination of the selection mechanism (pools) and the socialization mechanism (schools). As our data are correlational we are not able to formulate and test strict causal reasoning. Future research, based on longitudinal designs or experiments, might focus on these causal issues. One aspect we did not cover is that civic organizations create essential networks and opportunities for mobilization and participation in political activities (e.g., Verba, Schlozman, & Brady, 1995). The relation between networks and opportunities for participation, and if collective activities are more affected by embeddedness than individual ones, might present fruitful directions for future research.

Implications of Our Findings

In terms of practical implications, the paper first and foremost shows that *the* activist does not exist. People active in leisure organizations differ from those who are checkbook-members of interest-organizations, who in turn, are different from activists. Thus, different activists are attracted by different organizations, and, in all likelihood, different incentives will motivate them to sustain their activism. Yet, this needs future research. Another point relates to aging activists. The 45–64 cohort is the *most* active group, both in interest and activist organizations, whereas the 25–44 group is the *less* active group, again both in interest and activist organizations. Organizations should either be innovative and creative to get and hold the young people aboard, or change to a checkbook organization run by a small team of professionals. As our data reveals, young people *are* willing to voluntary contribute to civil society, yet, mainly as passive members or to perform individualized forms of politics and consumerism.

The less people trust politicians, the more collective noninstitutionalized activities they undertake, and the less likely they are to cast a vote. Passive members of interest and activist organizations put the *most* faith in institutionalized politics, while their active fellows put the *least* faith in institutionalized politics. Those who trust politicians can afford restricted investment in civics, and checkbook membership suffices. Contrary to those who distrust politicians, they feel the urge to invest time and energy, as democratic watchdogs they try to influence politics via noninstitutionalized politics. In fact, following the noninvolved, active activist-members are the least likely to cast a vote. For them, individualized and collective noninstitutionalized politics partly *substitute* the institutionalized politics they distrust, while for active members of interest organizations *collective* non institutionalized politics *add* to institutionalized politics.

Does checkbook activism "crowd out" other forms of affiliation? It depends. Compared to active members, checkbook members are affiliated with more rather than fewer organizations. Checkbook affiliation requires less time and energy, so people could affiliate with more organizations. Does checkbook activism then "crowd out" other forms of activism? Again, it depends. Checkbook members of interest organizations undertake indeed relatively fewer collective activities compared to active members of interest organizations, but still as much as active members of activist organizations. They undertake also relatively fewer individualized activities, yet, those actively involved in interest organizations do neither. If crowding out does takes place, it is for checkbook members of activist organizations—given the negative relation between membership and collective activities–yet they compensate their inactivity in collective activities by the largest involvement in individual activities. Hence, rather than crowding out, citizens' engagement is moving away from organized actions to individualized modes of politics (cf. Micheletti, 2003), especially for checkbook members of activist organizations. Underlying this, might be what Lichterman (1996) calls "personalism": people feel a personal sense of political responsibility rather than feeling restricted or obliged to a community or group. The role of organizations in coordinating, organizing, and mobilizing individualized activities clearly needs more research. The same goes for the challenge of organizers to visualize the effects of unseen individualized activities their constituency undertakes, so that they can be framed and claimed as a movement success.

References

Alexander, D. T., Barraket, J., Lewis, J. M., & Considine, M. (2012). Civic engagement and associationalism: The impact of group membership scope versus intensity of participation. *European Sociological Review, 28*, 43–58. doi: 10.1093/esr/jcq047

Almond, G., & Verba, S. (1963). *The civic culture: Political attitudes and democracy in five nations.* Boston, MA: Little, Brown.

Barnes, S. H., & Kaase, M. (1979). *Political action.* Beverly Hills, CA: Sage.

Corrigall-Brown, C. (2012). From the balconies to the barricades and back? Trajectories of participation in contentious politics. *Journal of Civil Society, 8,* 17–38. doi: 10.1080/17448689.2012.665650

Dalton, R. J. (2008). *Citizen politics: Public opinion and political parties in advanced industrial democracies.* Washington D.C.: CQ Press.

Flash Eurobarometer (2013). *Europeans' engagement in participatory democracy.* Retrieved on December 27, 2015 from http://www.eesc.europa.eu/?i=portal.en.publications.27060.

Howard, M. M., & Gilbert, L. (2008). A cross-national comparison of the internal effects of participation in voluntary organizations. *Political Studies, 56,* 12–32. doi: 10.1111/j.1467-9248.2007.00715.x

Klandermans, B. (1984). Mobilization and participation: Social-psychological expansisons of resource mobilization theory. *American Sociological Review, 49,* 583–600.

Klandermans, B., van Stekelenburg, J., van Troost, D., van Leeuwen, A., Walgrave, S., Verhulst, J., van Laer, J., & Wouters, R. (2011). Manual for data collection on protest demonstrations. Caught in the act of protest: Contextualizing contestation (CCC-project), Version, 3.0

Lichterman, P. (1996). *The search for political community. American activists reinventing commitment.* Cambridge, UK: Cambridge University Press.

Lichterman, P. (2005). *Elusive togetherness: Church groups trying to bridge America's divisions.* Princeton, NJ: Princeton University Press.

Louis, W. R., Amiot, C. E., Thomas, E. F., & Blackwood, L. (2016). The "Activist Identity" and activism across domains: A multiple identities analysis. *Journal of Social Issues, 72*(2), 242–263.

Micheletti, M. (2003). *Political virtue and shopping: Individuals, consumerism, and collective action.* New York, NY: Palgrave Macmillan.

Norris, P. (2003). *Democratic Phoenix.* New York, NY: Cambridge University Press.

Paxton, P. (1999). Is social capital declining in the United States? A multiple indicator assessment. *American Journal of Sociology, 105,* 88–127. doi: 10.1086/210268.

Putnam, R. D. (1993). *Making democracy work. Civic traditions in modern Italy.* Princeton, NJ: Princeton University Press.

Schussman, A., & Soule, S. A. (2005). Process and protest: Accounting for individual protest participation. *Social Forces, 84,* 1083–1108. doi:10.1353/sof.2006.0034.

Stolle, D., Hooghe, M., & Micheletti, M. (2005). Politics in the supermarket: Political consumerism as a form of political participation. *International Political Science Review, 26,* 245–269. doi: 10.1177/0192512105053784.

Van der Meer, T. W. G., & Van Ingen, E. J. (2009). Schools of democracy? Disentangling the relationship between civic participation and political action in 17 European countries. *European Journal of Political Research, 48,* 281–308. doi: 10.1111/j.1475-6765.2008.00836.x.

Van Deth, J. W. (2014). A conceptual map of political participation. *Acta Politica, 49,* 349–367. doi: 10.1057/ap.2014.6.

Van Deth, J. W., Montero, J. R., & Westholm, A. (Eds.). (2007). *Citizenship and involvement in European democracies. A comparative analysis.* New York, NY: Routledge.

Van Stekelenburg, J., Walgrave, S., Klandermans, B., & Verhulst, J. (2012). Contextualizing contestation: Framework, design, and data. *Mobilization: An International Quarterly, 17,* 249–262.

Verba, S., Schlozman, K. L., & Brady, H. E. (1995). *Voice and equality: Civic voluntarism in American politics.* Cambridge, MA: Harvard University Press.

Wollebæk, D., & Selle, P. (2002). Does participation in voluntary associations contribute to social capital? The impact of intensity, scope, and type. *Nonprofit and Voluntary Sector Quarterly, 31,* 32–61. doi: 10.1177/089976400231100.

JACQUELIEN VAN STEKELENBURG is Associate Professor in the Sociology Department at the Vrije Universiteit Amsterdam. She studies the social psychological dynamics of protest participation. She edited (with Roggeband and

Klandermans) *The Future of Social Movement Research: Dynamics, Mechanisms and Processes* (2013). She is currently working on a comparative study on street demonstrations (with Klandermans and Walgrave) and a study on emerging networks and feelings of belonging.

BERT KLANDERMANS is Professor in Applied Social Psychology at the Vrije Universiteit, Amsterdam. He has published extensively on the social psychology of protest and social movement participation. He authored the now classic *Social Psychology of Protest* (1997). He coedited (with Conny Roggeband) *Handbook of Social movements across disciplines* (2007). He is the editor of *Sociopedia.isa*—an online database of review articles—in collaboration with the *International Sociological Association*. He is coeditor of Blackwell/Wiley's *Encyclopedia of Social Movements* and *The Future of Social Movement Research. Dynamics, Mechanisms, and Processes* (2013). He received the Harold Lasswell Award of the International Society of Political Psychology for his lifelong contribution to political psychology (2013) and the John D. McCarthy Award from Notre Dame University for his contribution to the study of social movements and collective action (2014).

AGNES AKKERMAN is Professor of Sustainable Cooperation in Labor Relations Department at Sociology of Groningen University and Associate Professor in the Department of Sociology at Vrije Universiteit, Amsterdam. Her research interests include voice and protest at the workplace and spill-over effects of workplace conflict.

Journal of Social Issues, Vol. 72, No. 2, 2016, pp. 315–334
doi: 10.1111/josi.12168

Acting in Solidarity: Cross-Group Contact between Disadvantaged Group Members and Advantaged Group Allies

Lisa Droogendyk[*] **and Stephen C. Wright**
Simon Fraser University

Micah Lubensky
The Global Forum on MSM & HIV

Winnifred R. Louis
The University of Queensland

The actions of advantaged group activists (sometimes called "allies") are admirable, and they likely make meaningful contributions to the movements they support. However, a nuanced understanding of the role of advantaged group allies must also consider the potential challenges of their participation. Both in their everyday lives and during their activist work, advantaged group allies are especially likely to have direct contact with disadvantaged group members. This article considers when such contact may harm rather than help resistance movements by disadvantaged groups. We also suggest that to avoid these undermining effects, advantaged group allies must effectively communicate support for social change, understand the implications of their own privilege, offer autonomy-oriented support, and resist the urge to increase their own feelings of inclusion by co-opting relevant marginalized social identities.

> *"I mean nothing against any sincere whites when I say that as members of black organizations, generally whites' very presence subtly renders the black organization automatically less effective. Even the best white members will slow down the Negroes' discovery of*

---

[*]Correspondence concerning this article should be addressed to Lisa Droogendyk, Psychology Department, Robert C. Brown Hall, Simon Fraser University, Burnaby BC V5A 1S6, Canada [e-mail: ldroogen@sfu.ca].

> *what they need to do, and particularly of what they can do—for themselves, working by themselves, among their own kind, in their own communities . . . "*
>
> – Malcolm X

> *"I must confess that over the past few years I have been gravely disappointed with the white moderate. . . . Shallow understanding from people of good will is more frustrating than absolute misunderstanding from people of ill will."*
>
> – Martin Luther King, Jr.

When members of disadvantaged groups engage in resistance, members of the advantaged group sometimes join in and support their efforts. During the women's suffrage movement in North America and Europe, some male politicians were openly supportive. Similarly, some White South Africans worked alongside Mandela and other Black activists to end Apartheid. More recently, some heterosexual parents have become strong supporters of same-sex marriage after learning their child was gay or lesbian (e.g., Johnson & Best, 2012), and this year as African Americans in U.S. cities protested the killing of Black people by police, some Whites and even a few White police officers have shown support for the Black Lives Matter movement (Wing, 2015). The actions of these advantaged group activists (at times called "allies") are admirable, and they likely make meaningful contributions to the movements they support. However, a nuanced understanding of the role of advantaged group allies must also consider the potential challenges of their participation. This article uses social psychological research and theorizing to consider when advantaged group allies may harm rather than help resistance movements by disadvantaged groups. Both in their everyday lives and during their activist work, advantaged group allies are especially likely to have direct contact with disadvantaged group members. Ironically, these interactions may sometimes (although not always) weaken the collective action engagement of disadvantaged group members. Throughout our analysis, we highlight a distinction between two subgroups within a given disadvantaged group—disadvantaged group members who are themselves activists and those who are nonactivists.

What Is an Advantaged Group Activist?

Curtin and McGarty (2016) describe activists as committed participants in a social movement, with a "relatively enduring orientation" to the social issue or problem. Here, we focus on *advantaged group allies* (AGAs)—advantaged group activists who are committed participants in action to improve the treatment and/or status of a disadvantaged group (e.g., Russell & Bohan, 2016; Smith & Redington, 2010). Some AGAs may be committed to engaging in action on behalf of a variety of disadvantaged groups (e.g., see Louis, Amiot, Thomas, & Blackwood, 2016; Ravarino, 2008). For others, activism may center around one particular disadvantaged group (e.g., straight parents of gay or lesbian children active in support of same-sex marriage). Our current analysis focuses on the fact that AGAs' involvement in these social movements is likely to create frequent opportunities for cross-group contact, which may psychologically impact members of the disadvantaged group.

Everyday Interactions: The Challenge of Positive Cross-Group Contact

AGA's daily lives may include routine, friendly interactions with disadvantaged group members (e.g., as a neighbor or coworker). Although likely to improve intergroup attitudes, recent research and theorizing also suggest that such positive contact may be disempowering for disadvantaged group members (e.g., Dixon, Levine, Reicher, & Durrheim, 2012; Saguy, Tausch, Dovidio, & Pratto, 2009; Wright, 2001). While echoing these concerns, we suggest that interactions with AGAs can also be structured to empower disadvantaged group members.

The vast majority of the contact literature focuses on how it can improve intergroup attitudes and reduce prejudice, especially among advantaged group members (see Pettigrew & Tropp, 2006; Wright, 2009, for reviews). However, although improving intergroup attitudes and the fight for social equality may appear to be complementary goals that could be pursued simultaneously, Wright and Lubensky (2009) argued that the underlying psychology supporting these goals may not be complementary at all. A growing literature supports this contention, suggesting that the kind of positive cross-group contact most likely to reduce prejudice can simultaneously undermine disadvantaged group members' collective action participation (e.g., Dixon et al., 2012; Saguy et al., 2009; Wright & Baray, 2012). A number of mechanisms may account for these negative effects. First, positive contact is often structured to focus attention away from collective identities (e.g., Gaertner & Dovidio, 2000; Miller, 2002). However, collective identification is a critical precursor to engaging in collective action (Stürmer & Simon, 2004; Tajfel & Turner, 1979; van Zomeren, Postmes, & Spears, 2008). Second, positive contact breaks down negative stereotypes of the out-group (Allport, 1954; Wright, Brody, & Aron, 2005). Indeed, the primary intended outcome of positive cross-group contact is to generate positive attitudes toward the out-group. However, holding a negative view of the advantaged out-group—for example, by identifying the advantaged group as responsible for the oppression faced by the disadvantaged group—can be critical for maintaining the strong perceptions of injustice and collective control essential for collective action engagement (Reynolds, Oakes, Haslam, Nolan, & Dolnik, 2000; Simon & Klandermans, 2001; Stott & Drury, 2004; Wright & Tropp, 2002).

To our knowledge, none of this research or theorizing has focused specifically on cross-group contact involving AGAs. However, cross-group interactions may become more likely as advantaged group members become allies and enter the communities and personal lives of disadvantaged group members. Ironically, these interactions may threaten disadvantaged group members' interest in collective action. This threat may be particularly relevant to disadvantaged group members who are nonactivists, as disadvantaged group activists and nonactivists likely differ in a variety of ways that account for their differential engagement in collective action. In particular, nonactivists likely identify less strongly with their disadvantaged in-group, perceive less injustice in the treatment or position of their group, and have a weaker sense of collective control (see Wright, 2010). As a result, nonactivists may be especially likely to be negatively influenced by cross-group contact with advantaged group activists.

The Promise of Cross-Group Contact

Despite the apparent conflict between positive contact and collective action engagement, there is also evidence that under the right circumstances, cross-group contact can be empowering. Specifically, cross-group contact may enhance a disadvantaged group member's collective action engagement when the advantaged group member deliberately moves beyond contact that is merely friendly and positive, and engage in *supportive contact*: positive cross-group contact in which the advantaged group member explicitly communicates opposition to inequality and/or support for the disadvantaged group and their goals (Droogendyk, Louis, & Wright, under review). For example, the advantaged group member might openly challenge the status quo or express support for resistance by the disadvantaged group.

Supportive contact could increase disadvantaged group members' collective action engagement by strengthening critical psychological mechanisms described earlier. By openly opposing existing intergroup inequality, the advantaged group member would focus attention on group memberships and represent the disadvantaged group as deserving and positive. Thus, rather than reducing the salience of group identity, the interaction might strengthen identification with the disadvantaged group. Open recognition of inequality by an advantaged group member could also strengthen perceptions of injustice. If injustice is apparent even to some who directly benefits from it, this is strong evidence of the reality of that injustice (e.g., Czopp & Monteith, 2003).

Our recent research (Droogendyk et al., under review) offers direct support for these claims. As there is a paucity of research on supportive contact, we describe this work here in some detail. Comparing supportive contact to other realistic positive cross-group contact experiences, we found that supportive cross-group contact can be empowering for disadvantaged group members.

One study involved international students in Australia. Although a significant source of funding to universities, this group is also the target of discrimination (e.g., Reitmanova, 2008). International students were asked to recall a domestic student with whom they had a friendly relationship, who was either clearly supportive of international students, showed little support, or was ambiguous in terms of their support (leaving the participant unsure whether the person was or was not supportive). Those recalling a clearly supportive domestic student friend reported higher willingness to engage in collective action than those who recalled a domestic student friend who was low or unclear in their support for international students. In addition, recalling supportive contact increased collective action engagement by heightening perceptions of injustice. In this context, supportive contact was empowering primarily because it drove home the reality of the injustice faced by international students.

In another study, first-generation Canadian university students engaged in a friendship-building interaction with a Canadian-born student (actually a confederate) and subsequently overheard the confederate make a comment regarding inequalities faced by first-generation Canadians. The comment was either explicitly supportive of first-generation Canadians (expressing opposition to intergroup inequality), or ambiguous (offering no information about the partner's feelings regarding intergroup inequality). In addition, these two groups were compared to a control group that had no interaction with a Canadian-born student. Compared to first-generation Canadians in both the control and ambiguous comment conditions, those whose partner expressed support reported more willingness to engage in collective action and actually engaged in more collective action by requesting more buttons to be used to raise awareness of the intergroup inequality. Again, heightened perceptions of injustice mediated the relationship between supportive contact and collective action.

These two studies offer initial evidence of the empowering impact of *supportive contact,* compared to both no contact and to positive/friendly contact that does not include a clear statement in support of social change.

Importance of Communication

The concept of supportive contact has obvious implications for the behavior of AGAs. Specifically, it points to the critical role of *communicating support* during cross-group contact. Contact with advantaged group members who are ambiguous about their support (i.e., offering no information about support, or sending unclear messages) appears to offer no benefits for disadvantaged group members' collective action engagement. In fact, ambiguity is generally deleterious for collective action engagement (Becker et al., 2013; Wright, 1997), in part because it may raise doubts about whether action against a seemingly friendly advantaged group is really justified. Thus, AGAs need to include clear, explicit messages of support for social change to ensure that their friendly cross-group interactions do not serve to undermine disadvantaged group members' collective action engagement.

Offering such explicit support may not be easy. Talking about issues of intergroup inequality can be challenging for advantaged group members, who have to deal with anxiety about appearing biased, feelings of embarrassment or guilt about their own privilege, and social norms to avoid "taboo" topics (e.g., Shelton, 2003; Tropp, Stout, Boatswain, Wright, & Pettigrew, 2006; Vorauer, 2006). And, regardless of one's good intentions, these conversations do not always go smoothly (e.g., Shelton, Richeson, Salvatore, & Trawalter, 2005). These concerns may be most acute during everyday interactions, where disadvantaged interaction partners are either nonactivists, or their movement involvement is unknown. In these casual, passing contact situations AGAs may be particularly hesitant to offer the kinds of clear expressions of support that we have described above, especially if they must initiate the conversation (Johnson, 2006; Tropp et al., 2006). Concerns around raising issues of structural discrimination, privilege, and intergroup inequality will be particularly acute when it is unclear whether one's interaction partner is interested in these topics. Thus, interactions with disadvantaged group members who are not known to be active members of a movement may closely resemble those shown to be most problematic—friendly and positive, but without clear communications related to intergroup inequality (Droogendyk et al., under review). In contrast, while interactions between AGAs and disadvantaged group activists are not immune to such concerns, it may be easier for AGAs to discuss intergroup inequality and offer explicit support during these interactions. While working together as part of a social movement to reduce inequality, conversations about social justice and group-based inequality may arise naturally and be much less "taboo." Additionally, AGAs' ongoing involvement with a movement may allow them to build meaningful personal relationships, in which supportive statements would appear more appropriate and genuine.

Finally, it is worth noting that not all supportive contact is likely to be equally effective. Rattan and Ambady (2014) show that even when advantaged group members attempt to offer cross-group support, they may not accurately intuit which kinds of messages are most beneficial and lead to feelings of empowerment (see also Brown & Ostrove, 2013). Clearly, more research is needed to investigate what kinds of messages AGAs usually send and whether these messages are received in ways that can produce the increases in empowerment found in our research.

The Challenge of Doing the Work: Misguided Activism

The challenge to AGAs does not end with the need to engage in clearly supportive cross-group contact in everyday interactions—it also extends to how they conduct themselves in their activist work. The stories and writings of disadvantaged group activists are replete with examples of AGAs who may have the right intentions, and express their concern and dissatisfaction with current injustices and inequalities but who nevertheless ended up doing as much harm as good. Social psychological theory and research may offer valuable insights into the processes that underpin these misguided efforts as well as offering explanations for the responses of disadvantaged group members affected by them.

The "Intergroup Helping" Problem

> *"If we are discussing racial inequalities... and White voice rise to the top of the conversation... how is that any social change? White voices have long been the arbiters of social understanding and norms."*
>
> – Jay Dodd, *Huffpost*

> *"When I see white people smiling for pictures at protests, carrying the biggest sign that takes up the most space, bringing in unnecessary violence, and talking about how 'we are all victims and all just need to get along' during demonstrations about the targeting of black people... I can't help but think that maybe they're just here to make themselves feel better about their own prejudice... I'm not saying don't support and/or participate, I'm saying make sure how you do so makes sense for you as a white person and doesn't harm the cause you claim to support."*
>
> – Mwende Katwiwa, *FreeQuency*

The sentiment expressed in these quotations highlights one of the ways enthusiastic AGAs can serve to detract from, rather than enhance, social movements. AGAs may fail to seek guidance from disadvantaged group activists, may take over work that would have otherwise been done by members of the disadvantaged group, may co-opt and in so doing obfuscate or trivialize the movement's message, may actively seek to become a leader or spokesperson within a movement, and may offer unwanted and/or unneeded advice on strategy and tactics. Some poignant examples are evident in the activism that has emerged in numerous U.S. cities in response to the many African Americans who have been killed by police officers (including many actions that have occurred under the banner of the *Black Lives Matter* movement). These actions have inspired many important and valuable conversations, including one about the role that White Americans should play, as numerous Black activists have objected to the behavior of some Whites who seek to join protests and other social action (De Graaf, 2014; Fagan & Ho, 2014).

At first glance, it seems incongruous, even ironic, that AGAs would ultimately undermine a movement by dominating it, when their apparent intentions are to help reduce inequality. However, social psychological research and theorizing on intergroup helping (e.g., Nadler, 2002; Nadler & Halabi, 2015; van Leeuwen & Täuber, 2010) offers valuable insights into the underlying psychology of advantaged group helpers and why these kinds of dominating/co-opting behaviors might emerge.

A key contention of recent theorizing on intergroup helping (e.g., Nadler & Halabi, 2015) is that helping is not benign—it can often reflect, and thus reify rather than undermine, the existing status differences between the groups. Even an offer of help implies that the helper has resources the recipient lacks and needs, and accepting help can be seen as an admission of lower status and power. In addition, being self-reliant is a valued attribute, at least in independent and individualist-oriented cultures. Recipients of help may appear to lack this kind of self-reliance and competence. Finally, the act of helping is understood to be highly laudable. Those who help should be praised, even honored, for their efforts. Helpers may feel that they have a legitimate right to expect gratitude and some degree of deference from those they assist (Halabi, Nadler, & Dovidio, 2013). Thus, to the degree that AGAs conceptualize their actions as helping the disadvantaged, the more likely they are to fall prey to processes that lead them to see themselves (and by extension their in-group) as more powerful, more capable, and more worthy of respect than the group they seek to help. It is not a long route from this sense of personal and in-group superiority to the kinds of dominating behaviors described earlier.

Even more disconcerting is the possibility that AGAs may sometimes be influenced by processes that van Leeuven and colleagues (2010) describe as "strategic" helping. Even helping that genuinely benefits the disadvantaged group can be partially motivated by a desire to protect the reputation or status of the advantaged in-group (e.g., Van Vugt & Hardy, 2010). Importantly for the current analysis, when advantaged group members recognize that the in-group is to some degree responsible for the injustice experienced by the disadvantaged group, they are motivated to provide help in order to restore the in-group's reputation and relieve feelings of collective guilt (e.g., Leach, Snider, & Iyer, 2002; van Leeuwen, 2007). However, these motives are likely to lead to *dependency-oriented help* (e.g., Nadler & Halabi, 2015) in which advantaged group helpers attempt to provide the full solution for the disadvantaged group's problem. For example, behaviors like taking over work that could be done by members of the disadvantaged group, seeking to act as a spokesperson or leader, and offering unwanted and/or unneeded advice would be consistent with this concept of dependency-oriented helping.

Finally, inappropriate forms of helping can also stem from AGAs' failure to recognize their own privilege. For most advantaged group members, the default view of intergroup inequality is to focus on the plight of the disadvantaged, seldom considering the flipside—the privilege of the advantaged (Case, Iuzzini, & Hopkins, 2012; Powell, Branscombe, & Schmitt, 2005). Contemplating privilege can be uncomfortable. Privilege implies that one has received something unearned and appears to call into question the legitimacy of one's position, one's accomplishments, and perhaps even one's integrity. Nonetheless, privilege is real and one of the ironic outcomes of possessing it is that one is not compelled to think about having it (e.g., Case, 2012; Johnson, 2006). Thus, AGAs may understand their helping as an effort to "raise up" those who are disadvantaged, without even examining how they are privileged by their race, their gender, their sexual orientation, their socioeconomic status, etc. and how the struggle they seek to support must also involve "tearing down" the privilege that their group holds. For these AGAs what needs to be examined and remedied is the lives and problems of the out-group. Their own lives and the lives of their in-group are the "normal" or the "desirable." We offer a few examples of negative outcomes resulting from this perspective. Of course, failure to recognize privilege can create a wide range of problems. We certainly do not mean to trivialize this by offering only these few.

First, a failure to examine one's own group-based privilege can lead to enacting that privilege in precisely the ways described above—expecting to be offered a position of responsibility, to be listened to, and to be seen as valuable without having to first demonstrate that value. Failure to examine their group-based privilege would leave AGAs unprepared to have that privilege openly questioned or denied to them within the social movement.

Second, disadvantaged group activists often face uncertainty around the terms of an advantaged group member's support. As Black feminist scholar Bell Hooks (2000) comments, "Support can be occasional. It can be given and just as easily withdrawn. Solidarity requires sustained, ongoing commitment" (p. 67). At the root of the problem of *uncommitted activism* is a lack of understanding of privilege—a lack of awareness of how different life is for members of a disadvantaged group. For privileged AGAs, activism can be an occasional activity to be engaged in when they have extra time or motivation. They can then disappear back to the safety of their own lives for days, weeks, or months. Disadvantaged group members do not have the luxury of taking time off from inequality and injustice. Part-time activism can be reasonably interpreted by disadvantaged group members as evidence of AGAs failure to understand this reality.

Finally, AGAs who are unaware of their privilege may fail to consider how group membership can influence the consequences of activism. For example, they may plan events that seem reasonable to them, and encourage disadvantaged group members to participate. However, time, financial resources, and support networks may make their plan safe and reasonable for them, while not being reasonable or safe for some members of the disadvantaged group. Similarly, AGAs may inadvertently engage in behaviors during actions organized by disadvantaged group activist that are only mildly costly to them, but put their disadvantaged group "comrades" at more serious risk. Doreen Silversmith, an Indigenous Canadian, describes such a case: "At the reclamation site, some settler activists came and wanted to fight the police. They yelled, threw things and egged the other side on, getting our people all worked up. We have to live there. Remember, no White people were arrested in that raid but 50 of our people have been charged" (Canon & Sunseri, 2011). In observing a recent political protest, one of the authors (Wright) was reminded of the difference between the experiences of a White, middle class, middle aged, professional *choosing* to be arrested compared to the likely experience of a young, First Nations activist being arrested for the same act of defiance. Would an AGA choose arrest if all of his/her privileges were somehow removed? Although this is anecdotal, we believe it makes clear the need for AGAs to be aware of the privileges they continue to hold even as they seek to help those who do not share those privileges.

Responses of the Disadvantaged Group to Dominant and Dependency-Oriented Help

> *"We ask you not for an invitation to your rallies and to sit at your tables, we ask you not to save us, but to back us up. . . . Or get the hell out of the way."*
> – Xhopakelxhit, Ancestral Pride

> *"Who ever walked in behind anyone to freedom? If we can't go hand in hand, I don't want to go."*
> – Hazel Scott

Although dependency-oriented helping can be very effective at resurrecting the damaged reputation of the advantaged group and relieving feelings of guilt, the implied message of this kind of help is that the disadvantaged group lacks the efficacy to accomplish their collective goals. The psychological consequences of this message for the recipients are typically negative, and may be especially negative when dependency-oriented help is provided in a very public way, as this public display further threatens the group's reputation (see Nadler & Porat, 1978). Thus, the public dominating actions by AGAs described above are particularly problematic.

Our analysis suggests two possible responses to this public dependency-oriented help. The first is represented in the quotations at the beginning of this section, and involves suspicion, frustration, and the rejection of the help. Disadvantaged group activists in particular (as opposed to nonactivists) may be likely to respond this way because the dominant behaviors of AGAs clash with the *cognitive alternatives* that inspired their own activism. Being able to imagine a different and better world—a cognitive alternative to the current inequality—has been described as a critical prerequisite to collective action (Jetten, Iyer, Branscombe, & Zhang, 2013; Tajfel & Turner, 1979). A movement that is co-opted and led by members of the group that currently holds power is inconsistent with this vision of a new and more equal world—no matter how benevolent the intentions of these "leaders." In addition, Reicher and Haslam (2012) argue that *how* the status quo will be replaced can also be important, and that a cognitive alternative involves "imagining an alternative social world . . . but also involves a sense of how we might get there" (p. 55). If disadvantaged group activists are indeed motivated by a shared vision of how the desired social change will be achieved, it is unlikely that this vision would involve a movement dominated by members of the current advantaged group. Thus, rejecting the dependency-oriented help offered by AGAs may itself be an act of resistance.

However, disadvantaged group members may not always resist the dominant behavior of AGAs. Acceptance of dependency-oriented help by AGAs is often closely tied to perceptions of collective control and may be especially likely among disadvantaged group members who are not activists. Wright (2001) describes two components of collective control. First, individuals must believe that change is possible—that there is some degree of *instability* in the intergroup relations (see Tajfel & Turner, 1979). Disadvantaged group nonactivists may believe the system to be relatively stable, and as a result may welcome the leadership and other intrusions of advantaged group members who espouse egalitarian values, seek social justice, and appear to offer a more benevolent alternative to the current power holders. Second, feelings of collective control also involve a belief that one's group has the *agency* or collective efficacy to take advantage of instability in the system— that the group has suitable resources and abilities to effect change (e.g., van Zomeren et al., 2008). Again, if disadvantaged group members believe their group lacks the resources to instigate or maintain a social movement, they may welcome and be grateful for dependency-oriented help (Nadler, 2002). Whether it results from perceptions of stability or a lack of collective efficacy, a lack of perceived collective control necessitates the acceptance of help that continues to reinforce and instantiate group-based status inequalities, although more benevolent than the hostility and discrimination offered by the current system. Importantly, a social movement that becomes dominated by AGAs due to a lack of perceived collective control may itself serve to reinforce those low feelings of collective control and further reduce the chances of future disadvantaged group-led resistance.

Alternatively, some disadvantaged group *activists* may initially tolerate the dominant behaviors of AGAs, while seeking to educate and reform them by encouraging them to take on alternative roles that involve what Nadler and Halabi (2015) call *autonomy-oriented help*—help that offers needed resources but allows the disadvantaged group to describe and carry out their own solutions. Although perhaps constructive, this process of educating and reforming is likely to be distracting and frustrating and may take resources away from other needed action. As one Black feminist blogger commented, "[People of color] if they're honest will admit that sometimes it takes entirely too much energy and patience to support White people in their process of being an ally" (Feminist Griote, 2013). Having to stretch already-limited resources and energy in this way may also reduce perceptions of efficacy.

Finally, identification with the disadvantaged in-group moderates responses to dependency-oriented help, with high identifiers more likely to reject and low identifiers to accept it (Nadler & Halabi, 2015). Thus, AGAs offering dependency-oriented help may receive "mixed messages." They may be lauded and welcomed by disadvantaged group members who have lower in-group identification (likely nonactivists), but will face criticism and rejection from activists, who are likely to have strong in-group identification. Having one's efforts to help rejected is unpleasant and can lead to feelings of resentment, to withdrawal of future support and can exacerbate group tensions (see Halabi et al., 2013).

In summary, cross-group helping seems highly laudable and an analysis uninformed by the psychology of intergroup helping would find it odd that advantaged group members who have a genuine interest in reducing inequality would engage in help that undermines rather than enhances collective efforts by the disadvantaged to achieve this goal. Similarly, an uninformed observer might see it as foolish and ungracious for disadvantaged group activists to criticize and reject the generous support of advantaged group members. However, informed by social psychological theories both of these actions become understandable and predictable. Fortunately, theory and research also offers a solution. AGAs need to focus on offering autonomy-oriented help—help that does not impede the disadvantaged group's ability to describe and carry out their own solutions. This kind of help represents a much smaller threat to the disadvantaged group's reputation, and it affirms their efficacy and is therefore much more likely to be sought and accepted. Moreover, it is more in keeping with the true intent of a movement designed to reduce inequality by moving resources and power from the privileged to the disadvantaged group.

The "Identity" Problem

> *"Genuine allies know that when people claim their differences . . . such as an Indigenous person or a person of color, within the context of challenging the oppressive power structure, that this should not be perceived and argued as being . . . disruptive to the larger goal and needed solidarity."*
>
> – Lynn Ghel

> *"'I wish there was an 'S' for 'Straight' in the acronym.' (Yes, people say this.) Rather than "fighting with us," how about you just try to help out as needed? This means not drowning out LGBT voices."*
>
> – Parker Marie Molloy

We propose that some critiques leveled by disadvantaged group activists against AGAs reflect concerns around collective identity and categorization, and that a social psychological analysis may be fruitful in articulating the processes exposed by these critiques. Research has demonstrated a connection between participation in action on behalf of a disadvantage group and an advantaged group member showing strong identification with that group (e.g., van Zomeren et al., 2011). Given that advantaged group members are usually unable to physically join the disadvantaged group (e.g., become Black or Gay or Indigenous), this identification with the disadvantaged group may be represented in more symbolic ways. Although this growing identification with the out-group increases interest in engaging in activism for the out-group, it also seems reasonable that the more AGAs come to see themselves (even symbolically) as members of the disadvantaged group, the more they will feel justified in taking the kinds of dominating actions described in the previous section. For example, "As a member of the group (rather than an outsider), I should have the right to speak for and lead the group." Thus, in some cases dominating actions by AGAs may result not from a sense of group superiority, but rather from a misguided sense that one has earned symbolic membership in the disadvantaged in-group.

Of course, this co-optation of their group identity can be unimpressive, even offensive, to members of the disadvantaged group. As one Indigenous activist eloquently puts it, "Just because you know some songs or are rejecting your heritage does not mean you can somehow become one of us. Never going to happen" (Ancestral Pride). In a very poignant example, Black activists in the *Black Lives Matter* protests in the United States responded with frustration and dismay as White supporters joined the protest and stand at the front with their hands in the air chanting "Hands Up, Don't Shoot." This chant and stance were initially taken by young Black protesters to symbolize their fear that they would be the next target of a police shooting. When White protesters mimic this behavior, it implies that they are just as likely to be shot by the police. This simply is not true. Unarmed Whites are much less likely to be shot by police. However, more importantly, the movement was supposed to be about the plight of Blacks, and many have argued that the visual of White people standing with their hands up misrepresents the problem and undermines the message (e.g., FreeQuency). So, while increasing psychological identification with the disadvantaged group out-group may inspire action by AGAs, it may also inspire behavior that will offend and be rejected by the disadvantaged group.

Given the difficulties of trying to take on the disadvantaged group identity, AGAs may instead seek to find a common identity that they can share with dis-advantaged group. Thus, they may (inadvertently) seek to alter the social identity that drives collective action from one that is exclusive to the disadvantaged group to one that can be shared by anyone who holds the same values, or attitudes, or commitment to the cause. For example, a Black activist identity, which defines Blackness as existing in opposition to Whiteness, may be replaced by a focus on an identity like "Anti-racists" which changes the intergroup struggle to position those who are fighting against racial inequality against those who are complicit with it. There is compelling evidence that of these kinds of shared in-group identities centered around opinions or causes can be very effective in garnering and solidifying the support and participation of advantaged group members (see McGarty, Bliuc, Thomas, & Bongiorno, 2009; Thomas & McGarty, 2009). This is not surprising given that these social identities are consistent with advantaged group member's preferences for focusing on cross-group communalities rather than group differences (Saguy, Dovidio, & Pratto, 2008). While acknowledging that shared group identities can play an important role in social change, here we offer a word of caution about their specific impact during interactions between AGAs and disadvantaged group members.

First, Mummendey and colleagues' in-group projection model points to one problem with replacing of the disadvantaged group identity as the focus of col-lective action with a more inclusive identity that includes both advantaged and disadvantaged groups (Mummendey & Wenzel, 1999). Research supports the con-tention that when multiple groups are part of a larger social category, all subgroups will seek to project the content of their local identities onto the identity of the larger social category and thus to have their own group define the normative representation of this larger shared identity. However, the advantaged subgroup is likely to be far more successful in doing so, resulting in the larger shared group identity being more reflective of the advantaged subgroup (e.g., Wenzel, Mummendey, & Waldzus, 2007; see also Hornsey & Hogg, 2000). This allows members of the advantaged group to feel more prototypical and perhaps to see themselves as most capable of acting as leaders for this shared group. So, because anyone can be an "anti-racist" and Whites come to this anti-racist coalition with more structural power and status, there is the potential for White anti-racists to come to see themselves as the legitimate leaders and spokespeople for this coalition. Again, we are back to dominating AGAs.

Finally, we propose that in addition to avoiding these pitfalls of altering group identities, there may be direct benefits for AGAs to remain highly aware of their advantaged group identity. Earlier in discussing the importance of recognizing one's privilege, we noted that engaging in activism frequently comes with tangible costs, but that these costs are much more pronounced for disadvantaged group members. It is also clear that confronting injustice can also come with social costs such as disapproval, denigration, and further discrimination (Bashir, Lockwood, Chasteen, Nadolny, & Noyes, 2013; Good, Moss-Racusin, & Sanchez, 2012), and again these social costs are borne more strongly by the disadvantaged, who may be disliked for speaking up, and unlikely to be taken seriously (e.g., Kaiser, Hagiwara, Malahy, & Wilkins, 2009; Kaiser & Miller, 2003). Conscious recognition of one's advantaged group status and its accompanying privilege may help AGAs recognize that the cost of confronting is lower for them, and encourage them to play a special role in challenging prejudice and discrimination by members of their in-group (e.g., Smith & Redington, 2010). Thus, recognition of their status as an out-group member might not only remind AGAs to seek the guidance and leadership of the disadvantaged group activists, it might also remind them of their obligation and special capacity to confront in-group members who stand in the way of social change (e.g., Greenwood, 2015). This sentiment is nicely demonstrated in the words of Dr. Omi Osun Joni L. Jones (2010) who encourages White allies to,

> "Be loud and crazy so Black folks won't have to be! Speak up! Say it! Name it! If you are male, YOU be the one to tell your department chair that the women's salaries in your department must be brought line with those of the men. If you are white, YOU be the one to advocate for the qualified grad student of color applicant over the qualified white grad student applicant."

To our knowledge there is no research addressing responses of disadvantaged group members to the redefinition of the relevant social identity from their local in-group to one that includes others committed to their values or cause. However, it seems reasonable to assume that their reactions might be very similar to their responses to offers of dependency-oriented help. For example, disadvantaged group members who are only weakly identified with their in-group, and perhaps are already identified with the larger mainstream community—those who are dual identified (e.g., Gaertner & Dovidio, 2000)—might be particularly welcoming of a broader definition of the relevant in-group. For example, a group like "anti-racists" might mesh well with and reinforce their existing dual identity, where a movement more tightly tied only to their disadvantaged group identity might not.

However, disadvantaged group members who are highly identified with their local in-group and whose clear vision of an alternative system has inspired active struggle (i.e., disadvantaged group activists) might be much less likely to endorse this redefinition of the in-group. As the quote by Malcom X at the opening of this article indicates, those who are actively committed to the in-group struggle are likely to recognize that inclusion of advantaged out-group members as part of the relevant in-group could call into question who the rightful leaders and architects of the movement should be, and that broadening the goals and scope of the movement might reduce its impact on the disadvantaged group whose concerns should be at the center of the problem. Again, the *Black Lives Matter* protests offer a very relevant example. As well-meaning White AGAs joined the movement, some thought to broaden the scope of the movement to be more representative of their "anti-racist" perspective by adapting the moniker to *All Lives Matter*. To those offering this adaptation, this new representation of the movement as emphasizing equality and respect for all seemed at worst innocuous and at best more inclusive. However, it was reacted to swiftly and vociferously by many who point out that *All Lives Matter* obfuscates the real problem—Black people are killed at a much higher rate than members of other groups. As Black American activist blogger Luvvie Ajayi explains, "We know that all lives matter. WE KNOW. But we have to say #BlackLivesMatter to remind people of our humanity, which is far too often forgotten. So for White people to feel like this proclamation somehow diminishes THEIR humanity is to confirm that very self-centeredness that we're fighting against" (Awesomely Luvvie, 2014).

Similarly, a larger and more inclusive identity which includes members of the advantaged out-group might also undermine the feelings of efficacy and illegitimacy that are key to vigorous collective action (see Tajfel & Turner, 1979; Wright, 2010). The argument here is similar to the one raised by Wright and Lubensky (2009) as to why cross-group contact might undermine collective action participation. A more inclusive in-group that includes advantaged group members alters and obfuscates the relevant out-group that can be clearly pointed to as the "oppressors" responsible for current injustices (see also Corenblum & Stephan, 2001). The belief that the advantaged and disadvantaged groups are in clear opposition to each other is part of the construction of a *politicized identity* (Simon & Klandermans, 2001; Stott & Drury, 2004), which is valuable in supporting perceptions of control and injustice, and distinguishes activists from nonactivists. Thus, acceptance of a new broader identity may undermine the collective action engagement of those who would otherwise be most dedicated—disadvantaged group activists. It seems important that AGAs avoid the allure of modifying and expanding relevant social identities so that they can feel included, as these alternative identities may in fact serve to further marginalize those the movement seeks to benefit.

Concluding Thoughts and Some Suggestions for Advantaged Group Allies

Our analysis focused on potential pitfalls stemming from the actions of advantaged group allies, but it is important to emphasize that we are by no means suggesting that advantaged group members avoid engaging in activism to benefit disadvantaged groups. Although there is a clear need for future research on appropriate AGA behavior, we offer some tentative suggestions. AGAs should actively consider how their presence and actions might influence the motivations, identities and resolve of the disadvantaged group members they seek to work alongside. If AGAs incorporate effective communication of support for social change as part of their cross-group interactions, their presence may benefit disadvantaged group members' collective action engagement. Additionally, we suggest that AGAs should seek to better understand their own privilege, which may increase the likelihood that they will offer autonomy-oriented support, rather than engaging in dominant behaviors consistent with dependency-oriented help. AGAs should also avoid the temptation to increase their own feelings of inclusion by expanding or modifying disadvantaged social identities. Instead, they should recognize their group-based privilege and leverage it to confront members of their in-group and social institutions that oppose social change. If done correctly, there is certainly potential for the activism of advantaged group members to make meaningful contributions to the creation of a more equal society.

References

Allport, G. W. (1954). *The nature of prejudice*. Reading, MA: Addison-Wesley.

Ancestral Pride (N.D.). *Everyone calls themselves an ally until it's time to do some real ally shit [Pamphlet]*. Retrieved on September 19, 2015 from warriorpublications.files. wordpress.com/2014/01/ancestral_pride_zine.pdf.

Awesomely Luvvie (2014, December). The stages of what happens when there's an injustice against Black people [Blog post]. Retrieved on September 19, 2015 from www.awsomelyluvvie. com/2014/12/stages-injustice-against-black-people.html.

Bashir, N. Y., Lockwood, P., Chasteen, A. L., Nadolny, D., & Noyes, I. (2013). The ironic impact of activists: Negative stereotypes reduce social change influence. *European Journal of Social Psychology, 43*, 614–626.

Becker, J. C., Wright S. C., Lubensky, M. E., & Zhou, S. (2013). Friend or ally: Whether cross-group contact undermines collective action depends on what advantaged group members say (or don't say). *Personality and Social Psychology Bulletin, 39*, 442–455.

Brown, K. T., & Ostrove, J. M. (2013). What does it mean to be an ally? The perception of allies from the perspective of people of color. *Journal of Applied Social Psychology, 43*, 2211–2222.

Canon, M. J., & Sunseri, L. (Eds.) (2011). *Racism, colonialism, and indigeneity in Canada: A reader*. Don Mills, ON: Oxford University Press.

Case, K. A. (2012). Discovering the privilege of whiteness: White women's reflections on anti-racist identity and ally behavior. *Journal of Social Issues*, *68*, 78–96.

Case, K. A., Iuzzini, J., & Hopkins, M. (2012). Systems of privilege: Intersections, awareness, and applications. *Journal of Social Issues*, *68*, 1–10.

Corenblum, B., & Stephan, W. G. (2001). White fears and native apprehensions: An integrated threat theory approach to intergroup attitudes. *Canadian Journal of Behavioural Science/Revue Canadienne des Sciences du Comportement*, *33*, 251–268.

Curtin, N., & McGarty, C. (2016). Expanding on psychological theories of engagement to understand activism in context(s). *Journal of Social Issues*, *72*(2), 227–241.

Czopp, A. M., & Monteith, M. J. (2003). Confronting prejudice (literally): Reactions to confrontations of racial and gender bias. *Personality and Social Psychology Bulletin*, *29*, 532–544.

De Graaf, M. (2014, November). The controversial rules for white people who were told 'not to take up space' at Michael Brown vigil in Toronto. *Daily Mail*. Retrieved on September 19, 2015 from www.dailymail.co.uk/news/article-2852167/Please-refrain-taking-space-controversial-rules-white-people-Michael-Brown-vigil-Toronto.html#ixzz3l65FJUQK.

Dixon, J., Levine, M., Reicher, S., & Durrheim, K. (2012). Beyond prejudice: Are negative evaluations the problem and is getting us to like one another more the solution? *Behavioral and Brain Sciences*, *35*, 411–425.

Droogendyk, L., Louis, W. R., & Wright, S. C. (under review). *Empowering disadvantaged group members to engage in collective action: The role of supportive contact and shared supportive emotions.*

Fagan, K., & Ho, V. (2014, December 13). White voices dominate Bay Area protests of racial inequality. *San Francisco Chronicle*. Retrieved on September 19, 2015 from www.sfgate.com/bayarea/article/White-voices-dominate-Bay-Area-protests-of-racial-5953977.php

Feminist Griote (2013, April 23). White people fatigue syndrome [Blog post]. Retrieved from thefeministgriote.com/white-people-fatigue-syndrome

FreeQuency (n.d.). On white people, solidarity, and (not) marching for Mike Brown [Blog post]. Retrieved on September 19, 2015 from freeqthamighty.tumblr.com/post/95573664816/on-white-people-solidarity-and-not-marching

Gaertner, S. L., & Dovidio, J. F. (2000). *Reducing intergroup bias: The Common Ingroup Identity Model*. Philadelphia, PA: Psychology Press.

Good, J. J., Moss-Racusin, C. A., & Sanchez, D. T. (2012). When do we confront? Perceptions of costs and benefits predict confronting discrimination on behalf of the self and others. *Psychology of Women Quarterly*, *36*, 210–226.

Greenwood, R. M. (2015). Remembrance, responsibility, and reparations: The use of emotions in talk about the 1921 Tulsa Race Riot. *Journal of Social Issues*, *71*, 338–355.

Halabi, S., Nadler, A., & Dovidio, J. F. (2013). Positive responses to intergroup assistance: The roles of apology and trust. *Group Processes and Intergroup Relations*, *16*, 395–411.

Hooks, B. (2000). *Feminist theory: From margin to center*. Cambridge, MA: South End Press.

Hornsey, M., & Hogg, M. (2000). Intergroup similarity and subgroup relations: Some implications for assimilation. *Personality and Social Psychology Bulletin*, *26*, 948–958.

Jetten, J., Iyer, A., Branscombe, N. R., & Zhang, A. (2013). How the disadvantaged appraise group-based exclusion: The path from legitimacy to illegitimacy. *European Review of Social Psychology*, *24*, 194–224.

Johnson, A. G. (2006). *Privilege, power, and difference* (2nd ed.). Boston, MA: McGraw Hill Publishing.

Johnson, J. L., & Best, A. L. (2012). Radical normals: The moral career of straight parents as public advocates for their gay children. *Symbolic Interaction*, *35*, 321–339.

Jones, O. O. J. L. (2010). *6 Rules for Allies*. Keynote speech delivered at the Seventeenth Annual Emerging Scholarship in Women's and Gender Studies Conference. Austin, TX.

Kaiser, C. R., Hagiwara, N., Malahy, L. W., & Wilkins, C. L. (2009). Group identification moderates attitudes toward ingroup members who confront discrimination. *Journal of Experimental Social Psychology*, *45*, 770–777.

Kaiser, C. R., & Miller, C. T. (2003). Derogating the victim: The interpersonal consequences of blaming events on discrimination. *Group Processes & Intergroup Relations*, *6*, 227–237.

Leach, C. W., Snider, N., & Iyer, A. (2002). "Poisoning the consciences of the fortunate": The experience of relative advantage and support for social equality. In I. Walker & H. J. Smith (Eds.), *Relative deprivation: Specification, development, and integration* (pp. 136–163). New York, NY: Cambridge University Press.

Louis, W. R., Amiot, C. E., Thomas, E.F., & Blackwood, L. (2016). The "activist identity" and activism across domains: A multiple identities analysis. *Journal of Social Issues, 72*(2), 242–263.

McGarty, C., Bliuc, A., Thomas, E. F., & Bongiorno, R. (2009). Collective action as the material expression of opinion-based group membership. *Journal of Social Issues, 65*, 839–857.

Miller, N. (2002). Personalization and the promise of contact theory. *Journal of Social Issues, 58*, 387–410.

Mummendey, A., & Wenzel, M. (1999). Social discrimination and tolerance in intergroup relations: Reactions to intergroup difference. *Personality & Social Psychology Review, 3*, 158–174.

Nadler, A. (2002). Inter–group helping relations as power relations: Maintaining or challenging social dominance between groups through helping. *Journal of Social Issues, 58*, 487–502.

Nadler, A., & Halabi, S. (2015). Helping relations and inequality between individuals and groups. In M. Mikulincer, P. R. Shaver, J. F. Dovidio, & J. A. Simpson (Eds.), *APA handbook of personality and social psychology, Volume 2: Group processes* (pp. 371–393). Washington, DC: American Psychological Association.

Nadler, A., & Porat, I. (1978). When names do not help: Effects of anonymity and locus of need attributions on help seeking behavior. *Personality & Social Psychology Bulletin, 4*, 624–626.

Pettigrew, T. F., & Tropp, L. R. (2006). A meta-analytic test of intergroup contact theory. *Journal of Personality and Social Psychology, 90*, 751–783.

Powell, A. A., Branscombe, N. R., & Schmitt, M. T. (2005). Inequality as ingroup privilege or outgroup disadvantage: The impact of group focus on collective guilt and interracial attitudes. *Personality and Social Psychology Bulletin, 31*, 508–521.

Rattan, A., & Ambady, N. (2014). How "It Gets Better": Effectively communicating support to targets of prejudice. *Personality and Social Psychology Bulletin, 40*, 555–566.

Ravarino, J. M. (2008). Men acting for change: An investigation of men's experiences as social justice allies in preventing men's violence against women. *Dissertation Abstracts International Section A, 69*, 2158.

Reicher, S. D., & Haslam, S. A. (2012). Change we can believe in: The role of social identity, cognitive alternatives, and leadership in group mobilization and transformation. In B. Wagoner, E. Jensen, & J. A. Oldmeadow (Eds.), *Culture and social change: Transforming society through the power of ideas* (pp. 53–73) Charlotte, NC: Information Age Publishing.

Reitmanova, S. (2008). Unequal treatment of international students in Canada: Handling the case of health insurance coverage. *College Quarterly, 11*. Retrieved from http://www. collegequarterly.ca/2008-vol11-num02-spring/reitmanova.html

Reynolds, K. J., Oakes, P. J., Haslam, S. A., Nolan, M. A., & Dolnik, L. (2000). Responses to powerlessness: Stereotyping as an instrument of social conflict. *Group Dynamics: Theory, Research, and Practice, 4*, 275–290.

Russell, G. M., & Bohan, J. S. (2016). Institutional allyship for LGBT equality: Underlying processes and potentials for change. *Journal of Social Issues, 72*(2), 335–354.

Saguy, T., Dovidio, J. F., & Pratto, F. (2008). Beyond contact: Intergroup contact in the context of power relations. *Personality and Social Psychology Bulletin, 34*, 432–445.

Saguy, T., Tausch, N., Dovidio, J. F., & Pratto, F. (2009). The irony of harmony: Intergroup contact can produce false expectations for equality. *Psychological Science, 20*, 114–121.

Shelton, J. N. (2003). Interpersonal concerns in social encounters between majority and minority group members. *Group Processes and Intergroup Relations, 6*, 171–185.

Shelton, J. N., Richeson, J. A., Salvatore, J., & Trawalter, S. (2005). Ironic effects of racial bias during interracial interactions. *Psychological Science, 16*, 397–402.

Simon, B., & Klandermans B. (2001). Politicized collective identity: A social psychological analysis. *American Psychologist, 56*, 319–331.

Smith, L., & Redington, R. M. (2010). Lessons from the experiences of white antiracist activists. *Professional Psychology, Research, and Practice, 41*, 541–549.

Stott, C., & Drury, J. (2004). The importance of social structure and social interaction in stereotype consensus and content: Is the whole greater than the sum of its parts? *European Journal of Social Psychology, 34*, 11–23.

Stürmer, S., & Simon, B. (2004). Collective action: Towards a dual-pathway model. *European Review of Social Psychology, 15*, 59–99.

Tajfel, H., & Turner, J. C. (1979). An integrative theory of intergroup conflict. In W. G. Austin & S. Worchel (Eds.), *The social psychology of intergroup relations* (pp. 33–48). Monterey, CA: Brooks/Cole.

Thomas, E. F., & McGarty, C. A. (2009). The role of efficacy and moral outrage norms in creating the potential for international development activism through group-based interaction. *British Journal of Social Psychology, 48*, 115–134.

Tropp, L. R., Stout, A. M., Boatswain, C., Wright, S. C., & Pettigrew, T. F. (2006). Trust and acceptance in response to references to group membership: Minority and majority perspectives on cross-group interactions. *Journal of Applied Social Psychology, 36*, 769–794.

van Leeuwen, E. (2007). Restoring identity through out-group helping: Beliefs about international aid in response to the December 2004 tsunami. *European Journal of Social Psychology, 37*, 661–671.

van Leeuwen, E., & Tauber, S. (2010). The strategic side of out-group helping. In S. Stürmer & M. Snyder (Eds.), *The psychology of prosocial behavior: Group processes, intergroup relations, and helping* (pp. 81–99). Malden, MA: Wiley-Blackwell.

Van Vugt, M., & Hardy, C. L. (2010). Cooperation for reputation: Wasteful contributions as costly signals in public goods. *Group Processes and Intergroup Relations, 13*, 101–111.

van Zomeren, M., Postmes, T., & Spears, R. (2008). Toward an integrative social identity model of collective action: A quantitative research synthesis of three socio-psychological perspectives. *Psychological Bulletin, 134*, 504–535.

van Zomeren, M., Postmes, T., Spears, R., & Bettache, K. (2011). Can moral convictions motivate the advantaged to challenge social inequality? Extending the Social Identity Model of Collective Action. *Group Processes and Intergroup Relations, 14*, 735–753.

Vorauer, J. D. (2006). An information search model of evaluative concerns in intergroup interaction. *Psychological Review, 113*, 862–886.

Wenzel, M., Mummendey, A., & Waldzus, S. (2007). Superordinate identities and intergroup conflict: The ingroup projection model. *European Review of Social Psychology, 18*, 331–372.

Wing, N. (2015, January 13). If most police officers are 'good cops,' these are even better. *Huffington Post.* Retrieved on September 19, 2015 from http://www.huffingtonpost.com/2015/01/13/police-support-protests_n_6419220.html

Wright, S. C. (1997). Ambiguity, social influence and collective action: Generating collective protest in response to tokenism. *Personality & Social Psychology Bulletin, 23*, 1277–1290.

Wright, S. C. (2001). Strategic collective action: Social psychology and social change. In R. Brown & S. L. Gaertner (Eds.), *Intergroup processes: Blackwell handbook of social psychology* (Vol. 4, pp. 409–430). Oxford, UK: Blackwell.

Wright, S. C. (2009). Cross-group contact effects. In S. Otten, T. Kessler, & K. Sassenberg (Eds.) *Intergroup relations: The role of emotion and motivation* (pp. 262–283). New York, NY: Psychology Press.

Wright, S. C. (2010). Collective action and social change. In J. F. Dovidio, M. Hewstone, P. Glick, & V. M. Esses (Eds.), *Handbook of prejudice, stereotyping, and discrimination* (pp. 577–596). London, UK: Sage.

Wright, S. C., & Baray, G. (2012). Models of social change in social psychology: Collective action or prejudice reduction, conflict or harmony. In J. Dixon & M. Levine (Eds.), *Beyond prejudice: Extending the social psychology of intergroup conflict, inequality and social change* (pp. 225–247). Cambridge, UK: Cambridge University Press.

Wright, S. C., Brody, S. M., & Aron, A. (2005). Intergroup contact: Still our best hope for improving intergroup relations. In C. S. Crandall, & M. Schaller (Eds.), *Social psychology of prejudice: Historical and contemporary issues* (pp. 115–142). Seattle, WA: Lewinian Press.

Wright, S. C., & Lubensky, M. E. (2009). The struggle for social equality: Collective action versus prejudice reduction. In S. Demoulin, J. P. Leyens, & J. F. Dovidio (Eds.), *Intergroup misunderstandings: Impact of divergent social realities* (pp. 291–310). New York, NY: Psychology Press.

Wright, S. C., & Tropp, L. R. (2002). Collective action in response to disadvantage: Intergroup perceptions, social identification, and social change. In I. Walker, & H. J. Smith (Eds.), *Relative deprivation: Specification, development, and integration* (pp. 200–236). New York, NY: Cambridge University Press.

LISA DROOGENDYK (PhD Simon Fraser University, 2015) is currently a post-doctoral researcher and psychology instructor at Simon Fraser University, and will be a Professor of Psychology at Sheridan College beginning in August 2016. Her research is focused on collective action, especially intersections between cross-group contact and collective action, and outcomes of environmental activism.

STEPHEN C. WRIGHT (PhD McGill University, 1991) is Professor of Social Psychology at Simon Fraser University. His research focuses on intergroup relations, with specific interests in: collective action and resistance; intergroup helping and advantaged group allies; and prejudice and its reduction (cross-group friendships and extended contact).

MICAH LUBENSKY (PhD University of California, Santa Cruz, 2004) is Community Mobilization Manager at the Global Forum on MSM & HIV (MSMGF), in Oakland, USA. Micah's work primarily involves coordinating global collaboration by networks of gay/bisexual men and other men-who-have-sex-with-men (MSM) and transgender communities on HIV prevention and care, HIV policy advocacy, and Human Rights documentation.

WINNIFRED R. LOUIS (PhD McGill University, 2001) is an Associate Professor in the School of Psychology at The University of Queensland. Her research interests focus on the influence of identity and norms on social decision-making.

Journal of Social Issues, Vol. 72, No. 2, 2016, pp. 335–354
doi: 10.1111/josi.12169

Institutional Allyship for LGBT Equality: Underlying Processes and Potentials for Change

Glenda M. Russell[*]
University of Colorado

Janis S. Bohan
Metropolitan State University of Denver

Discussions of outgroup activism in support of lesbian, gay, bisexual, and transgender (LGBT) equality reflect two shortcomings. First, such discussions generally present uncritically positive views of ally activism; second, research on ally activism has overly focused on individual allies. The aim of this article is twofold: to suggest that action toward LGBT equality may often be influenced by sexual prejudice and may thus recapitulate longstanding power dynamics between majority and sexual minority groups, and to expand our understanding of ally behavior beyond individuals by presenting an ethnographic study exploring the development of institutional ally identity in a mainstream church that underwent a marked shift from an explicit anti-LGBT to an expressly LGBT-supportive stance. The study employed critical discourse analysis to examine interview, textual, and participant-observation data. Dimensions of individual and institutional ally activism, and potential pitfalls in each, are explored. Suggestions for promoting more constructive collective action are offered.

Discussions of ally activism in the context of collective action for lesbian, gay, bisexual, and transgender (LGBT) equality have generally been characterized by an unreservedly positive view of both the process by which such activism occurs and the change potential it embodies (Russell, 2011). This positive view is reflected in both empirical (e.g., Asta & Vacha-Haase, 2013; Cortese, 2006; Duhigg,

---

[*]Correspondence concerning this article should be addressed to Glenda Russell, Ethnography and Evaluation Research, Center to Advance Research and Teaching in Social Sciences, University of Colorado Boulder, 3100 Marine Street, 580 UCB Boulder CO 80301, USA. Tel: 303-447-9600 [e-mail: gmrussell5@hotmail.com].

We are grateful to Cathy Xiong and Veronica Vang, who assisted in the team analysis of the data for this study, particularly with the documents related to the reconciling congregation process.

Rostosky, Gray, & Wimsatt, 2010; Fingerhut, 2011; Hall, 2009; Horne, Rostosky, & Riggle, 2011; Tillman-Healy, 2001) and more popular descriptions (e.g., Ayers & Brown, 2005; Maran & Watrous, 2005) of heterosexual allies and their work. Most research in this area has aimed to identify qualities and experiences associated with ally behaviors, but has not examined in greater depth the potentially negative concomitants of such work (e.g., Duhigg et al., 2010; Fingerhut, 2011; Stotzer, 2009). Furthermore, such discussions have largely focused on individual allies, albeit sometimes as allies acting in groups (e.g., Vernaglia, 1999), and have rarely considered in depth the process by which institutions, here referring to organizational entities, establish a pro-LGBT stance and act as allies on behalf of LGBT issues. This article addresses these limitations by calling into question the consistently positive characterization of ally activism through an exploration of previous research and extends this analysis to an institution level, using the case of a mainstream Protestant church that underwent a dramatic shift from an explicitly anti-LGBT stance to a position of visible support for the LGBT community.

To ground our discussion, we turn first to Russell's (2011) report on a long-term, ongoing study of heterosexual allies that began in the early 1990s. Based on that study, Russell articulated a distinction between two broad categories of motives that led individuals to engage in work on behalf of LGBT equality: motives based on professional roles or on personal relationships with particular LGBT persons, and motives rooted in fundamental values or principles, such as justice, civil rights, and moral or religious ideals.

The role/relationship set of motives are expressed by allies who move toward collective action for a variety of personal reasons. Arguably, the most visible allies expressing this set of motives are those whose support for LGBT rights derives from a personal relationship with a family member, colleague, or friend. The national organization PFLAG (previously, Parents, Families, and Friends of Lesbians and Gays), which has historically focused on allies who are parents or other family members, represents perhaps the best-known group of such allies. The visibility of that organization, and likely the emotional power for LGBT people of feeling accepted by family members, has contributed to an emphasis on individuals who are allies in direct response to the presence of LGBT individuals in their lives (e.g., Broad, Alden, Berkowitz, & Ryan, 2008; Broad, Crawley, & Foley, 2004). A prominent framework for explaining the importance and effects of such relationships, both in general terms (Tropp & Pettigrew, 2005) and in terms of LGBT issues (e.g., Herek & Glunt, 1993), is seen in research on intergroup contact, which suggests that direct personal contact between advantaged and disadvantaged groups serves, especially in the context of sustained contact between co-equals with shared goals, to reduce intergroup hostility and bias.

The second overarching category of ally behavior identified by Russell (2011), namely actions motivated by basic values, reflects the motivating power of principles such as a commitment to civil rights, religious beliefs that support equal treatment of all, principles of justice, and recognition of privilege. At their foundation, these value-based motives sometimes have little to do with LGBT issues in particular; instead, they are grounded in worldviews that might apply equally to a range of issues. The motive for allies in this second group lies in their wish to live up to the principles they view as central to their lives and their activism (see also Klar & Kasser, 2009). Such principled stances are akin to those underpinning opinion-based activism (e.g., McGarty, Bliuc, Thomas, & Bongiorno, 2009; Wright, 2009) in contrast to identity-based activism (Reicher, Cassidy, Wolpert, Hopkins, & Levine, 2006).

Russell's (2011) distinction between two broad types of motivations, which had been foreshadowed in earlier work (e.g., Russell, 1996; Russell, Dixon, & Levine, 2002; Russell & Ruckert, 2004; Russell, 2006), is consistent with Vernaglia's (1999) identification of two sorts of motives among her small group of PFLAG parents, and is also akin to Rattan and Ambady's (2014) differentiation between an emphasis on providing social support and an emphasis on creating social change. The recognition of variation in allies' motives provides a framework for considering ally activism in a less uniform way and for examining differences in why and how allies participate in action for LGBT equality, as well as in the outcomes of that participation.

The research described above mirrors most of the research on heterosexual allies to date in that the focus and level of analysis center on individual allies. The virtually exclusive focus on the individual is perhaps ironic when one considers that allies represent a central concept in *collective* action (Wright & Lubensky, 2009). Missing from the literature are studies focused on institutional levels of analysis. Even when research ostensibly addresses institutional relationships—as, for example, families (Arm, Horne, & Levitt, 2009) or work settings (Brooks, & Edwards, 2009; Draughn, Elkins, & Roy, 2002), it takes the individual as the unit of analysis.

Thus, the current study expanded on previous research on individual allies' motives by considering the development of allyship in a religious institution, providing an opportunity to explore Russell's (2011) distinction more thoroughly, this time in an institutional context. The present study was an in-depth ethnographic examination of a mainstream Protestant congregation whose identity, as expressed in its actions, shifted from an overtly anti-LGBT identity to one as a staunch and visible supporter of LGBT issues. The focus of the study was not primarily on the relationship between religion and attitudes toward sexual orientation, a complex topic in its own right (e.g., Whitley, 2012). Rather, this study examined the evolution of one particular church's pro-LGBT identity and identified certain processes that bespoke a failure to interrogate implicit biases and a persistent power imbalance. By examining this dynamic through the lens of first- and second-order change (e.g., Watzlawick, Weakland, & Fisch, 1974), we began to recognize additional dimensions related to the aforementioned distinction between relationship- and values-based ally activism. Furthermore, by viewing the earlier research on allies together with the findings of the present study, we were able to explore how these intersecting dimensions can be manifested at an individual level and in an institutional setting where individual and institutional dynamics are both in play.

In addition, this study allowed us to consider recent critiques of the role and nature of intergroup contact in the process of social change. Research on intergroup contact has a long history that has, in general, framed such contact in positive terms. However, some recent research has challenged this acritical rendition of intergroup contact as a strategy for achieving social justice aims (e.g., Dixon, Durrheim, Kerr, & Thorne, 2013; Hopkins & Kahani-Hopkins, 2006; Tropp, Hawi, Van Larr, & Levin, 2012), and other work has encouraged reconsideration of common approaches to the study of intergroup contact (e.g., Hopkins & Kahani-Hopkins, 2006; Shelton, 2000). For example, much of the research on intergroup contact in the context of social justice has focused on the goal of prejudice reduction (Dixon et al., 2013). Yet, as Hopkins and Kahani-Hopkins (2006) pointed out, the prejudice-reduction model of social change centers the perspective of the privileged group, with members of the disadvantaged group included only in their role as victims of discrimination. Such an approach to social change fails to take into account the perspective of the marginalized groups and disregards their interactional concerns vis-à-vis the majority. Additionally, recent critiques have pointed to potentially reactionary effects for disadvantaged groups when intergroup contact primarily serves the aims of the advantaged majority, especially in the absence of significant overt hostility. Such paradoxical effects may include decreased political awareness and decreased commitment to social change on the part of the minority group (Dixon et al., 2013). These critiques alerted us to potential pitfalls associated with considerations of intergroup contact and helped to clarify our findings.

Method

Participants and Procedures

The specific church that was the subject of this study, which we will call "City Church," was selected because of the dramatic transition it had undergone in a relatively short span of time from overt condemnation of LGBT people to its current status as a visibly LGBT-supportive congregation. This shift in the church's perspective and role seemed ideal as material for a study of the emergence of institutional allyship; hence, we conducted an ethnographic study of the church's trajectory. We begin by providing some context for this church.

City Church is located in a small university city in Colorado. This church belongs to the worldwide United Methodist Church (UMC), which condemns the practice of homosexuality as, to quote the governing *Book of Discipline*, "incompatible with Christian teaching" (Otterman, 2013, May 5). Hence, the UMC prohibits the celebration of same-sex unions, the ordination of LGBT clergy, and the use of church funds to support LGBT causes (Otterman, 2013, May 5).

The timeframe of our inquiry, which comprises retrospective and contemporaneous approaches, spans the period from 1982 to the present. During that time, the broad sociopolitical climate for LGBT people in the United States underwent dramatic and complicated changes. Early in the period, when openness about one's sexual orientation or gender identity was rare, a youth pastor at City Church came out as gay and was fired (Merrick, 2001; Trillin, 1982). Although LGBT issues were virtually invisible in City Church's home city leading up to that event, significant changes followed. In 1987, the city's voters endorsed adding sexual orientation to the nondiscrimination ordinance. Yet, at the national level, during this period and for more than a decade after, LGBT people were an important focus of the so-called "culture wars" (Herman, 1997), with LGBT rights contested at local, state, and national levels around the United States. In City Church's state, that focus peaked in 1992, 5 years after the minister's firing, when an anti-LGBT amendment to the state's constitution, Amendment 2 (A2), was passed by voters—although it was handily rejected by voters in City Church's home city. A2's passage generated pronounced distress, anger, and sadness, but also increased activism and visibility (Russell, 2000; Russell, Bohan, McCarroll, & Smith, 2010). The latter reaction included a dramatic increase in LGBT and LGBT-supportive groups around the state, as A2 galvanized many LGBT people and allies.

Against this background and in the wake of A2, a PFLAG chapter was founded in the focal city and began meeting at City Church. Soon thereafter, several members of the congregation began the process of moving City Church toward designation by the UMC as a "reconciling congregation," i.e., one that welcomes LGBT congregants. The reconciling process culminated in a 1997 affirmative vote by the congregation. In this, City Church seemed ahead of national attitudes toward LGBT issues, but in sync with those of the city, as evidenced by the aforementioned decision to grant legal protection to LGBT people and the vote against A2. However, the worldwide UMC denomination maintained its official condemnatory position toward LGBT people. Perhaps due to this doctrinal restriction, City Church's commitment to LGBT-positive action was expressed largely outward, toward notable support for the LGBT community outside the church. The primary internal expression of support was an annual celebratory worship service recognizing the anniversary of the church's reconciling status.

We initiated the present study some years after City Church's decision to become a reconciling congregation, with the aim of tracing the story of this congregation's movement toward institutional allyship. We began the retrospective part of our study in 2002, when we interviewed several key members of the congregation. In 2007, we began attending LGBT-oriented programs at City Church, and in that same year, we began a systematic review of a large volume of documents related to the reconciling process, which had been archived by City Church and were made available to us. These materials included minutes, curricula, notes, reports, church bulletins, and other print materials related to the work of the "Reconciling Committee" that led the reconciling process; all of these materials were included in our analyses. In addition, we reviewed other types of data, including newspaper and other print media coverage of City Church, especially its relationship to LGBT issues; transcripts of interviews with seven members of the congregation who had been involved in the church's discussion of LGBT issues; sermons and other documents posted on the church website; and transcripts of radio interviews featuring City Church clergy.

Additionally, beginning in 2006 and continuing to the present, we have attended 28 City Church events that included some LGBT-related content as participant-observers. These events included Sunday services with specific LGBT content announced in advance; services celebrating the church's reconciling status; events sponsored by outside LGBT groups in which City Church clergy participated; and church-sponsored events featuring LGBT-related content with subsequent dialogue between the presenter and audience members. Our participation in and notes from these events provided additional context for our analysis of the aforementioned texts.

Results

Data Analysis

We submitted these data to critical discourse analysis (van Dijk, 1993; Riggins, 1997), a multidisciplinary approach that examines the "intricate relationships between talk, text, social cognition, power, society, and culture" (van Dijk, 1993, p. 253). Discourse analysis entails thorough reading designed to identify implicit messages in target texts and to posit connections between those texts and larger sociocultural issues. We analyzed the documents and interview transcripts using a team approach and consensus coding (see Russell, 2000, for a thorough description). Briefly, consensus coding entails developing a set of themes or codes through careful reading and discussion of the data by the authors and other members of the research team. Each of these codes is then further refined with continuing discussion and analyses, including by reference to relevant research and popular literature. No effort is made to identify "facts" through this process; rather, guiding themes are sought that may clarify complex data and promise useful applications.

First- and Second-order Change at City Church

Given that prior research on allies had been silent on the issue of institutional allyship, our initial intent was to use a grounded theory approach to develop hypotheses and theories to interpret the events we encountered. However, as we moved more deeply into the data analysis, we came to recognize the utility of a change model previously proposed by Watzlawick et al. (1974) and Bartunek (1984), among others. Basic to this model of change are the concepts of first- and second-order change. Briefly, first-order change is relatively superficial; it aims to modify existing practices but does not challenge institutional structures or hierarchies of power and privilege. Second-order change, by contrast, is foundational change; it works to alter structures and challenge hierarchies of power. This model became a framework for subsequent coding, and it also proved invaluable in identifying and elaborating the synergy between the present study and results from Russell's (2011) earlier study on allies.

Our analysis revealed considerable complexity underlying City Church's transition from anti-LGBT to LGBT-supportive status. We came to realize that the visible transformation that had inspired us to study this church's trajectory actually disguised an underlying failure to challenge entrenched power dynamics and an apparent inability to enact anything more than first-order change. What we had anticipated would be a case study in intergroup contact as a foundation for positive social change was, in large part, a years-long case study of the efforts of a core group of heterosexual-cisgender[1] individuals to decrease anti-LGBT prejudice among other members of City Church. Indeed, the presence of active resistance from some members of the congregation may have facilitated a focus on these visible adversaries to the apparent exclusion of attention to LGBT voices. Committee members wondered, for instance, about how to "keep from being judgmental, ourselves, toward the 'opposition'."

Overall, the records of the reconciling process reveal that the undertaking was conducted by heterosexual-cisgender allies whose motives were rooted primarily in personal relationships. Several people mentioned LGBT family members during the course of their discussions, underscoring the suggestion of one leading member of the committee, who wrote in the church newsletter, "if my daughter had not come out, I would have remained complacent." With rare and short-lived exceptions, the perspectives of LGBT people were not actively sought by the committee as they engaged in deliberations and planned educational programming. Indeed, LGBT people were rarely even mentioned in the committee's discussions; the few references that occurred implicitly depicted LGBT people in passive (vs. agentic) terms; "I felt a need to stick up for gay people who were marginalized," one committee member stated. Often, such discussions had to do with organizing

---

[1]The term "cisgender" refers to people whose gender identity is consistent with their assigned sex at birth; it is used in contrast to "transgender" or "trans." Thus, the term "heterosexual-cisgender" refers to individuals who identify their sexual orientation as heterosexual and their gender identity as consistent with their assigned gender, in contrast to those who identify as sexual minorities (i.e., lesbian, gay, bisexual, and/or trans).

social events for LGBT people. The process reflected here, wherein allies assume primary agency in situations related to prejudice and oppression, parallels observations made by Bergsieker, Shelton, and Richeson (2010) regarding interracial interactions. Furthermore, instead of centering the experiences of LGBT people, the committee's efforts focused primarily on the institution's status—that is, on making City Church a reconciling congregation, evoking Dixon et al.'s (2013) critique of efforts focused on prejudice reduction without attention to minority group perspectives. Thus, the committee devoted far more time to the concerns of congregation members who worried that City Church would be seen as a "gay church" than to the concerns of LGBT people.

Additionally, the record revealed very little attention paid to heterosexual privilege, overt or subtle biases, or exclusionary decision making among supporters of reconciliation. Implicit heteronormative assumptions were reflected in frequent references to how the committee (and, presumably, the reconciling status) could help LGBT people, coupled with the absence of any discussion of ways in which the heterosexual-cisgender members of City Church might benefit from the inclusion of LGBT people in the life of the church. The reconciling process was framed as a kindness to LGBT people; one committee member was clear about this: "We're surrogate parents for some people." In short, fundamental systems of power, privilege, and oppression and existing institutional structures were neither acknowledged nor questioned. Attention was focused on first-order change: superficial changes that were compatible with existing power dynamics, with no substantive challenge to institutional structures, including the willingness to abide, if grudgingly, by basic religious precepts that devalue LGBT people. "If there's going to be social change," a leading committee member opined, "it'll come from mainstreaming change." This sentiment was likely in keeping with prevalent "liberal" attitudes toward the inclusion of LGBT people at the time and in this city. At that point in time, the LGBT movement was strongly, if not solely, focused on achieving marriage equality, a quintessentially mainstream goal.

Then, City Church entered a new phase in their growth toward full inclusion. The initiation of this shift appears to have coincided with the arrival of a new ministerial staff. The new clergy had backgrounds of broad and long involvement in a variety of social justice movements, "as near as sleeping outdoors in support of homeless youth next door, as far away as fighting apartheid in South Africa," they noted in a church blog. Their commitment to LGBT issues appeared to be a part of a larger vision that derived from a religiously grounded view of justice and human rights. In effect, the new ministers' actions embodied Russell's (2011) principle-based motivation for allyship.

The first indication of this new direction came at the 2011 anniversary of the church's reconciling status, when the new senior pastor apologized to LGBT people for their long-standing mistreatment at the hands of the Christian church, including his own denomination. For the first time during City Church's transition to an explicitly LGBT-supportive position, to our knowledge, this minister took the experiences of LGBT people as his authority, declaring that it was the church that had sinned. The following year, after reiterating his apology, the pastor announced that he and the two other City Church clergy felt "called by God and by conscience to perform marriage ceremonies and to bless holy unions for all persons regardless of sexual orientation or gender identification." Given the historical context and the UMC's doctrinal stance on LGBT issues, his statement was radical. At that point, same-sex marriage remained illegal in most of the United States, and City Church's state did not yet recognize even civil unions. Furthermore, other UMC ministers had been tried and even defrocked for performing same-sex unions (e.g., Goodstein, 2013, December 19). The ministers' new direction appeared to challenge the willingness of City Church to yield authority to UMC doctrine in matters relating to LGBT people. Thus, although the trajectory seemed broadly in sync with the direction of cultural change vis-à-vis LGBT rights in the United States and with changes in some other churches, as marriage equality was by now spreading in the United States and other countries, City Church was clearly out of sync with its home state and the worldwide church to which it belongs.

In addition to the new stance relative to LGBT issues, other significant changes also appeared at City Church, such as greater attention to racism, food insecurity, homelessness, and issues of power and privilege, which have become frequently expressed concerns at this church. Meanwhile, the clergy have reaffirmed their commitment to celebrate same-sex marriages, despite the fact that the governing body of the UMC has voted multiple times to retain the same anti-LGBT language (Paulson, 2014, June 24). In short, under the leadership of a group of principle-based allies who were willing to confront institutional bias and to challenge existing power hierarchies, City Church seemed to be moving toward second-order change.

Discussion

Taken together, these findings suggest a number of dimensions along which ally activism might be described, with one end of each representing ally behavior that tends to reinforce and the other end representing ally behavior that tends to challenge existing power dynamics between the hetero-cisgender-normative status quo and sexual minorities. Ally activism representing the former end may perpetuate unexamined negative biases against sexual minorities, effectively delimiting the nature and degree of change that is possible. For example, allies who view their task as "parenting" LGBT people may fail to examine matters of privilege and tend to focus instead on social connection rather than on social change (Rattan & Ambady, 2014). This approach may result in pro-LGBT change that is superficial, even procedural, rather than substantive. Additionally, the unrecognized re-enactment of existing power dynamics may be expressed in allies' striving to befriend LGBT persons and yet failing to seek their input or query their needs, conveying the assumption that the advantaged group knows best what the disadvantaged group needs. By contrast, ally activism representing the other end of these dimensions, i.e., activism grounded in broader sociopolitical analysis, is more likely to entail active examination of privilege and intentional analysis of modern forms of sexual prejudice (Herek's 2004 term encompassing all forms of bias against LGBT people) and of the traditional power dynamics that are perpetuated by subtler manifestations of bias. In this latter form, ally activism fosters second-order change in individuals and institutions, which challenges and alters existing structures. For example, intentional examination of the dynamics of heterosexual-cisgender privilege creates space for determinative involvement by LGBT people in identifying the paths that change might take.

Dimensions of Ally Activism

As we worked to summarize the findings from this study, we became aware of their close connection to the distinction proposed in Russell's (2011) work. Furthermore, we came to recognize that both the distinction between relationship/role-based and values-based allies and that between first- and second-order change evoke other dimensions found in the broader literature on social change that have often been used to describe processes of collective activism and other efforts toward social justice. In what follows, we will explore several such dimensions and their links to results from the current study and Russell's 2011 work, and then discuss implications of this synthesis for genuinely egalitarian action on behalf of LGBT equality.

Table 1 presents a number of dimensions that have been used in previous work to describe the poles of certain forms of oppression, privilege, and social activism. We note that these concepts represent dimensions rather than absolute categories; hence, they reflect general tendencies or potentials, not categorical entities or fixed relationships. We suggest that among the previously explored constructs listed in the table, items in the column labeled "first-order change" represent one sort of ally activism on behalf of LGBT equality, qualities reminiscent both of the relationship/role-based motives identified in Russell's (2011) prior research on allies and of the early stage of change seen in the City Church study. The column labeled "second-order change," on the other hand, lists qualities more predictably found among principle-based allies in the first study and during the emergence of second-order change in the City Church study. Rather than discuss each dimension listed in the table individually, we will attempt to weave them into a narrative that sketches the nature of ally work among allies representing each of these two general positions. We will follow this discussion with an exploration of some implications for social activism on behalf of LGBT equality suggested by each.

Table 1. Dimensions of Collective Activism for LGBT Equality

First-order change	Second-order change
Superficial change	Potential for deeper change
Supports much of the status quo	Challenges the status quo
Power relationships unchallenged	Power relationships challenged
Privilege unexamined and unquestioned	Privilege examined and questioned
Primacy of role/relationship-based allies	Primacy of principle-based allies
Absence of voices of target group	Voices of target group heard
Limited analysis of social stigma	Greater analysis of social stigma
Focus on old-fashioned –isms	Attention also to modern –isms
Explicit attitudes challenged	Explicit and implicit attitudes challenged
Goal is policy change	Goal is social climate change
Identity politics	Value-based politics
Support through social connection	Support through social change
Noblesse oblige	Shared value in social change
Target group members as tokens	Target group members as equals
Target group narratives reflect suffering, oppression, internalized oppression	Target group narratives also reflect resilience, personal agency, transformation
Empathic sorrow	Empathic joy

The connection between Russell's differentiation of primarily relationship-based and primarily value-based allyship and the concept of first- versus second-order change is rich with implications. The first group's activism is grounded primarily in relationships with particular individuals or in personal experiences, not in an analysis of the dynamics of social stigma. Furthermore, the specificity of focus with which these individuals approach their role as allies—i.e., as an expression of support for loved ones or to fulfill personal roles or needs—requires no broader social or political analysis. Thus, the efforts of relationship-based allies are not likely to be directed toward profound structural change, as they implicitly regard themselves as benevolent representatives of that structure, able to employ it for the goals at hand, rather than as its critics. In this role, they are likely to focus relatively little on supporting a broad social justice agenda and relatively more on providing nurturing, protective, perhaps heroic support in the face of violations to individual people or groups (Rattan & Ambady, 2014). Sorrow, or even pity, for members of the target group may well be expressed in the desire to rescue the targets and punish the perpetrators of such treatment, an observation that is consistent with Pittinsky's (2012) description of actions based on empathic sorrow.

In such circumstances, members of the target group may easily be tokenized, and narratives of suffering (Russell, Bohan, & Lilly, 2000) may be embraced because such narratives serve well the motivation to protect and rescue members of the target group. In the process, traditional systems of power and privilege are recapitulated, as nontarget allies retain the power to define the problem and provide solutions that sustain their own position as knowledgeable and powerful agents of social change, even as members of the target group tend to be portrayed as victims, lacking in personal agency and unable to define for themselves the direction that change should take. The dynamic portrayed here is echoed in the work of Droogendyk, Wright, Lubensky, and Louis (2016), who argue that problematic motivations among allies can disrupt relationships between members of target and nontarget groups and can also limit the potential for constructive change.

By contrast, allies who approach their activism with a values- or principle-based identity perform such work exactly because they see sexual prejudice as an example of a broad violation of universal principles of justice and rights. These allies are thus more likely to have thought carefully about hegemonic systems of oppression and privilege, with their aim being precisely systemic change in hierarchies of power and privilege, even the undoing of existing structures. Attention to often subtle, implicit forms of bias expressed in sexual prejudice and other domains of oppression renders values-based allies more capable of applying complex social and political analyses to the dynamics of collective action and to their work within it. Given their more politically astute stance, principle-based allies are more likely to resist the subtle imposition of dominant understandings regarding what should be done and how change will proceed. They recognize the resilience and agency of LGBT people and strive to resist actions, overt or subtle, that tokenize, trivialize, or patronize members of the target group. Thus, the satisfaction of doing ally work rests on an awareness of shared values and the opportunity to enact those in collegial work with members of both target and non-target groups. Pittinsky's (2012) notion of empathic joy is reflected in this sort of ally work; here, allies move toward positive change *with*, rather than *for*, the minority group. Hence, they are more prone to strive for deep-seated social change than for the immediate gratification gained from providing individual assistance or rescue.

As we saw above, values-based allies had often worked on social justice issues in other domains, seeing their activism in LGBT issues as part of their commitment to eliminating bias across identities, in whatever form it appears. Thus, their primary focus is the expectation of collective social action aimed not only at reducing the immediate consequences of oppression but also at creating deep and long-standing social change across a wide range of domains.

Institutional Allyship at City Church

The first several lines in Table 1 serve as a brief synopsis of the core differences between first- and second-order change. This distinction and its elements encapsulate the trajectory of changes we witnessed at City Church. Early attempts to address blatant sexual prejudice were minimally challenging to the existing structure of the local congregation and the overseeing denomination. The changes that were envisioned and then enacted by the reconciling process were superficial: changes in language (claiming the appellation "Reconciling Congregation"), in symbolic presentation (rainbow décor at the annual celebration), in externally directed actions (support for independent LGBT organizations and programs), and to a small degree, in liturgical content (annual LGBT-specific sermons).

The documents portraying the Reconciling Committee's work revealed no attempt to question the appropriateness of a largely heterosexual committee's determining the course forward vis-à-vis LGBT equality in the church, and no impulse to question their own privilege and heterosexism or that embedded in the materials the committee used. The archival records show that committee members reflected on the sexual prejudice of certain other members of the congregation without noticing their own reference to LGBT people in the third person, as if none could possibly be present in the congregation even then. They worried that some heterosexual congregants might feel left out if the church moved toward reconciling status, without considering the fact that LGBT people already felt left out, even actively excluded. The committee invested extensive effort in educational programming, i.e., in prejudice reduction through the provision of information, thus focusing their attention on the congregation rather than on the LGBT people they intended to welcome to it. Committee members assumed that they knew what LGBT people wanted and needed from the church: reconciliation. They assumed that if LGBT people were "welcomed," they would feel at home—as new heterosexual members might. They failed to ask LGBT people what it would take for them to feel that they were a substantive part of the church, on their own terms— and in the process, limited the opportunity for authentic collective action. Finally, they collectively consented to the limitations imposed by the worldwide UMC's doctrinal language, choosing not to perform same-sex ceremonies or to recruit LGBT clergy. Instead, the committee reached outward to the larger community, offering existing structures (literally, in the form of buildings, and figuratively, in the form of social and political support) for the local LGBT community. These were important changes, to be sure, and they may well have represented necessary precursors to the next steps, some years later.

During the recent second phase of the church's transition relative to LGBT issues, the new ministers have broached second-order change. They have openly and directly challenged the structural constraints of the worldwide church, at risk to their own careers. In a City Church blog responding to the UMC's 2012 decision to retain anti-LGBT language in the *Book of Discipline*, the ministers wrote, "[N]othing has saddened, embarrassed and angered us more than witnessing United Methodist institutional leaders fall horribly short of implementing Jesus' call to radical inclusion and love when it comes to our LGBT sisters and brothers. . . . [E]ven more important than the internal institutional struggles of our denomination, is our commitment to continue living in faithful obedience to the Biblical story of God's unconditional love for all." In taking this stand, the ministers expressly centered the experiences of LGBT people as valid and worthy, and explicitly challenged the power of the worldwide church. Their message seems to be having an effect on others at City Church. Following the aforementioned 2012 UMC decision, the chair of City Church's Welcoming and Affirming Committee (formerly the Reconciling Committee; the name change is itself telling) was quoted in a news release: "We won't pretend that this week's votes weren't enormously disappointing but we don't intend to be defined, defeated or deterred by those votes."

Furthermore, this commitment to values-based allyship extends well beyond LGBT issues, and the new ministers have repeatedly charged members of the congregation to examine their own privileged status by granting centrality to this and other issues of social justice. For example, after Trayvon Martin, a young unarmed black man wearing a hooded sweatshirt, was killed by a neighbor participating in a "neighborhood watch" program, one of the City Church pastors delivered his sermon wearing a hooded sweatshirt. In addition, the church is now the site of frequent free meals for anyone who wishes to partake, and the pastors regularly participate in events designed to raise money and enhance awareness of the needs of homeless people. The extent of their commitment to such issues is revealed by their currently considering leasing a large parcel of very valuable church-owned land to a program for homeless youth. Furthermore, public educational fora, sermons, and blogs addressing matters of power and privilege are more common, no longer relegated to the annual celebration of City Church's reconciling status.

Other shifts have also been evident. There has been increasing emphasis on locating issues related to specific marginalized groups within a broader social justice framework—a move that suggests reduced focus on positions related solely to individual identity claims, such as welcoming LGBT people, and enhanced attention to work rooted in larger values that apply to a range of marginalized groups, such as involvement in actions serving a variety of disadvantaged communities. Correspondingly, the focus of discussions about marginalized groups now entails relatively less emphasis on social connection, such as organizing social events for LGBT people or serving a weekly meal to people living on the streets, and greater emphasis on social justice, such as working to reduce homelessness and racism. Moreover, the church's efforts center the voices of oppressed groups, avoiding the tendency to "rescue." A blog about racism in the local community by one of the pastors provides an example. "Those of us who are white," he wrote, "can offer our gifts, talents and experiences following the leadership of People of Color." Such shifts suggest a movement away from intergroup contact for its own sake—and even for the sake of prejudice reduction—and toward the possibility of concrete engagement in social change efforts (Dixon et al., 2013; Tropp et al., 2012).

Because this promise of second-order change is quite recent, it remains to be seen whether City Church's future activism will eventually embody the range of characteristics given in the right-hand column of Table 1. But the stage seems set for movement in that direction. Importantly, that stage setting required active attention to the voices of marginalized individuals, making genuinely collective action possible.

Implications

Implications for intervention. Our synthesis of observations drawn from an ethnographic study of institutional allyship, complemented by findings from an earlier study of individual allies, suggests that collective action regarding social inequities can both create positive social change and reinstate the power dynamics of existing relationships between majority and minority groups. Furthermore, both dynamics can occur at the level of individual ally work and at that of institutional efforts to promote social change. The lack of attention to the potential recapitulation of dysfunctional dynamics may prevent us from recognizing the subtle risks inherent in change efforts and also the full potential that emerges when these risks are addressed. The putative model presented above suggests strategies for optimizing collective action without inadvertently reinstating the power structures that we aim to dismantle.

The model proposed in Table 1, which is largely based on two qualitative studies, drawing from broad literatures on social change, power and privilege, and LGBT equality (e.g., Saguy, Tausch, Dovidio, & Pratto, 2009; Wright & Lubensky, 2009), is best viewed not as definitive but as heuristic. We make no claim to finality here; rather, we view this model as a tentative impetus to further reflection, research, and application. To the degree that it serves as a useful heuristic, it suggests several considerations for activists and researchers at individual, interpersonal, and institutional levels of social change work (Batts, 2002).

At the individual level, members of both groups in the LGBT—ally collective action partnership have the responsibility to examine their own actions, thoughts, and feelings that might influence whether social change will be substantive and enduring or superficial and circumscribed. LGBT people should consider the degree to which they personally enact positions that devalue LGBT identity (Russell & Bohan, 2006) and instead actively strive to counter the explicit and implicit anti-LGBT attitudes that persist in their lives. Some of the principles of liberation psychology (Russell & Bohan, 2007), as well as more recent empirical findings drawn from implicit attitudes research (e.g., Banaji & Greenwald, 2013), may be helpful here.

Heterosexual-cisgender-identified people have also incorporated and thereby enact LGBT-oppressive actions and attitudes. A stated commitment to LGBT equality cannot by itself eliminate a lifetime of participation in heteronormative assumptions and sexual prejudice. Thus, it is incumbent upon heterosexual-cisgender allies and the institutions with which they are affiliated to examine their sexual prejudice at both explicit and implicit levels. Drawing from the studies described above, allies might be particularly alert to phenomena that may predispose limited, first-order change, as well as to the potential for (usually subtle) reactions to the emergence of LGBT empowerment that may displace allies from positions of status. When such status is removed, nontarget individuals may experience a phenomenon that has been termed "privilege deprivation" (Russell & Bohan, 2014), which may reduce the potential for effective collective social change work.

At the interpersonal and institutional levels, LGBT people and heterosexual-cisgender allies should be attentive to practices that tokenize, infantilize, or marginalize LGBT people—and, conversely, those that unduly center heterosexual-cisgender people. It may be easier to recapitulate historical hierarchies if each group considers the other group only in terms of their target or nontarget identity; heterosexual-cisgender people may easily slip into dominant roles, and LGBT people may assume lower status roles with neither group noting the attribution of status. On the other hand, the differences in perspective that derive from including differing identities in the conversation allow for richer discussion, problem solving, and action. Thus, discussions of positionality should be common. As Tropp et al. (2012) suggested, "contact between low- and high-status groups should include opportunities for enhancing awareness and discussions of structural inequalities to protect the interests of low-status groups in cross-group interaction" (p. 268). The emphasis should be on challenging the status quo, and it should include cautions about narratives that center the victimization of LGBT people to the neglect of their resilience and power or that valorize ally status at the expense of LGBT agency.

The chart presented in Table 1 may serve as the beginning of a helpful checklist for individuals, groups, or organizations who are interested in addressing issues of power and oppression. It may also provide a framework for LGBT people and their allies to engage in conversations that enhance their collective action, in terms of both its process and its outcome.

Implications for future research.   Like so much research that looks at complex issues, the limitations inherent in this study leave many questions unanswered, including several having to do with the putative model presented here linking a broad set of factors with first- and second-order change. For example, are all of the factors listed here linked in a systematic way with one another? Are they all necessary to a full understanding of social change efforts? Is there some hierarchy of importance among them? In a related vein, what is the relationship between first- and second-order change? Is first-order change a necessary precursor, or can second-order change emerge on its own? If it can arise independently, what conditions—both internal to the organization and in the larger society—facilitate such an apparent leap? If not, what precludes it? The answers are not trivial. We may too easily settle for first-order steps, assuming them necessary, when further progress might be possible, or we may insist on second-order aims when individuals or institutions are not capable of that level of social change. Attempts to address such questions might take many forms, with mixed-methods approaches perhaps promising especially useful outcomes (Hopkins & Kahani-Hopkins, 2006).

A second set of questions warranting further attention concerns the absence of virtually any representation of the minority perspective in the materials we examined. Hopkins and Kahani-Hopkins (2006) pointed out that one cannot gain access to minority perspectives through top-down methods that bypass minorities' models of intergroup contact. The meaning of intergroup contact must be examined from the perspective of minority participants (Pettigrew & Tropp, 2000). Thus, future research might examine situations in which the evolution of institutional allyship involves the participation of roughly equivalent numbers of minority and majority participants, rendering genuinely collective action a realistic aim. Under such circumstances, it would be possible to address, if not necessarily to answer, the questions raised above regarding our putative model. Based on the results of the present study, it seems clear that the domain of institutional allyship is rife with important questions, and the potential for significant impact on movements for social justice seems equally clear.

References

Arm, J. R., Horne, S. G., & Levitt, H. M. (2009). Negotiating connection to GLBT experience: Family members' experience of anti-gay movements and policies. *Journal of Counseling Psychology, 56*, 82–96. doi: 10.1037/a0012813

Asta, E. L., & Vacha-Haase, T. (2013). Heterosexual ally development in counseling psychologists: Experiences, training and advocacy. *Counseling Psychologist, 41*, 493–529. doi: 10.1177/0011000012453174

Ayers, I., & Brown, J. G. (2005). *Straightforward: How to mobilize heterosexual support for gay rights.* Princeton, NJ: Princeton University Press.

Banaji, M. R., & Greenwald, A. G. (2013). *Blind spot: Hidden biases of good people.* New York, NY: Delacorte Press.

Bartunek, J. M. (1984). Changing interpretive schemes and organizational restructuring: The example of a religious order. *Administrative Science Quarterly, 29*, 355–372. doi: 10.2307.2393029

Batts, V. (2002). Is reconciliation possible? Lessons from combating "modern racism." Retrieved March 29, 2016, from http://sph.unc.edu/files/2013/07/ditf_is_reconciliation_possible.pdf

Bergsieker, H. B., Shelton, J. N., & Richeson, J. A. (2010). To be liked versus respected: Divergent goals in interracial interactions. *Journal of Personality and Social Psychology, 99*, 248–264. doi: 10.1037.a0018474

Broad, K. L., Alden, H., Berkowitz, D., & Ryan, M. (2008). Activist parenting and GLBTQ families. *Journal of GLBT Family Studies, 4*, 499–520. doi: 10.1080/15504280802191749

Broad, K. L., Crawley, S. L., & Foley, L. (2004). Doing "real family values": The interpretive practice of families. *Sociological Quarterly, 45*, 509–527. doi: 10.1111/j.1533-8525.2004.tb02301.x

Brooks, A. K., & Edwards, K. (2009). Allies in the workplace: Including LGBT in HRD. *Advances in Human Resources, 11*. Retrieved March 29, 2016, from http://adh.sagepub.com/content/11/1/136. doi: 10.1177/15234223083285000

Cortese, D. K. (2006). *Are we thinking straight? The politics of straightness in a lesbian and gay social movement organization*. New York, NY: Routledge.

Dixon, J., Durrheim, K., Kerr, P., & Thorne, M. (2013). 'What's so funny 'bout peace, love and understanding?' Further reflections on the limits of prejudice reduction as a model of social change. *Journal of Social and Political Psychology, 1*, 239–252. doi: 10.5964/jspp.v1i1.234

Draughn, T., Elkins, B., & Roy, R. (2002). Allies in the struggle: Eradicating homophobia and heterosexism on campus. *Journal of Lesbian Studies, 6*, 9–20. doi: 10.1300/J155v96n03_02

Droogendyk, L., Wright, S. C., Lubensky, M.E., & Louis, W. R. (2016). Acting in solidarity: Cross-group contact between disadvantaged group members and advantaged group allies. *Journal of Social Issues, 72*(2), 315–334.

Duhigg, J. M., Rostosky, S. S., Gray, B. E., & Wimsatt, M. K. (2010). Development of heterosexuals into sexual-minority allies: A qualitative exploration. *Sexuality Research and Social Policy, 7*, 2–14. doi: 10.1007/s13178-010-0005-2

Fingerhut, A. W. (2011). Straight allies: What predicts heterosexuals' alliance with the LGBT community? *Journal of Applied Social Psychology, 41*, 2230–2248. doi: 10.1111/j.1559-1816.2011.00807.x

Goodstein, L. (2013, December 19). Defrocking of minister widens split over gays. New York Times. Retrieved December 20, 2013, from http://www.nytimes.com/2013/12/20/us/methodist-pastor-defrocked-over-gay-marriage-service.html

Hall, D. M. (2009). *Allies at work: Creating a lesbian, gay, bisexual and transgender inclusive work environment*. San Francisco, CA: Out and Equal Workplace Advocates.

Herek, G. M. (2004). Beyond "homophobia": Thinking about sexual prejudice and stigma in the twenty-first century. *Sexuality Research and Social Policy, 1*, 6–24. doi: 10.1525/srsp.2004.1.2.6

Herek, G. M., & Glunt, E. K. (1993). Interpersonal contact and heterosexuals' attitudes toward gay men: Results from a national survey. *Journal of Sex Research, 30*, 239–244. doi: 10.1080/00224499309551707

Herman, D. (1997). *The antigay agenda: Orthodox vision and the Christian right*. Chicago, IL: University of Chicago Press.

Hopkins, N., & Kahani-Hopkins, V. (2006). Minority group members' theories of intergroup contact: A case study of British Muslims' conceptualizations of 'Islamophobia' and social change. *British Journal of Social Psychology, 45*, 245–264. doi: 10.1348/014466605x8583

Horne, S. G., Rostosky, S. S., & Riggle, E. D. B. (2011). Impact of marriage restriction amendments on family members of lesbian, gay, and bisexual individuals: A mixed-method approach. *Journal of Social Issues, 67*, 358–375. doi: 10.1111/j.1540-4560.2011201702.x

Klar, M., & Kasser, T. (2009). Some benefits of being an activist: Measuring activism in its role in psychological well-being. *Political Psychology, 20*, 755–777. doi: 10.1111/j.1467-9221.2009.00724.x

Maran, M., & Watrous, A. (Eds.). (2005). *50 ways to support lesbian and gay equality*. Maui, HI: Inner Ocean Publishing.

McGarty, C., Bliuc, A-M, Thomas, E. F., & Bongiorno, R. (2009). Collective action as the material expression of opinion-based group membership. *Journal of Social Issues, 65*, 839–857. doi: 10.1111/j.1540-4560.2009.01627.x

Merrick, L. H. (2001). *Julian Rush—Facing the music: A gay Methodist minister's story*. Bloomington, IN: Universe.

Otterman, S. (2013, May 5). Caught in Methodism's split over same-sex marriage. New York Times. Retrieved May 7, 2013, from http://www.nytimes.com/2013/05/06/nyregion/caught-in-methodisms-split-over-same-sex-marriage.html

Paulson, M. (2014, June 24). Methodists reinstate pastor, deepening Church's rift over gays. New York Times. Retrieved June 24, 2014, from http://www.nytimes.com/2014/06/25/us/methodist-panel-reinstates-defrocked-pastor.html

Pettigrew, T. F., & Tropp, L. R. (2000). Does intergroup contact reduce prejudice? Recent meta-analytic findings. In S. Oskamp (Ed.), *Reducing prejudice and discrimination* (pp. 93–114). Mahwah, NJ: Erlbaum.

Pittinsky, T. L. (2012). *Us + them: Tapping the positive power of difference*. Boston, MA: Harvard Business Review Press.

Rattan, A., & Ambady, N. (2014). How "It gets better": Effectively communicating support to targets of prejudice. *Personality and Social Psychology Bulletin, 40*, 1–12. doi: 10.1177/0146167213519480

Reicher, S., Cassidy, C., Wolpert, L., Hopkins, N., & Levine, M. (2006). Saving Bulgaria's Jews: An analysis of social identity and the mobilization of social solidarity. *European Journal of Social Psychology, 36*, 49–72. doi: 10.1002/ejsp.291

Riggins, S. H. (Ed.). (1997). *The language and politics of exclusion: Others in discourse*. Thousand Oaks, CA: Sage.

Russell, G. M. (1996, June). *Research as documentary: A study of heterosexual allies*. Symposium Presented at Convention of the Society for the Psychological Study of Social Issues, Ann Arbor, MI.

Russell, G. M. (2000) *Voted out: The psychological consequences of anti-gay politics*. New York, NY: New York University Press.

Russell, G. M. (2011). Motives of heterosexual allies in collective action for equality. *Journal of Social Issues, 67*, 358–375. doi: 10.1111/j.1540-4560.2011.01703.x

Russell, G. M., & Bohan, J. S. (2006). The case of internalized homophobia: Theory and/as practice. *Theory and Psychology, 16*, 343–366. doi: 10.1177/0959354306064283

Russell, G. M., & Bohan, J. S. (2007). Liberating psychotherapy: Liberation psychology and psychotherapy with LGBT clients. *Journal of Gay and Lesbian Psychotherapy, 11*, 59–75. doi: 10.1300/J236v11n03_04

Russell, G. M., & Bohan, J. S. (2014). Toward a contextual understanding of psychology trainees' religious conflicts. *Psychology of Sexual Orientation and Gender Diversity, 1*, 293–301. doi: 10.1037/sgd0000072

Russell, G. M., Bohan, J. S., & Lilly, D. (2000). Queer youth: Old stories, new stories. In S. Jones (Ed.), *A sea of stories: The shaping power of narrative in gay and lesbian cultures* (pp. 69–92). New York, NY: Haworth.

Russell, G. M., Bohan, J. S., McCarroll, M. C., & Smith, N. (2010). Trauma, recovery, and community: Perspectives on the long-term impact of anti-LGBT politics. *Traumatology, 17*, 14–23. doi: 10.1177/1534765610362799

Russell, G. M., Dixon, S., & Levine, M. (2002, August). Motivations of heterosexual allies: Implications for public policy. In R. Georgemiller (Chair), *Psychosocial issues and LGBT psychology*. Paper Session Presented at Conference of the American Psychological Association, Chicago, IL.

Russell, G. M., & Ruckert, S. (2004, July). Multiple pathways to activism: The case of heterosexual allies. In G. M. Russell (chair), *Voices of heterosexual allies: Public discourse, activism, and research*. Symposium Presented at Conference of the American Psychological Association, Honolulu, HI.

Saguy, T., Tausch, T., Dovidio, J. F., & Pratto, F. (2009). The irony of harmony: Intergroup contact can produce false expectations for equality. *Psychological Science, 20*, 114–121. doi: 10.1111/j.1467-9280.2008.02261.x

Shelton, J. N. (2000). A reconceptualization of how we study issues of racial prejudice. *Personality and Social Psychology Review, 4*, 374–390. doi: 10.1207/S15327957PSPR0404_6

Stotzer, R. L. (2009). Straight allies: Supportive attitudes toward lesbians, gay men, and bisexuals in a college sample. *Sex Roles, 60*, 67–80. doi: 10.1007/s11199-008-9508-1

Tillman-Healy, L. M. (2001). *Between gay and straight: Understanding friendship across sexual orientation*. Walnut Creek, CA: AltaMira Press.

Trillin, C. (1982, January 25). U.S. journal: Boulder, Colorado: Let me find a place. New Yorker. Retrieved June 26, 2014, from http://www.newyorker.com/magazine/1982/01/25/let-me-find-a-place

Tropp, L. R., Hawi, D. R., Van Larr, C., & Levin, S. (2012). Cross-ethnic friendships, perceived discrimination, and their effects on ethnic activism over time: A longitudinal investigation of three ethnic minority groups. *British Journal of Social Psychology, 51*, 275–272. doi: 10.1111/j2044-8309.2011.02050.x

Tropp, L. R., & Pettigrew, T. F. (2005) Relationships between intergroup contact and prejudice among minority and majority status groups. *Psychological Science, 16,* 951–957. doi: 10.1111/j.1467-9280.2005.01643.x

van Dijk, T. A. (1993). Principles of critical discourse analysis. *Discourse in Society, 4,* 249–283.

Vernaglia, E. R. (1999). Parents as straight allies: A qualitative study of the experiences of heterosexual parents in the gay rights movement. *Boston College Dissertations and Theses,* AAI9961584.

Watzlawick, P., Weakland, J. H., & Fisch, R. (1974). *Change: Principles of problem formation and problem resolution.* Oxford, UK: W. W. Norton.

Whitley, B. E., Jr. (2012). Religiosity and attitudes toward lesbians and gay men: A meta-analysis. *International Journal for the Psychology of Religion, 19,* 21–38. doi: 10.1080/10508610802471104

Wright, S. C. (2009). The next generation of collective action research. *Journal of Social Issues, 65,* 859–879. doi: 10.1111/j.1540-4560.2009.01628.x

Wright, S. C., & Lubensky, M. (2009). The struggle for social equality: Collective action versus prejudice reduction. In S. Demoulin, J. P. Leyens, & J. F. Dovidio (Eds.), *Intergroup misunderstandings: Impact of divergent social realities* (pp. 291–310). New York: Psychology Press.

GLENDA M. RUSSELL is a research associate with Ethnography & Evaluation Research, Center to Advance Research and Training in the Social Sciences at the University of Colorado Boulder, and a psychologist in private practice in Boulder. Her research interests have included the psychological impact of anti-LGBT politics, ally activism, and multicultural psychotherapies.

JANIS S. BOHAN is Professor Emerita at Metropolitan State University of Denver. Her work has been primarily in the areas of women in the history of psychology, feminist psychology, psychology of sexual orientation, and postmodern critiques of psychology, especially as regards identity categories.

Journal of Social Issues, Vol. 72, No. 2, 2016, pp. 355–375
doi: 10.1111/josi.12170

Intergroup Relations in Latin America: Intergroup Contact, Common Ingroup Identity, and Activism among Indigenous Groups in Mexico and Chile

Huseyin Çakal[*]
University of Exeter

Anja Eller
National Autonomous University of Mexico

David Sirlopú
Universidad del Desarrollo

Andrés Pérez
National Autonomous University of Mexico

*In two correlational studies in Mexico (Study 1: N = 152, Mexican Indige-
nous people) and Chile (Study 2: N = 185, Chilean Indigenous people, Mapuche), we investigated how different dimensions of common ingroup identity (CII)
and intergroup contact between Indigenous people influence activist tendencies
and how past participation moderates this influence. In Study 1, CII as Mexican
and intragroup contact between Indigenous people predicted activist tendencies
via increased group efficacy. In Study 2, CII as Chilean positively predicted normative activism both directly and via group efficacy. In both studies intragroup
contact between Indigenous people directly and positively predicted future intentions to engage in political action and past activism moderated these associations.
These findings suggest that the negative effects of CII on activism do not readily map onto contexts where subgroup and CII overlap, and contact might have*

---

[*]Correspondence concerning this article should be addressed to Huseyin Çakal, Washington
Singer Laboratories, School of Psychology, University of Exeter, Perry Road, Prince of Wales Road,
Exeter, EX4 4QG, UK [e-mail: H.Cakal@exeter.ac.uk].

We are grateful to John Drury, University of Sussex, the guest editors, and two anonymous
reviewers for their valuable comments on an earlier version of the manuscript.

355

beneficial effects on activism. Implications for future research and policy are discussed.

Extant literature suggests that prejudice-reduction strategies, such as common ingroup identity (CII; Gaertner & Dovidio, 2000) and regular contact (Allport, 1954; Pettigrew, 1998) with advantaged groups, reduce the motivation to engage in political action among the members of disadvantaged groups (Dixon, Levine, Reicher, & Durrheim, 2012). Specifically, emphasis on a common identity that includes both the advantaged and disadvantaged groups, and positive contact across the intergroup divide, cause the disadvantaged to perceive the system as just. Such perceptions then might demotivate disadvantaged group members from seeking to redress the unequal system. In this article, we argue that in some contexts both common ingroup identities and contact may play crucial roles in instigating political action especially among the disadvantaged groups. First, people might perceive themselves as entitled to certain rights and privileges based on their membership of a group (van Zomeren, Postmes, & Spears, 2008), and would act to protect those privileges or reclaim them (Wenzel, 2000). Their social identity would thus facilitate access to political and psychological resources to engage in political action. Second, as a result of perceived commonalities, individuals from different disadvantaged groups may form strategic alliances and pool their resources against an authority (Glasford & Calcagno, 2012). Similarly, contact can facilitate a learning process through which people could discover such commonalities. In what follows, we report findings from two studies that investigate how CII and intragroup contact can energize members of different disadvantaged groups, that is, Indigenous peoples, to engage in political action.

Collective Action

Research on collective action, i.e., acting on behalf of one's group with the aim of improving or maintaining conditions for that group (Wright, 2009), has established identification with the group, perceptions of group efficacy, and anger resulting from being collectively and unjustly disadvantaged as the primary predictors of collective action (van Zomeren et al., 2008). More recent work has sought to integrate these processes with research on coping. According to the Dynamic Dual Pathway Model of Approach Coping with Collective Disadvantage (DDPMAC: van Zomeren, Leach, & Spears, 2012), collective action is a consequence of a dynamic appraisal-reappraisal process. At the primary appraisal stage, individuals assess a particular problem, for example, having no access to particular resources, as a result of their membership to a particular group, e.g., as Indigenous, Mexican, or African American, as self-relevant. The self-relevance of the problem then triggers two distinct processes of coping, problem-focused versus emotion-focused (van Zomeren et al., 2012).

During problem-focused coping, individuals are more willing to engage in activism and political action if they perceive that they have sufficient resources to cope with the problem (Klandermans, 1984, 1997). Research suggests that social networks are the primary point of access to such group-based resources (Ellemers, 1993; Louis, Amiot, Thomas, & Blackwood, 2016; van Zomeren et al., 2012) that include but are not limited to instrumental support for action, leadership, channels of communication, trust, and solidarity.

As for the emotion-coping pathway, perceptions of being unfairly and collectively disadvantaged leads to negative affect, that is, anger, at the group level, which, in turn, motivates individuals to engage in political action to remove their collective disadvantages as a group (van Zomeren, Spears, Fischer, & Leach, 2004). Accordingly, research has also demonstrated that group-related disadvantages only invoke negative affect if the individual identifies with the group (Mackie, Maitner, & Smith, 2009).

Recent research on activism argues that past participation in political action or even civic participation could influence future activism (van Stekelenburg, Klandermans, & Akkerman, 2016). In a similar vein, DDPMAC hypothesizes that both emotion-focused and problem-focused pathway are influenced by past participation in political action. Taking part in political action, for instance, is likely to (i) empower individuals and reinforce their subjective identification with the group (Drury & Reicher, 2009; Tausch & Becker, 2013), and (ii) to intensify their anger resulting from unjust collective disadvantage. Alternatively, participation in unsuccessful action could also backfire and lead to disidentification from the group (Becker, Tausch, Spears, & Christ, 2011; Tausch & Becker, 2013). Preliminary findings from research on CII and contact, however, imply that both CII and intergroup contact could ameliorate these psychological processes that lead to political action, and eventually dampen activism.

Common Ingroup Identity

CII (Gaertner & Dovidio, 2000) model predicts that it is possible to reduce intergroup bias via processes of de-categorization and re-categorization which result in a superordinate group that includes both ingroup and the outgroup. Individuals are first encouraged to de-categorize themselves as exclusive members of their ethnic, religious, or racial groups. In a subsequent process, they are induced to re-categorize themselves as members of a new superordinate group, such as, a national identity. CII model assumes that these categorization processes are not static and at any given time individuals identify with a multitude of social groups which may or not be exclusive of each other (Dovidio, Saguy, Gaertner, & Thomas, 2012). Once this re-categorization of "us" and "them" into "we" is underway, the negative bias toward "former" outgroup members is transformed into positive bias as they are now perceived as members of the new all-inclusive group. The

CII model has been criticized for its paradoxical predictions in relation to social change benefitting disadvantaged groups (but see Droogendyk, Wright, Lubensky, & Louis, 2016, for an alternative account of how individuals from both advantaged and disadvantaged groups can cooperate toward political activism within a common identity that rests on solidarity). Specifically, research has demonstrated that CII is associated with reduced perceptions of inequalities and discrimination among the disadvantaged. In the United States, identifying as American as opposed to White American reduced recognition of discrimination against African Americans and willingness to protest in favor of African Americans (Banfield & Dovidio, 2013). In the European context, identifying as European negatively predicted willingness to protest among the disadvantaged Kurds by reducing anger whereas identification with the Kurdish ingroup predicted stronger willingness to engage in protest behavior via anger and group efficacy (Ufkes, Dovidio, & Tel, 2014).

We argue that such paradoxical effects of CII partly depend on the social and political structure and how multiple identities interact (Curtin, Kende, & Kende, 2016). As such, the sedative or demobilising effects of CII are not readily applicable to contexts in which members of the disadvantaged group have been severely marginalized and discriminated against. In such cases membership of the mainstream group might provide the only way to access to political and psychological resources that are needed to challenge the system. A case in point is societal structures in which multiple layers of superordinate identity with blurred boundaries, for example, religious, linguistic, and racial, exist and overlap with each other. For instance, in the majority of Latin American societies, including Mexico and Chile where the present research was conducted, the mainstream society is a racial and cultural mix of Indigenous groups, groups of European descend, and a mixture of both, commonly referred as "Mestizo" (Stavans, 2013). This notion of the mainstream CII, while simultaneously recognizing proto-typicality of Indigenous elements, marginalizes various "unassimilated" indigenous groups whose members identify with their specific communities, for example, Mayan, Nahuatl, or Zapotec, as well as with a collective Indigenous identity (Jung, 2008).

Research also shows that while such groups are beginning to reclaim their cultural rights and assert their identity, Indigenous people in Latin America still remain among the most marginalized and socially excluded peoples on the globe. Stark differences exist among Indigenous and non-Indigenous in terms of access to economic, political, and social opportunities (Arias, Yamada, & Tejerina, 2004; Hall & Patrinos, 2004; Parker, Rubalcava, & Teruel, 2005). We therefore propose that it is possible to construe several dimensions of a CII in Mexican and Chilean societies. Correspondingly, we argue that CII as Indigenous is marginalized and stigmatized on the basis of its differences from the national CII as Mexican and/or Chilean. In both societies, therefore, identifying with the mainstream society as Mexican and/or Chilean might provide emotional and instrumental support, which in turn, might provoke approach-oriented emotions, e.g., anger, and perceptions of increased group efficacy. What is more, by categorizing oneself as an integral part of the mainstream society, one also asserts one's rights to access the necessary political structure to challenge the disadvantages that Indigenous people in these countries currently face.

Contact

Contact theory (Allport, 1954; Pettigrew, 1998; Pettigrew & Tropp, 2006) posits that under certain conditions, frequent and positive intergroup contact between individuals belonging to different groups improves attitudes, emotions, and behavior toward each other. Recent research, however, has shown that among the disadvantaged frequent and pleasant interactions with those in power might have paradoxical effects on social change and could potentially make it difficult for the disadvantaged to resist and challenge their "nice and benevolent" friends from the advantaged group as oppressors (Dixon et al., 2012; Tausch, Saguy, & Bryson, 2015).

In such cases these paradoxical effects are facilitated various psychological processes. Perhaps the first and foremost of these processes is the reduced perceptions of discrimination and inequality. In South Africa, more and positive contact with White South Africans decreased perceptions of inequality among Black South Africans who, in turn, showed less support for racial equality policies (Dixon, Durrheim, Tredoux, Tropp, & Eaton, 2010). Similarly, positive contact with the advantaged Jewish Israelis reduced perceptions of discrimination among the disadvantaged Israeli Arabs who, much like their Black South African counterparts, showed less support for social change (Saguy, Tausch, Dovidio, & Pratto, 2009). Sengupta and Sibley (2013) demonstrated that contact with the advantaged group increased beliefs in a meritocratic system and decreased support for policies aimed at supporting the impoverished Maori ingroup in New Zealand. However, Sengupta and Sibley (2013) also reported that those who had more intragroup contact with the other members of their disadvantaged group had more critical views of the meritocratic system, and thus showed more support for policies aiming to improve the conditions for the disadvantaged Maori. This implies that intragroup contact between members of disadvantaged groups, as opposed to intergroup contact between the advantaged and disadvantaged, could potentially motivate individuals to engage in political action against the common oppressor. In fact, recent research argues that even interaction might actually have a positive effect on political action (Curtin & McGarty, 2016; Thomas, McGarty, & Louis, 2014).

However, there is no research, known to us, that investigates the effect of contact between the members of different disadvantaged groups on joint collective action via established predictors of collective action, e.g., anger or group efficacy (van Zomeren et al., 2012). If intergroup contact can improve awareness of commonalities between the advantaged and disadvantaged groups (Saguy et al., 2009), and contact between members of a particular group could facilitate support for political action by informing individuals about their collective disadvantage, then intragroup contact could also facilitate similar processes among the members of different disadvantaged groups. Members of the disadvantaged groups might become cognizant of shared beliefs about the unfairness of the situation through regular contact with members of other disadvantaged groups, in this case other Indigenous people. They might also learn about similar-others' willingness to redress this inequality. As such, intragroup contact then can trigger (i) group-based appraisals of illegitimacy and unfairness of the collective disadvantage; and (ii) attributions of blame to external actors for the unfairness of the situation. Previous research has established that both processes provoke approach-oriented psychological processes and facilitates one's willingness to engage in political action. On one hand, knowing that other people, too, are discontent and angry with the collective disadvantage could emphasize the group-level nature of the emotional experiences related to collective disadvantage, that is, anger (Mackie et al., 2009; van Zomeren et al., 2004). On the other, perceiving that one is not alone in one's evaluation of the situation and one's desire to change could positively change one's beliefs about the group's capacity to challenge the conditions.

Based on our reading of this research and recent findings of Thomas et al. (2014) which show that social interaction positively influences political participation, we argue that intragroup contact between members of disadvantaged groups can (i) increase perceptions of group efficacy, (ii) intensify emotional experiences, i.e., anger and, therefore, (iii) motivate individuals to engage in political action and activism aimed at redressing the inequalities.

Present Study and Overview of Hypotheses

The Indigenous peoples of Mexico and Chile remain two of the least researched groups, so provide a fertile context to test our research hypotheses. Both Mexico and Chile have a colonial background and are home to Indigenous populations consisting of various groups, each with its own cultural and linguistic idiosyncrasies. Despite the rising tide of social movements and struggle for equality, the Indigenous people in both countries are traditionally the most excluded and disadvantaged segment of the society. As Indigenous, they also remain stigmatized and discriminated against. Thus, identifying as Mexican/Chilean might provide the only viable way to access the resources necessary for improving their conditions. Accordingly, we hypothesize that

> H1 CII as Mexican and/or Chilean will predict willingness to engage in political action over and above identification as Indigenous both directly and via anger and group efficacy.

Extrapolating from Sengupta and Sibley (2013) and Thomas et al. (2014), we contend that contact with other Indigenous people will intensify perceptions of shared group-based disadvantaged and instrumental support, in turn leading to increased activism. Therefore

> H2 Contact will predict political action tendencies both directly and via anger and group efficacy.

Finally, because Indigenous people have long suffered institutional discrimination and marginalization, and have had little success in reclaiming their rights as Indigenous, we predict that

> H3 Past participation in activism will moderate how CII and intragroup contact predict future political action tendencies via anger and group efficacy.
>
> H3a In situations where the CII as Indigenous and CII as national identity, i.e., Mexican and/or Chilean overlap, the moderating effect of past participation will be positive,
>
> H3b In situations where there is no or little overlap between two different types of CII the moderating effect of past participation will be negative.

We test these hypotheses in two studies that we report below.

Study 1: Method

Participants

One hundred and fifty-two Indigenous adults (95 females, $M_{age} = 37.07$, $SD = 14.76$) were recruited from Indigenous communities in Mexico City and interviewed by a male research assistant of Indigenous origin and received monetary compensation (equivalent of $3 in local currency) for their voluntary commitment of time.

Measures

Variables were measured on five point Likert-type scales. Higher values denote stronger identification, more contact, more anger, higher perceived group efficacy, and more willingness to engage in political action (CII, group efficacy, and political action items: 1, *strongly disagree*; 5, *strongly agree*; anger items 1, *not at all*; 5, *very much*; contact items: 1, *never*; 5, *very often*). CII as Indigenous is measured by two items adapted from Leach et al. (2008): "Being Indigenous is an important part of how I see myself ," and "I am very happy to be Indigenous" ($r = .70, p < .001$). We adapted the same items to measure CII as Mexican: "Being

Table 1. Descriptive Statistics and Correlations Between the Latent Variables in the Model (Study 1: All Variables Measured by 1–5 Likert Scales)

Variable	M	SD	1	2	3	4	5	6	7
CII as Indigenous	4.57	.92	1	$.59^{***}$	$.13^{*}$	$.39^{***}$	$.22^{***}$	.03	$.31^{***}$
CII as Mexican	4.66	.80		1	.10	$.48^{***}$	.02	$.14^{**}$	$.43^{***}$
Intragroup contact among indigenous	3.31	1.01			1	.21	$.28^{***}$	$.32^{***}$	$.21^{**}$
Group efficacy	4.34	.99				1	$.17^{*}$	.02	$.54^{***}$
Anger	3.06	1.54					1	$.27^{**}$	$.34^{**}$
Past participation in activism	2.22	1.20						1	.09
Political action tendencies	4.30	1.06							1

Note. $^{***}p < .001$; $^{**}p < .01$; $^{*}p < .05$.

Mexican is an important part of how I see myself," and "I am very happy to be Mexican" ($r = .88, p < .001$). Contact among Indigenous is measured by two items "How often do you have direct, face-to-face interactions with other Indigenous in daily life, i.e., during shopping etc.?" and "How often do you exchange house visits with other Indigenous people" ($r = .69, p < .001$). We adapted two items each from van Zomeren, Leach, and Spears (2010) to measure anger and group efficacy "When you think about the disadvantages and hardships that Indigenous people in Mexico face, how much anger/fury do you feel in general?" ($r = .80, p < .001$); "Working with other Indigenous communities we can improve the condition for Indigenous" and "We Indigenous people can improve our conditions" ($r = .93, p < .001$). We assessed past participation with three items: "In the last six months I have signed a petition/took part in a peaceful demonstration/ attended a meeting on Indigenous rights" ($\alpha = .92$). Political action tendencies were measured by two items ($r = .71, p < .001$; van Zomeren, Spears, & Leach, 2008): "I would be willing to sign a petition to improve the conditions for Indigenous people" and "I would be willing take part in a legal demonstration to improve the conditions for Indigenous people."

Study 1: Results and Discussion

We report the descriptive statistics of our variables in Table 1. We ran a structural equation model (SEM) with latent variables using MPlus (Muthen & Muthen, 2008). SEM is a commonly used set of statistical procedures that combine factor analysis and path modeling to test models with latent variables, that is, variables that cannot be measured directly, and consists of two components, measurement model and structural model. It uses observed variables, in other words, items that the participants respond to by indicating their preference on the given scale. A

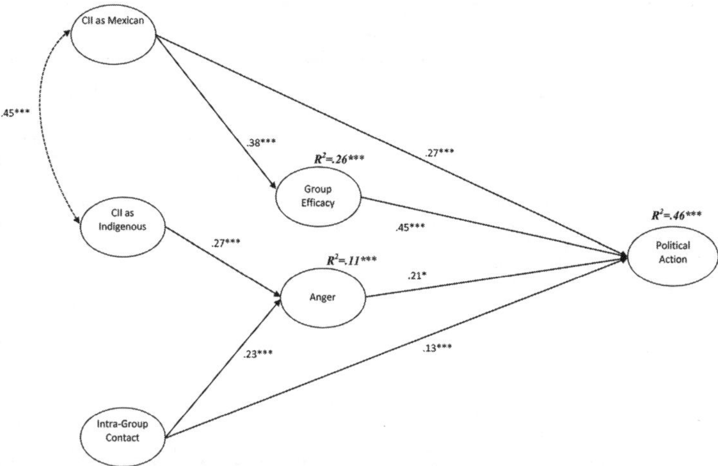

Fig. 1. Specified model using data from Mexican Indigenous ($n = 152$; (χ^2 (75) = 78.84, $p = 0.336$, $\chi^2/df = 1.06$; RMSEA = .017; CFI = .99; SRMR = .052). Only significant paths are reported. Path coefficients are standardized estimates, ***$p < .001$; **$p < .01$; *$p < .05$.

confirmatory factor analysis (CFA) then assesses if these specific set of items load onto the same factor, that is, convergent validity. This part of the model is generally called the "structural model." Once the CFA confirms that all the given items in a scale are performing similarly then the structural model assesses the associations between these latent variables. SEM is generally considered as a more advanced and precise form of ordinary regression as it has the capacity to report the unexplained variances, error terms, and the explained variances for all the components in the model as well as evaluating how well the estimates fit to the actual data by means of "fit indices" (Kline, 2011).

We did not have any missing data and we employed MLR (robust maximum likelihood estimation Schermelleh-Engel, 2003) estimator to estimate our model. The model fit was evaluated by χ^2 test, χ^2/df ratio, RMSEA, CFI, and SRMR (cut of points for these fit indices are a nonsignificant χ^2 value; χ^2/df ratio no higher than 3; CFI $\geq$ .95; RMSEA $\leq$ .06 or; SRMR $\leq$ .08 (Barrett, 2007; Bentler, 2007; Hu & Bentler, 1999). We ran a CFA to test our factor structure which revealed that all observed items in the model have factor loadings above $\beta = 0.60$ (Hair, Black, Babin, & Anderson, 2010).

Our specified model (SM) that includes all our variables of interest fit the data well (χ^2 (75) = 79.84, $p = .336$, $\chi^2/df = 1.06$; RMSEA = .016; CFI = .99; SRMR = .052; Figure 1) with a nonsignificant Chi-square value. We report the descriptive statistics in Table 1 and the path analytic results in Table 2. CII as Mexican was positively associated with political action ($\beta = .27$, $p < .001$) and group efficacy ($\beta = .38$, $p < .001$), which in turn, was also

Table 2. Direct and Indirect Effects of Predictor Variables on Mediating Variables and Political Action in Study 1

| | Direct effects | | Indirect effects via | | | |
| | | | anger | | group efficacy | |
Path	B	P	PE	CI	PE	CI
CII as Mexican-political action	.27	.001			.17	[.049,.255]
CII as Mexican-group efficacy	.38	.001				
Contact-political action	.13	.001	.054	[.022, .112]		
Contact-anger	.23	.001				
CII as indigenous-political action			.06	[.029, .121]		
CII as indigenous-anger	.27	.001				
Anger-political action	.21	.032				
Group efficacy—political action	.45	.001				

Notes. PE = point estimate.
CI = 95% confidence interval.

positively associated with political action ($\beta = .45, p < .001$). Intragroup contact among Indigenous was positively associated with anger ($\beta = .23, p < .001$) and political action tendencies ($\beta = .13, p < .001$). CII as Indigenous had a positive association with anger ($\beta = .27, p < .001$), which in turn, was positively associated with political action ($\beta = .21, p = .032$). Finally, we detected a significant association between CII as Mexican and CII as Indigenous ($r = .45, p < .001$).

Due to the correlational nature of our data, we are unable to rule out alternative causal accounts of the relations between variables in our model. Therefore, we compared our model with two alternative models. One could argue that group efficacy and contact between Indigenous people could strengthen the ingroup identification as Indigenous and weaken ingroup identification as Mexican, which in turn, might be associated with collective action tendencies via anger (Alternative Model 1: AM1). Alternatively, it is also possible that contact among Indigenous people could strengthen the identification with the Indigenous group while weakening CII at the national Mexican level, which in turn, might be associated with political action via group efficacy and anger (Alternative Model 2: AM2). We employed the Satorra-Bentler scaled χ^2 difference test that adjusts for the correction factor when the estimator is MLR (Kline, 2011, pp. 215–216) to compare model fit. The results revealed that both of the alternative models fit the data significantly less well than our SM, AM1: $\chi^2(73) = 128.03, p = .001$, $\chi^2/df = 1.75$; RMSEA = .061; CFI = .95; SRMR = .090; SM vs. AM1: $\Delta \chi^2(2) = 8.17, p = .013$; AM2: $\chi^2(72) = 125.50, p < .001, \chi^2/df = 1.74$, RMSEA = .070; CFI = .94; SRMR = .095; SM vs. AM2: $\Delta \chi^2(3) = 10.48, p = .014$. We therefore retained our SM as it was the most parsimonious and restricted of all three models.

We are also interested in the indirect effects of both types of CII and contact between the Indigenous on political action via anger and group efficacy. We used bootstrapping based on 5,000 resamples (Finney & DiStefano, 2012; Preacher & Hayes, 2008) and created standardized point estimates (PE) with bias-corrected confidence intervals (CIs) to deal with any bias resulting from small sample size. We report the effects whose CIs do not include zero (Table 2). There was a significant positive indirect effect of CII as Mexican on political action tendencies (PE = .165, 95% CI) via group efficacy. Both contact between the Indigenous (PE = .054, 95% CI) and CII as Indigenous (PE = .057, 95% CI) had a positive and significant effect on political action tendencies via anger.

Moderating Effects of Past Participation

Our theoretical model predicts that past participation in activism could influence how identification and intergroup contact influence future political action intentions. To test the moderating effect of past participation we created a latent interaction variable with the predictor variable of the path we are testing and past participation using the "xwith" (short form for "multiplied with") command in MPlus (Muthen & Muthen, 2008). We regressed our dependent variable of interest on this new latent interaction variable created by multiplying our predictor variable with our proposed moderator, past participation, in MPlus. We then obtained specific betas for the effect of the latent interaction variable we created on the dependent variable as well as betas for the effect of predictor variable on the dependent variable when the moderator variable is low (-1 SD or less), at mean (0), and when the moderator variable is high ($+1$ SD or more). Our results showed that past participation has a positive moderating effect on CII as Chilean-political action, and a negative moderating effect on CII as Indigenous-Group Efficacy and Group Efficacy-Political Action paths. We discuss these effects below.

The effect of past participation on political action was negative and significant ($\beta = -.12$, $p < .05$) but the effect of latent interaction variable (CII as Mexican x past participation) on political action was positive and significant ($\beta = .20, p < .05$). Moderation analysis showed that when past participation was low the association between CII as Mexican and action tendencies was not significant ($\beta = -.07$, ns). This association was positive and significant ($\beta = .27, p = .022$) when past participation was at the mean level. When past participation was high the association between CII and political action was strongly positive and significant ($\beta = .47, p < .001$).

The effect of past participation on group efficacy was not significant ($\beta = 0.10$, ns) but the effect of latent interaction variable (CII as Mexican $\times$ past participation) on group efficacy was negative and significant ($\beta = -.25, p < .001$). When past participation was low the association between CII as Mexican and group efficacy was positive and significant ($\beta = 0.45, p <$

.001). This association was positive but not significant ($\beta = .20$, ns) when past participation was at mean. When past participation was high the association between CII and group efficacy was not significant ($\beta = -.04$, ns).

For the CII as Indigenous and group efficacy path, the effect of latent interaction variable on group efficacy was negative and significant ($\beta = -.17$, $p = .038$). When past participation was low the association between CII as Indigenous and group efficacy was positive and significant ($\beta = .33$, $p = .032$). This association was not significant ($\beta = .16$, ns) when past participation was at mean levels. When past participation was high the association between CII as Indigenous and group efficacy disappeared ($\beta = -.02$, ns).

Finally, the effect of the latent interaction variable (group efficacy × past activism) on political action tendencies was negative and significant ($\beta = -.34$, $p < .001$). When past participation was low the association between group efficacy and political action was positive and significant ($\beta = .68$, $p < .001$). This association diminished in size but it was still significant ($\beta = .34$, $p = .018$) when past participation was at mean. When past participation was high the association between group efficacy and political action disappeared ($\beta = -.01$, ns).

Study 2: Method

Participants

One hundred and eighty-five Indigenous adults (72 females, $M_{\text{age}} = 36.73$, $SD = 13.34$) were recruited from Indigenous communities in Concepción (Southern Chile) by one male and one female research assistants of Indigenous origin. The participants took part in the study on a voluntary basis and did not receive any monetary compensation.

Measures

We used the same items as in Study 1. All our scales demonstrated satisfactory reliability (CII as Indigenous: $r = .72$, $p < .001$; CII as Chilean: $r = .70$, $p < .001$; contact among Indigenous: $r = .72$, $p < .001$; anger: $\alpha = .86$, $r = .75$, $p < .001$; group efficacy: $r = .67$, $p < .001$; political action: $r = .54$, $p < .001$; past participation: $\alpha = .79$).

Study 2: Results and Discussion

As in Study 1, CFA showed that that observed items have satisfactory loadings on their respective latent variables and our model fit the data well (χ^2 (75)= 120.28, $p = .007$, $\chi^2/df = 1.60$, RMSEA $= .059$, CFI $= .94$, SRMR $= .054$; Figure 2). We report the descriptive statistics in Table 3 and the path analytic

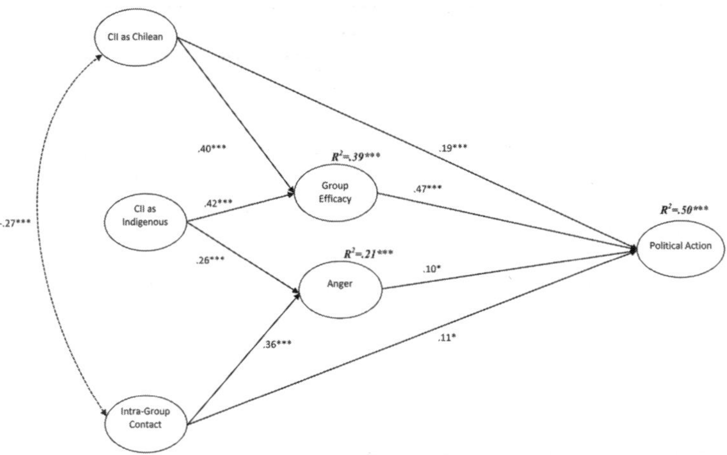

Fig. 2. Specified model using data from Chilean Indigenous ($n = 185$, χ^2 (75) = 120.28, $p = .007$, $\chi^2/df = 1.60$; RMSEA — .059; CFI — .94; SRMR = .054). Only significant paths are reported. Path coefficients are standardized estimates, ***$p < .001$; **$p < .01$; *$p < .05$.

Table 3. Descriptive Statistics and Correlations between the Latent Variables in the Model (Study 2)

Variable	M	SD	1	2	3	4	5	6	7
CII as indigenous	4.27	.99	1	.20**	.04	.50***	.27***	.11*	.48***
CII as Chilean	4.74	.69		1	−.26**	.45***	−.06	−.22**	.42***
Intragroup contact among indigenous	2.61	1.28			1	.09	.50***	.38***	.17***
Group efficacy	4.55	.76				1	.12	.02	.61***
Anger	3.22	1.43					1	.13	.19**
Past participation in activism	2.53	1.30						1	.11
Political action	4.56	.71							1

Note. ***$p < .001$; **$p < .01$; *$p < .05$.

results in Table 4. Similar to Study 1, CII as Chilean was positively associated with political action ($\beta = .19$, $p < .001$) and with group efficacy ($\beta = .40$, $p < .001$) that, in turn, was also positively associated with political action ($\beta = .47$, $p < .001$). CII as Indigenous had a positive association with group efficacy ($\beta = .42$, $p < .001$) and anger ($\beta = .26$, $p < .001$) that, in turn, was positively associated with political action ($\beta = .10$, $p < .05$); Intragroup contact among Indigenous was positively associated with anger ($\beta = .36$, $p < .001$) and political action ($\beta = .11$, $p = .041$).

We also tested the same alternative models as in Study 1 and found that both of the alternative models fit the data significantly less well than our SM (AM1: χ^2

Table 4. Direct and Indirect Effects of Predictor Variables on Mediating Variables and Political Action in Study 2

| | Direct effects | | Indirect effects via | | | |
| | | | anger | | group efficacy | |
Path	B	P	PE	CI	PE	CI
CII as Chilean-political action	.19	.001			.146	[.052, .225]
CII as Chilean-group efficacy	.40	.001				
Contact-political action	.11	.041	.040	[.009, .101]		
Contact-anger	.36	.001				
CII as indigenous-political action					.188	[.064, .291]
CII as indigenous-anger	.26	.001				
CII as indigenous-group efficacy	.42	.001				
Anger-political action	.10	.039				
Group efficacy –political action	.47	.001				

Notes. PE = point estimate.
CI = 95% confidence interval.

$(73) = 151.79, p < .001, \chi^2/df = 2.08, \text{RMSEA} = .079, \text{CFI} = .89, \text{SRMR} = .074;$ SM vs. AM1: $\Delta \chi^2 (2) = 9.16, p = .010;$ AM2: $\chi^2 (72) = 149.02, p < .001, \chi^2/df = 2.04, \text{RMSEA} = .054, \text{CFI} = .96, \text{SRMR} = .076$ SM vs. AM2: $\chi^2(3) = 9.27, p = .026$). Therefore, we retained our proposed model.

Tests of indirect effects using the same procedure as in Study 1, showed a significant positive indirect effect of CII as Chilean on political action (PE = .146, 99% CI) via group efficacy. As in Study 1, contact between Indigenous had a positive and significant effect on political action (PE = .040, 95% CI) via anger. Unlike Study 1, the results also revealed that CII as Indigenous had an indirect effect on political action via group efficacy (PE = .188, 95% CI) but not via anger.

Moderating Effects of Past Participation

Using the same approach as in Study 1, we tested the moderating effects of past participation. Unlike Study 1, the results showed that past participation has a negative moderating effect on CII as Chilean-Political Action, CII as Indigenous-Political action path, and on Group Efficacy-Political Action paths. On the other hand, past participation positively moderated the CII as Indigenous-Group Efficacy path. The effect of past participation on activism was not significant ($\beta = 0.06$, ns) but the effect of latent interaction (CII as Chilean $\times$ past participation) variable on activism was negative and significant ($\beta = -.15, p = .046$). Moderation analysis showed that when past participation was low (-1 SD) the association between CII as Chilean and activism was positive and significant ($\beta = .37$, $p < .001$). This association diminished in size ($\beta = .22$, $p = .011$) when past participation was at the mean level. When past participation was high ($+1$ SD) the association between CII and activism disappeared ($\beta = .08$, ns).

Looking at the association between CII as Indigenous and activism, the effect of latent interaction variable on activism was negative and significant ($\beta = -0.29$, $p < .001$). When past participation was low the association between CII as Indigenous and political action was positive and significant ($\beta = .35$, $p < .001$). This association diminished ($\beta = 0.06$, ns) when past participation was at mean and became negative ($\beta = -.22$, ns) but failed to reach the level of significance when past participation was high.

The effect of past participation on group efficacy was not significant ($\beta = 0.04$, ns) but the effect of latent interaction variable (CII as Chilean $\times$ Past participation) on group efficacy was negative and significant ($\beta = -0.15$, $p = .033$). When past participation was low the association between CII as Chilean and group efficacy was positive and significant ($\beta = 0.54$, $p < .001$). This association diminished in size ($\beta = 0.38$, $p = .013$) when past participation was at mean. When past participation was high the association between CII and group efficacy was no longer significant ($\beta = 0.23$, ns).

For the CII as Indigenous and group efficacy path, the effect of latent interaction variable on group efficacy was positive and significant ($\beta = 0.22$, $p < .001$). When past participation was low the association between CII as Indigenous and group efficacy was positive and significant ($\beta = .32$, $p = .034$). This association increased in size ($\beta = 0.54$, $p < .001$) when past participation was at mean. When past participation was high the association between CII as Indigenous and group efficacy became stronger ($\beta = 0.76$, $p < .001$).

As for the association between group efficacy and political action, the effect of latent interaction variable (group efficacy $\times$ past participation) on political action tendencies was negative and significant ($\beta = -0.25$, $p < .001$). Specifically, when past participation was low the association between group efficacy and political action was positive and significant ($\beta = 0.60$, $p < .001$). This association diminished in size but was still significant ($\beta = 0.35$, $p = .014$) when past participation was at the mean. When past participation was high the association between group efficacy and political action disappeared ($\beta = 0.10$, ns).

General Discussion

We investigated how different forms of CII and contact could energize political action by facilitating emotional and instrumental support, and facilitating access to political and social resources, that, in turn, provoke group-level experiences of anger and perceptions of increased group efficacy. In addition, we explored how these psychological processes are influenced by past participation in political action. We believe our findings extend the debate on factors promoting versus inhibiting political activism especially among less accessible groups. Emphasizing the importance of context in explaining the impact of CII on social change our findings suggests that (i) alternative forms of CII could provide access to psychological resources necessary for activism, that is, group efficacy; (ii) intragroup contact among the disadvantaged could energize political action via the emotional path of anger; (iii) past participation in political activism could either have a dampening or energizing effect on these processes. Below, we discuss our findings and their implications for future research on CII, contact, and research on collective action.

We tested for the energizing effects of CII on activism. Counter to existing evidence on sedative effects, we found robust evidence in favor of CII's energizing effects on political action. We predicted that CII as Mexican (Study 1) and CII as Chilean (Study 2) would be positively associated with intentions to engage in activism over and above CII as Indigenous. This makes sense because in both contexts, Indigenous people have been marginalized on the basis of their Indigenous identity. Our findings are inconsistent with the large body of research that suggests CII might dampen motivations to mobilize by decreasing perceptions of inequality and discrimination whereas subgroup identity energizes such motivations. Contrary to our expectations, however, CII as Indigenous was indirectly associated with political action tendencies via group efficacy in Study 2 in which we also found no meaningful association between CII as Chilean and CII as Indigenous. There was, however, a negative association between intragroup contact and CII as Chilean (see Figure 2). In the absence of more data, we can only speculate that, compared to the Mexican Indigenous peoples, Mapuche people have been involved in a more sustained conflict with the colonisers (De la Maza, 2014; Merino, Mellor, Saiz, & Quilaqueo, 2009; Stocker, 2013). Combined with extensive discrimination and regular intragroup contact this conflictual context might drive the Mapuche away from the mainstream society, and influence the emotional and instrumental support they draw from their own community. We believe this finding is in line with earlier work on psychological resources needed for mobilization (Kitschelt, 1986; van Zomeren et al., 2004)

We also provided fresh evidence in support of the moderating role of past participation on the problem-focused path to collective action. We found that past participation in political action moderated how CII and group efficacy relate to activist tendencies. This influence seems to depend on the wider societal context. In Study 1, more activism in the past positively moderated the impact of CII as Mexican on activist tendencies whereas in Study 2 the impact of both types of CII was negatively moderated. Research argues that both efficacy and anger are associated with normative political action (Tausch et al., 2011) and undertaking collective action can increase both perceptions of efficacy and anger (van Zomeren et al., 2012). Our findings, however, show that participation could negatively feed into problem-focused path-weakening perceptions of group efficacy whereas the emotion-focused path seems to be unaffected by the level of past participation. Thus, results imply that the impact of past participation on the CII - future intentions to participate in political action path seems to depend on the overlap between mainstream CII and CII as Indigenous. When there is a greater overlap between the more inclusive CII and less inclusive CII, as indicated by strong correlation between CII as Mexican and CII as Indigenous in Study 1, past participation positively moderates the effect of the more inclusive CII on activist tendencies. When, however, the overlap is smaller or does not exist, as indicated by the nonsignificant correlation between CII as Chilean and CII as Indigenous, this effect is negative.

We found partial support for our predictions regarding the effects of contact on political engagement and activism. We hypothesized that contact among the disadvantaged Indigenous would energize political action by increasing anger and group efficacy. Intragroup contact was associated with future collective action tendencies both directly and via anger. This is in line with research on the impact of social interaction on political engagement (Thomas et al., 2014). Previous research also implies that this might be due to a learning process through which members of the disadvantaged group learn about other individuals' grievances and their emotional reactions to these grievances which provide feedback on one's emotional experiences related to disadvantage. There is, however, no support for the empowering role of contact via increased group efficacy. As our data suggest, such empowerment, if there is any, is direct rather than via the mediating role group efficacy. We echo Kende (2016) and argue that these results call for conceptual clarity and contextualization for research also on the paradoxical effects of contact and CII. In particular, more research is needed on what types of contact energize political action. When it happens between the advantaged and the disadvantaged, intergroup contact does seem to dampen motivations to engage in action aimed at challenging inequalities. As our results suggest, however, intragroup contact between different disadvantaged groups seem to drive intentions to mobilize.

Finally, we emphasize that the majority of existing research on CII has been conducted in WEIRD societies (Western Educated Industrialized Rich and Democratic; Henrich, Heine, & Norenzayan, 2010). Findings from the current studies suggest that the so-called paradoxical effects of CII are not readily generalizable to contexts in which the disadvantaged has been consistently discriminated and marginalized. In such societies where the group boundaries between the advantaged and disadvantaged are blurred, such as Mexico and Chile, and where the mainstream society is made of individuals of mixed origins, the impact of collective Indigenous identity on political action seems to depend on past participation. In some contexts such as those studied here, identifying with the mainstream society and engaging in political action as equal members of the mainstream society might seem to be the only way out of the deadlock for the disadvantaged communities. This might be due to perceiving the past efforts as worthwhile or not and the specific reactions of the state and the mainstream society to such efforts. Therefore, we need more data exploring these processes. More research exploring the specific mechanisms of this CII related empowerment in non-WEIRD contexts is particularly welcome.

Notwithstanding the novelty of our findings, we also acknowledge their limitations. First, our causality claims should be interpreted with care due to the correlational nature of our data. Second, our samples are nonrepresentative. As such, our findings cannot be generalized to the entire Indigenous populations in both countries. We do however emphasize that we recruited from two of the least accessible populations for research. Understandably, it is unusually difficult to obtain representative samples in such situations. Third, we did not measure actual behavior, that is, activism as is the case for most research on collective action. Given the difficulty of direct observation of behavior in collective action research, this is understandable.

Policy Implications

Both studies employ data from two uncommonly studied populations in social psychology. Both in Mexico and Chile, the state has attempted to assimilate Indigenous peoples into the mainstream society without considering their opinions, albeit via different approaches. In Mexico, the state has been more inclusive, though assimilationist, while in Chile the state has mainly been isolationist. In both countries, however, Indigenous people have suffered the usurpation of their lands and resources. Accordingly, this situation has led them to form social movements to redress their collective disadvantage. In Mexico, these movements led to conditional autonomy and notable gains of rights. In Chile, repressive policies seem to have pushed the Indigenous people further away from the mainstream society. It seems, however, that no matter whether the state adopts inclusive or isolationist policies regarding Indigenous people are often implemented as if the country were homogenous. In that regard, the findings we present can account for a constant concern for identity and recognition among Indigenous people and how intragroup contact and CII might lead to mobilization to achieve this recognition. This research therefore provides important insights into the level of interest of Indigenous groups to the right of self-determination, and their determination to active participation in political decisions that affect their people. Thus, as our findings suggest, more inclusionary policies are needed to involve Indigenous people in the decision-making process and to accommodate their demands regarding education, land reforms, and other cultural rights.

References

Allport, G. W. (1954). *The nature of prejudice*. Garden City, NY: Doubleday.

Arias, O., Yamada, G., & Tejerina, L. (2004). Education, family background and racial earnings: Inequality in Brazil. *International Journal of Manpower*, *25*, 355–374.

Banfield, J. C., & Dovidio, J. F. (2013). Whites' perceptions of discrimination against Blacks: The influence of common identity. *Journal of Experimental Social Psychology*, *49*, 833–841. doi:10.1016/j.jesp.2013.04.008.

Barrett, P. (2007). Structural equation modeling: Adjudging model fit. *Personality and Individual Differences, 42*, 815–824. doi:10.1016/j.paid.2006.09.018.

Becker, J. C., Tausch, N., Spears, R., & Christ, O. (2011). Committed dis(s)idents: Participation in radical collective action fosters disidentification with the broader in-group but enhances political identification. *Personality and Social Psychology Bulletin, 37*, 1104–1116. doi:10.1177/0146167211407076.

Bentler, P. (2007). On tests and indices for evaluating structural models. *Personality and Individual Differences, 42*, 825–829. doi:10.1016/j.paid.2006.09.024.

Çakal, H., Hewstone, M., Schwar, G., & Heath, A. (2011). An investigation of the social identity model of collective action and the "sedative" effect of intergroup contact among Black and White students in South Africa. *British Journal of Social Psychology, 50*, 606–627. doi:10.1111/j.2044-8309.2011.02075.x.

Curtin, N., Kende, A., & Kende, J. (2016). Navigating multiple identities: The simultaneous influence of advantaged and disadvantaged identities on politicization and activism. *Journal of Social Issues, 72*(2), 264–285.

Curtin, N., & McGarty, C. (2016). Expanding on psychological theories of engagement to understand activism in context(s). *Journal of Social Issues, 72*(2), 227–241.

De la Maza, F. (2014). Between conflict and recognition: The construction of Chilean indigenous policy in the Araucania region. *Critique of Anthropology, 34*, 346–366. doi:10.1177/0308275×14531836.

Dixon, J., Durrheim, K., Tredoux, C., Tropp, L. R., & Eaton, L. (2010). A paradox of integration? Interracial contact, prejudice reduction, and perceptions of racial discrimination. *Journal of Social Issues, 66*, 401–416.

Dixon, J., Levine, M., Reicher, S., & Durrheim, K. (2012). Beyond prejudice: Are negative evaluations the problem and is getting us to like one another more the solution? *Behavioral and Brain Sciences, 35*, 411–425. doi:10.1017/S0140525×11002214.

Dovidio, J. F., Saguy, T., Gaertner, S. L., & Thomas, E. L. (2012). From attitudes to (In)action: The darker side of "we". In J. Dixon & M. Levine (Eds.). *Beyond prejudice: Extending the social psychology of intergroup conflict, inequality, and social change* (pp. 248–269). Cambridge, MA: Cambridge University Press.

Droogendyk, L., Wright, S. C., Lubensky, M.E., & Louis, W. R. (2016). Acting in solidarity: Cross-group contact between disadvantaged group members and advantaged group allies. *Journal of Special Issues, 72*(2), 315–334.

Drury, J., & Reicher, S. (2009). Collective psychological empowerment as a model of social change: Researching crowds and power. *Journal of Social Issues, 65*, 707–725. doi:10.1111/j.1540-4560.2009.01622.x.

Ellemers, N. (1993). The influence of socio-structural variables on identity management strategies. *European Review of Social Psychology, 4*, 27–57. doi:10.1080/14792779343000013.

Finney, S. J., & DiStefano, C. (2012). Nonnormal and categorical data in structural equation modeling. In G. R. Hancock & R. O. Mueller (Eds.), *Structural equation modeling: A second course* (2nd ed., pp. 269–312). Charlotte, NC: Age Publishing.

Gaertner, S. L., & Dovidio, J. F. (2000). *Reducing intergroup bias: The common ingroup identity model*. Philadelphia, PA: Psychology Press.

Glasford, D. E., & Calcagno, J. (2012). The conflict of harmony: Intergroup contact, commonality and political solidarity between minority groups. *Journal of Experimental Social Psychology, 48*, 323–328. doi:10.1016/j.jesp.2011.10.001.

Hair, J. F., Black, W., Babin, B., & Anderson, R. E. (2010). *Multivariate data analysis* (7th ed.). Upper Saddle River, NJ: Prentice-Hall.

Hall, G. H., & Patrinos, H. A. (Eds.) (2004). *Indigenous peoples, poverty, and development*. Cambridge, MA: Cambridge University Press.

Henrich, J., Heine, S. J., & Norenzayan, A. (2010). The weirdest people in the world? *Behavioral and Brain Sciences, 33*, 61–83. doi:10.1017/S0140525×0999152X.

Hu, L., & Bentler, P. M. (1999). Cutoff criteria for fit indices in covariance structure analysis: Conventional criteria versus new alternatives. *Structural Equation Modeling, 6*, 1–55. doi:10.1080/10705519909540118.

Jung, C. (2008). *The moral force of indigenous politics*. Cambridge, UK: Cambridge University Press.

Kende, A. (2016). Separating social science research on activism from social science as activism. *Journal of Social Issues, 72*(2), 399–412.

Kitschelt, H. P. (1986). Political opportunity structures and political protest: Anti-Nuclear movements in four democracies. *British Journal of Political Science, 16*, 57. doi:10.1017/S000712340000380X.

Klandermans, B. (1984). Mobilization and participation: Social-Psychological expansions of resource mobilization theory. *American Sociological Review, 49*, 583–600. doi:10.2307/2095417.

Klandermans, B. (1997). *The social psychology of protest*. Oxford, UK: Blackwell.

Kline, R. B. (2011). *Principles and practice of structural equation modelling* (3rd ed.). Guildford, UK: The Guildford Press.

Leach, C. W., van Zomeren, M., Zebel, S., Vliek, M. L. W., Pennekamp, S. F., Doosje, B., Spears, R. (2008). Group-level self-definition and self-investment: A hierarchical (multicomponent) model of in-group identification. *Journal of Personality and Social Psychology, 95*, 144–165. doi:10.1037/0022-3514.95.1.144.

Louis, W. R., Amiot, C. E., Thomas, E. F., & Blackwood, L. (2016). The "activist identity" and activism across domains: A multiple identities analysis. *Journal of Social Issues, 72*(2), 242–263.

Mackie, D. M., Maitner, A. T., & Smith, E. R. (2009). Intergroup emotions theory. In T. D. Nelson (Ed.), *Handbook of prejudice, stereotyping, and discrimination* (pp. 285–308). Mahwah, NJ: Erlbaum.

Merino, M. E., Mellor, D. J., Saiz, J. L., & Quilaqueo, D. (2009). Perceived discrimination amongst the indigenous Mapuche people in Chile: Some comparisons with Australia. *Ethnic and Racial Studies, 32*, 802–822. doi:10.1080/01419870802037266.

Muthen, L. K., & Muthen, B. O. (2008). *Mplus software package*. Los Angeles, CA: Muthen & Muthen.

Parker, W. S., Rubalcava, L., & Teruel, Y. G. (2005). Schooling, inequality and language barriers. *Economic Development and Cultural Change, 54*, 71–94. doi:10.1086/431257.

Pettigrew, T. F. (1998). Intergroup contact theory. *Annual Review of Psychology, 49*, 65–85. doi:10.1146/annurev.psych.49.1.65.

Pettigrew, T. F., & Tropp, L. R. (2006). A meta-analytic test of intergroup contact theory. *Journal of Personality and Social Psychology, 90*, 751–783. doi:10.1037/0022-3514.90.5.751.

Preacher, K. J., & Hayes, A. F. (2008). Asymptotic and resampling strategies for assessing and comparing indirect effects in multiple mediator models. *Behavior Research Methods, 40*, 879–891. doi:10.3758/BRM.40.3.879.

Saguy, T., Tausch, N., Dovidio, J. F., & Pratto, F. (2009). The irony of harmony: Intergroup contact can produce false expectations for equality. *Psychological Science, 20*, 114–121. doi:10.1111/j.1467-9280.2008.02261.x.

Schermelleh-Engel, K. (2003). Evaluating the fit of structural equation models: Tests of significance and descriptive goodness-of-fit measures. *Methods of Psychological Research Online, 8*, 23–74.

Sengupta, N. K., & Sibley, C. G. (2013). Perpetuating one's own disadvantage: intergroup contact enables the ideological legitimation of inequality. *Personality & Social Psychology Bulletin, 39*, 1391–403. doi:10.1177/0146167213497593.

Stavans, I. (2013). *The United States of mestizo*. Montgomery, AI: New South Books.

Stocker, E. (2013). Chile: The nation that's still waging war on Native Americans. *The Independent*. Retrieved on December 8, 2015 from http://www.independent.co.uk/news/world/americas/chile-the-nation-thats-still-waging-war-on-native-americans-8996336.html.

Tausch, N., & Becker, J. C. (2013). Emotional reactions to success and failure of collective action as predictors of future action intentions: a longitudinal investigation in the context of student protests in Germany. *The British Journal of Social Psychology, 52*, 525–542. doi:10.1111/j.2044-8309.2012.02109.x.

Tausch, N., Becker, J. C., Spears, R., Christ, O., Saab, R., Singh, P., & Siddiqui, R. N. (2011). Explaining radical group behavior: Developing emotion and efficacy routes to normative and non-normative collective action. *Journal of Personality and Social Psychology, 101*, 129–48. doi:10.1037/a0022728.

Tausch, N., Saguy, T., & Bryson, J. (2015). How does intergroup contact affect social change. *Journal of Social Issues, 71*, 536–553. doi: 10.1111/josi.12127.

Thomas, E. F., McGarty, C., & Louis, W. R. (2014). Social interaction and psychological pathways to political engagement and extremism. *European Journal of Social Psychology, 44*, 15–22. doi:10.1002/ejsp.1988.

Ufkes, E. G., Dovidio, J. F., & Tel, G. (2014). Identity and collective action among European Kurds. *British Journal of Social Psychology, 54*, 176–186. doi:10.1111/bjso.12084.

van Stekelenburg, J., Klandermans, B., & Akkerman, A. (2016). Does civic participation stimulate political activity? *Journal of Social Issues, 72*(2), 286–314.

van Zomeren, M., Leach, C. W., & Spears, R. (2010). Does group efficacy increase group identification? Resolving their paradoxical relationship. *Journal of Experimental Social Psychology, 46*, 1055–1060. doi:10.1016/j.jesp.2010.05.006.

van Zomeren, M., Leach, C. W., & Spears, R. (2012). Protesters as "Passionate Economists": A dynamic dual pathway model of approach coping with collective disadvantage. *Personality and Social Psychology Review, 16*, 180–199. doi:10.1177/1088868311430835.

van Zomeren, M., Postmes, T., & Spears, R. (2008). Toward an integrative social identity model of collective action: A quantitative research synthesis of three socio-psychological perspectives. *Psychological Bulletin, 134*, 504–35. doi:10.1037/0033-2909.134.4.504.

van Zomeren, M., Spears, R., Fischer, A. H., & Leach, C. W. (2004). Put your money where your mouth is! Explaining collective action tendencies through group-based anger and group efficacy. *Journal of Personality and Social Psychology, 87*, 649–64. doi:10.1037/0022-3514.87.5.649.

van Zomeren, M., Spears, R., & Leach, C. W. (2008). Exploring psychological mechanisms of collective action: Does relevance of group identity influence how people cope with collective disadvantage? *The British Journal of Social Psychology, 47*, 353–372. doi:10.1348/014466607×231091.

Wenzel, M. (2000). Justice and identity: The significance of inclusion for perceptions of entitlement and the justice motive. *Personality and Social Psychology Bulletin, 26*(2), 157–176. doi:10.1177/0146167200264004.

Wright, S. C. (2009). The next generation of collective action research. *Journal of Social Issues, 65*, 859–879. doi:10.1111/j.1540-4560.2009.01628.x.

HUSEYIN ÇAKAL holds a MSc in Sociology, University of Manchester, and a DPhil in Social Psychology, University of Oxford. He is a Research Fellow at the University of Exeter. His research investigates collective action, intergroup contact, and robot-human interactions.

ANJA ELLER is a professor of Social Psychology at the National Autonomous University of Mexico. She is broadly interested intergroup relations, intergroup contact, identity and categorization, and embarrassment.

DAVID SIRLOPÚ is an assistant professor in the Faculty of Psychology at Universidad del Desarrollo (Concepción, Chile). His research interests are intergroup relations and acculturation processes on Latino American immigrants and majority society. He has also conducted research involving mentally disabled and nondisabled people in school settings with inclusion programs. He lectures on social psychology and community psychology both at the undergraduate and postgraduate level.

ANDRÉS PÉREZ has recently completed his undergraduate studies in Psychology at the National Autonomous University of Mexico, Mexico.

Journal of Social Issues, Vol. 72, No. 2, 2016, pp. 376–398
doi: 10.1111/josi.12171

How Activists Respond to Social Structure in Offline and Online Contexts

Lisa K. Hartley[*]
Curtin University

Girish Lala and Ngaire Donaghue
Murdoch University

Craig McGarty
Murdoch University and Western Sydney University

The social identity model of collective action (SIMCA) proposes that collective action flows from identity, perceived injustice, and efficacy beliefs but do these drivers apply for activists in all situations? Intuitively, the social structure that confronts activists should influence when and how they act. In two studies, we consider how activists incorporate the opinions of other people, groups, and institutions as part of their own reality or social structure. In Study 1, quantitative data from 248 activists campaigning for reconciliation between Indigenous and other Australians showed less support for SIMCA when activists faced a divided social movement. In Study 2, qualitative data from 40 online activists suggested that interactions involved identity presentation, used to sharpen and present views of the world and an idealized social structure. Together, findings highlight the practical importance for activists to have a consensual position about social structure, and of activists' efforts to reach that consensus.

An important question for activists and social movement organizations (SMOs) is how to foster sustained collective action (Curtin & McGarty, 2016; Louis, 2009). Social psychology has a wealth of knowledge about the factors that motivate activists to engage in collective action (e.g., Stürmer & Simon, 2004; Stürmer, Simon, Loewy, & Jörger, 2003). Van Zomeren, Postmes, and Spears

---

[*]Correspondence concerning this article should be addressed to Lisa K. Hartley, Centre for Human Rights Education, Curtin University, GPO Box U1987, Perth, Western Australia, 6845, Australia. Tel: +61 8 9266 1678 [e-mail: Lisa.Hartley@curtin.edu.au].

(2008) have conducted an integrative meta-analysis of collective action research that yielded the social identity model of collective action (SIMCA, see also the EMSICA model of Thomas, Mavor, & McGarty, 2012; Thomas, McGarty, & Mavor, 2009). This model points to three drivers of collective action: social identity, a sense of grievance or injustice (reflected in group-based emotions), and instrumental concerns (efficacy).

But do these drivers of collective action themselves vary in their importance (Livingstone, 2013)? Although activists may generally be convinced that their own cause is true and just, that cause may be contested by other people, including the general population, the government of the day, or even the SMOs and political parties that the activists belong to. Put another way, activists operate in a set of conditions created by institutions and social forces that impose consequences on members of society. Sometimes these consequences may be direct and sometimes they involve inferences about what is possible or desirable. We refer to this pattern of relationships as social structure. Social structure is thus the thing that changes when social change occurs but also constrains social action (as per Giddens, 1984, whose approach to social structure informs our treatment). As activists are so often involved in bringing about or resisting social change, it follows that social structure needs to be incorporated into our analyses of activism.

Intuitively, the opinions of other people are part of the reality or social structure that activists operate in. In many circumstances, changing public opinions is the immediate direct objective of activism: in order, say, to win an election, or stop a war. The opinions of other people thus provide the context of activism. Activists make judgments about whether their ideas are supported or opposed by others and about the prospects of changing those opinions. Thus, perceived social structure should make a difference to how and when activists take action and this is the proposition that we explore here. That is, to understand activism we need to understand the impact of perceptions of social structure on collective action processes. In this article, we explore this proposition in relation to predicting offline forms of collective action (Study 1) and for shaping perceptions of shared opinion, structure, and action in online activism (Study 2).

Previous scholars have emphasized the need to understand the impact of perceptions of social structure on collective action processes (e.g., Klandermans, 1997; Reicher, 2004; van Stekelenburg, Klandermans, & van Dijk, 2009; Wright, 2009). Simon and Klandermans (2001) conceptualize social structure as triangulation: a competition between groups for support from a third party that could be the government or the general public. Perceived social structure is also incorporated in social identity theory (Tajfel & Turner, 1979) through the idea that responses to a social structure depend upon belief systems about the relevant intergroup context (Tajfel, 1982). There are, however, other ways for social structure to be constituted and activists' understanding of their social position are likely to inform (and indeed transform) the actions they take.

Work in both political science (e.g., public opinion theory; Wilson, 1962) and social psychology (Jost, Pelham, Sheldon, & Sullivan, 2003; Moscovici, 1988) points to the role of consensus at the broader societal level in shaping individual and social behaviour (just as Sani & Reicher, 1998 show that intractable dissensus can lead to group schisms). Similarly, van Zomeren et al. (2004) proposed that people take action when they feel that relevant others share their opinion (perceived opinion support) and/or that relevant others are prepared to act in the same way (perceived social action support). The common thread across this literature is that the degree of consensus within a given social context can have implications for whether or not someone is likely to engage in group-based actions. We, thus, conceptualize the opinions of other people, groups, and institutions as part of the reality or social structure that activists operate in. Accordingly, opinions are both part of the background that activists work in but they may also be the specific aspect of reality that activists are working to change.

In Study 1, we explored activists' responses to consensus as perceived social structure in two different contexts. In one case, the activists were positioned as the vanguard of a social movement where the cause they championed was supported by the government and much of the broader population (consensus position). In the second case, the same activists confronted an issue where they championed a minority position in opposition to the government and in the face of dissensus in their own social movement. Do the factors identified by van Zomeren, Postmes et al.'s (2008) SIMCA predict commitment to action in both cases in the same way where levels of perceived consensus vary?

Activists are defined as those who actively work for social or political causes (Curtin & McGarty, 2016). While "active work" is often seen as desire to act, in online contexts interaction ("talk") often drives judgments about what is effective behavior and is the predominant, and sometimes only, visible outcome ("action"). Part of the reality faced by activists in the online globalized world is that they have a diffuse and, at times, open communication environment that may make consensus hard to achieve. How do online activists perceive this potential tension between talking about an issue and acting on that issue, and do those perceptions offer insights into the importance of social structure for activists? In Study 2, we questioned activists involved in a wide range of social and political issues about their reasons for engaging online, and explored how that engagement shaped perceptions of shared opinion, structure, and action. Together, the two studies work toward explaining the importance to activists of a consensualized position about social structure, and their efforts to reach that consensus (e.g., within their in-group and with third parties).

Study 1

In this study, we compared the predictors of action for activists campaigning for reconciliation between Indigenous and other Australians in relation to two government policies designed to inequality between Indigenous and non-Indigenous Australians. The first policy involves assisting the economic development of Indigenous communities to remove the inequality in health status and life expectancy by the year 2030. Close the Gap (CTG) was originally proposed by activist organizations (collectively, known by some, as the Reconciliation movement) and implemented by the government. It was supported by the clear majority of Australians (70% according to a survey conducted for Amnesty International, 2009).

In contrast, the second policy, the Northern Territory Emergency Response (NTER), is an interventionist government policy that was introduced in June 2007 in response to a report indicating high rates of sexual abuse and neglect of children in Indigenous communities in Australia's Northern Territory. The measures implemented included an income management regime, imposition of compulsory leases, and community-wide bans on alcohol consumption and pornography. This initiative was criticized as being discriminatory and coercive, with some Indigenous rights activists and their organizations calling for its immediate abolition, and others supporting its continuation with some reforms. Opinion polls conducted at the time of its implementation suggest it had majority public support, with 61% supporting the intervention, 23% disapproving, and 16% being undecided (Newspoll and The Australian, 2007).

These policies provide a stark contrast in terms of social structure. The CTG program was championed by the Reconciliation movement. We would expect active members of Reconciliation organizations to embrace the policy as normative for their group. On the other hand, the NTER is problematic for members of these organizations. The policy received trenchant criticism but the official position of many Reconciliation organizations was to reform rather than to abolish the NTER.

These two policies allowed us to test three activist stances. The first community vanguard stance was expected to apply to all activists in relation to promoting the CTG policy. The second stance, characterized as pragmatic opposition, was expected to apply to activists who supported the organization's official position of reforming the NTER. The third stance, we term marginalized opposition, applies to activists who, contrary to the official opposition of their SMO, wished to see the NTER abolished in its entirety.

We tested the SIMCA model for the three different stances. We expected the component factors of SIMCA to be relevant in each case but for the strength of the links to vary as a result of differing social structures. We now consider those factors in more detail.

According to self-categorization theory, when social identity becomes salient, people see themselves as more interchangeable with other members of their group (Turner, Hogg, Oakes, Reicher, & Wetherell, 1987). A salient (social movement) group identity should therefore render collective action more likely. However, intragroup disagreements over central aspects of a group's norms, values, or behaviors, can create group schisms resulting in fragmentation or dissolution of a social movement (Sani & Reicher, 1998). We would thus expect Social Movement (SM) identity to be a weak predictor of action intentions for the marginalized opposition stance.

People are more likely to take collective action in the face of perceived injustice (Leach, Iyer, & Pedersen, 2006). Anger tends to be a good indicator of perceived injustice, but this context is complicated because most Reconciliation activists are allies who belong to the advantaged category and may feel anger or guilt for the advantage experienced by others. To address this issue, we actually measured both anger and guilt in relation to advantage but, for the test of the SIMCA model, we focus here on anger given the evidence linking anger to action that seeks to address inequality (e.g., Iyer, Schmader, & Lickel, 2007; Leach et al., 2006; Thomas et al., 2009).

Recent work also re-emphasizes the importance of the practical issues confronting potential supporters of social change. When choosing to engage in action, people weigh up the potential costs and benefits and other practical concerns that can influence participation (Klandermans, 1997). Van Zomeren and colleagues argue that the construct of group efficacy captures this instrumental aspect of collective action (van Zomeren, Spears, & Leach, 2008). Group efficacy is the belief that the group's actions will be effective in achieving desired goals and has been shown to be useful in predicting collective action in some contexts but not others. Hornsey et al. (2006) explain this inconsistency by arguing that group members do not always undertake action to achieve the stated aim of their group but can pursue other aims such as to solidify connections within the group and mobilize support from other areas of society and that efficacy measures need to accommodate these aspects.

We expected the SIMCA model to have variable applicability in view of our position that a lack of consensus can be an obstacle for collective action. As such, the model should work best for CTG where activists were positioned as the vanguard of a popular social movement, less well for the pragmatic minority stance (reforming the NTER), and least well for the marginalized minority stance (abolishing the NTER) where the social movement was divided.

Method

Participants

Two hundred and sixty activists filled out an online survey (196 female, 60 male, 4 did not indicate their gender) and were aged between 20 and 83 years ($M = 48$ years, $SD = 16.50$). Participants who had not spent time on any movement or SMO activities in the past or submitted substantially incomplete answers were excluded from the analyses leaving a final sample size of 248 (187 female, 57 male, 4 did not indicate their gender). On average, participants spent 5.3 hours per month in movement activities and 6.4 hours per month in SMO activities suggesting that the final sample was highly active.

The final sample were aged between 20 and 83 years ($M = 48$ years, $SD = 16.01$), and were highly educated with over 80% having completed a bachelor degree or above. The sample was drawn from every Australian state and territory. Eighty-one percent were born in Australia, with 70% self-identified as having an Anglo-Australian heritage and 4% as Aboriginal or Torres Strait Islander heritage. Participants tended to support left-wing political parties, with 50% supporting the Australian Greens Party and 27% supporting the Australian Labor Party.

The participants were recruited from the email list of Australia's largest non-Indigenous organization in the Reconciliation movement. An advertisement was included in a monthly email newsletter that invited people to fill out the survey by clicking on a Web link. To increase the participation rate, participants were offered a chance to win either a digital camera or an MP3 player.

Research on online "click-through" rates (the total number of people who click through on Web-based advertisements divided by the exposure population reach of the advertisement) suggests the average rate is 0.9% (e.g., Chandon, Chtourou, & Fortin, 2003). Considering the advertisement reached approximately 5,000 people, our research yielded a healthy click-through rate of approxima tely 5%.

Measures

SM identity. Social identity measures comprised five modified items from Leach et al. (2008: one item from each subscale): "I feel a bond with other members of the Reconciliation movement"; "I am glad to be a member of the Reconciliation movement"; "I often think about the fact that I am a member of the Reconciliation movement"; "I have a lot in common with the average member of the Reconciliation movement"; and "People who are members of the Reconciliation movement are very similar to each other" ($1 =$ strongly disagree and $7 =$ strongly agree; $\alpha = .82$).

CTG position. Participants were asked to indicate whether they support or oppose action to CTG between Indigenous and non-Indigenous Australians in health, employment, education, and other outcomes ("I support action to Close the Gap"; "I oppose action to Close the Gap"; and "I do not take either of these positions").

NTER position. Participants were asked to indicate whether they think that there should be an immediate abolition of the NTER or whether it should be continued, with improvements where necessary ("I think the Northern Territory

Emergency Response should be stopped so its objectives can be achieved by other means"; "I think the Northern Territory Emergency Response should be continued, with improvements where necessary"; and "I do not take either of these positions"). The two positions are referred to as Abolish NTER and Reform NTER.

Perceived consensus: CTG and NTER. Participants were asked to indicate their perceived level of consensus within the Reconciliation movement (SM) and the SMO for each of these two issues (1 = no consensus and 7 = complete consensus).

CTG and NTER collective action intentions. Participants were asked to rate the likelihood of engaging in the following actions to support their opinion about efforts to CTG and their opinion about the NTER: "challenge other people"s views that oppose my own"; "sign an online petition"; "put up a poster"; "join a protest march"; and "write a letter to or meet with a politician" (1 = very unlikely and 7 = very likely; α = .80 and .86, respectively).

Close the gap and NTER efficacy. Adapting Hornsey et al. (2006), participants were asked to indicate the extent to which they thought engaging in collective action would be effective in: "Influencing government leaders and policy makers"; "Influencing public opinion"; "Helping to build a movement that supports your position on this issue"; "Expressing values that you hold" (1 = not at all effective and 7 = very effective). There were no differences in the predictive value of each of these items separately and thus they were combined to form one single efficacy scale (α = .74 and .79, respectively).

Anger. A single item asked participants: "In your opinion, which group of Australians is more advantaged; non-Indigenous Australians or Indigenous Australians" (1 = Indigenous advantaged and 7 = non-Indigenous Australians advantaged). Using a list of emotion terms, taken from Leach et al. (2006), participants were then asked to indicate the degree to which they felt each emotion (0 = not at all and 5 = extremely) about the answer they gave about advantage/disadvantage. Three anger items were used: angry, outraged, and furious (guilt was also measured in the same way but is not reported here; α = .90).

Sociodemographics. Participants were asked to state their age; gender; education level; Australian state or territory of residence; country of birth; Aboriginal or Torres Strait Islander heritage; heritage other than Aboriginal or Torres Strait Islander (open-ended); federal political party support. Participants were asked to record how many hours per month they spend participating in activities in line with the Reconciliation movement and how many hours per month they spend participating in activities related to their SMO.

Table 1. Correlations and Means (*SD*) for Measured Variables Supporters of Close the Gap (*N* = 244)

	M (*SD*)	1.	2.	3.	4.	5.	6.
1. Collective action	5.8 (1.6)	–					
2. Group efficacy	5.0 (1.1)	.26**	–				
3. SM identity	5.0 (1.0)	.26**	.15*	–			
4. SMO identity	5.2 (0.9)	.10	.11	.55**	–		
5. Anger	3.6 (1.1)	.27**	.19**	.25**	.31**	–	
6. SM consensus	4.3 (1.7)	.26*	.18**	.15	−.02	.14*	–
7. SMO consensus	5.0 (1.7)	.10	.17*	−.04	.09	−.11	.60**

Notes. *p < .05, **p < .01.

Table 2. Correlations and Means (*SD*) for Measured Variables for Supporters of Abolish NTER (Above the Diagonal; *N* = 140) and Reform NTER (Below the Diagonal; *N* = 58)

	M (*SD*)	1.	2.	3.	4.	5.	6.	7.
M (SD)		5.7 (1.2)	4.8 (1.2)	5.1 (1.0)	5.2 (0.9)	3.8 (1.0)	5.0 (1.4)	5.5 (1.3)
1. Collective action	4.4 (1.3)	–	.15	.18*	.10	.28**	.18*	.22*
2. Group efficacy	4.3 (1.4)	.64**	–	.17	.10	.22*	.33**	.31**
3. SM identity	4.9 (0.8)	−.09	−.02	–	.62**	.17	.28**	.14
4. SMO identity	5.2 (0.7)	−.03	−.09	.31*	–	.25**	.14	.07
5. Anger	3.2 (1.2)	.02	.14	.15	.29*	–	.07	.05
6. SM consensus	3.2 (1.6)	.28*	.20	.25	−.12	.13	–	−.49**
7. SMO consensus	4.0 (1.9)	.19	.14	.18	−.10	.07	.70	–

Notes. *p < .05, **p < .01.

Results

Preliminary analyses.   Descriptive statistics are shown in Table 1 for CTG and Table 2 for the NTER stances. There was broad support for efforts to CTG (98%, while 2% chose neither position). As expected, there was much more division about the NTER. The majority of the activists wanted to abolish NTER (57%), while 23% wanted to reform NTER and 20% chose neither position.

Mean differences in perceived consensus.   Not surprisingly, activists who supported CTG perceived there to be a high degree of consensus about that position in the SM, *M* = 6.16, *SD* = 1.2, and SMO, *M* = 6.17, *SD* = 1.2. By contrast, there was dissensus about the NTER policy positions within the SM and SMO. The Abolish NTER supporters perceived their own stance to be more consensual within the SM, $M = 4.95$, $SD = 1.4$, than did Reform NTER supporters, $M = 3.22$, $SD = 1.6$, $F(1,197) = 53.35$, $p < .001$, $\eta^2 = .21$. Similar patterns were revealed for perceived consensus within the SMO, with Abolish NTER supporters perceiving there to be significantly more consensus within the SMO for the Abolish NTER position, $M = 5.52$, $SD = 1.4$ compared to the Reform position, $M = 4.01$, $SD = 1.9$, $F(1,174) = 34.16$, $p < .001$, $\eta^2 = .17$.

Tests of models. We used Hayes and Preacher's (2014) MEDIATE (identical to INDIRECT in this context) macro within SPSS to test SIMCA for each of the three stances. For the pro-CTG stance, as shown in Figure 1(a), social movement identity predicted efficacy, and anger, The direct effects of identity, anger and efficacy for collective action were also significant and a 95% confidence intervals (CI) from a bias-corrected bootstrap with 5,000 samples did not include zero suggesting that the effect of identity was mediated by efficacy [0.01, 0.08] and anger [0.02, 0.13]. For the Abolish NTER stance in Figure 1(b, social movement identity predicted anger but only anger and not efficacy or identity predicted collective action intentions. The 95% CI for the indirect effect for efficacy [-0.01, 0.07] included zero suggesting no mediation, but that for anger [0.01, 0.14] did not (consistent with mediation). For the Reform NTER stance (Figure 1c), social movement identity predicted neither anger nor efficacy and only efficacy predicted action intentions and again the CIs for the indirect effects through efficacy [-0.43, 0.30] and anger [-0.20, 0.03] included zero providing no clear evidence of mediation. In sum, none of the stances provide good support for the SIMCA model but the paths for the CTG stance were in line with the broad expectations of the model. For the Abolish and Reform NTER stances, only anger and efficacy, respectively, were predictors of action.

Discussion

Study 1 demonstrates that very different relationships predict action toward government policies relating to Indigenous-non-Indigenous inequality, and perceptions of social structure appears to play a part in the form of perceived consensus. Although our correlational design does not allow us to prove that different causal processes apply for the two samples, our results do refute the proposition that the same processes apply in the three activist stances. That is, although correlation does not imply causation, causation does imply large correlations (leaving aside the very real prospect of suppressor variables) and the large correlations obtained here are variable. Future research may seek to address this limitation by experimentally exploring the relationship between these variables.

The novelty of this study is notable. Nested within dynamic, real debates about the issue of intergroup inequality, we have combined insights from the collective action literature, and in particular van Zomeren, Postmes et al.'s (2008) SIMCA

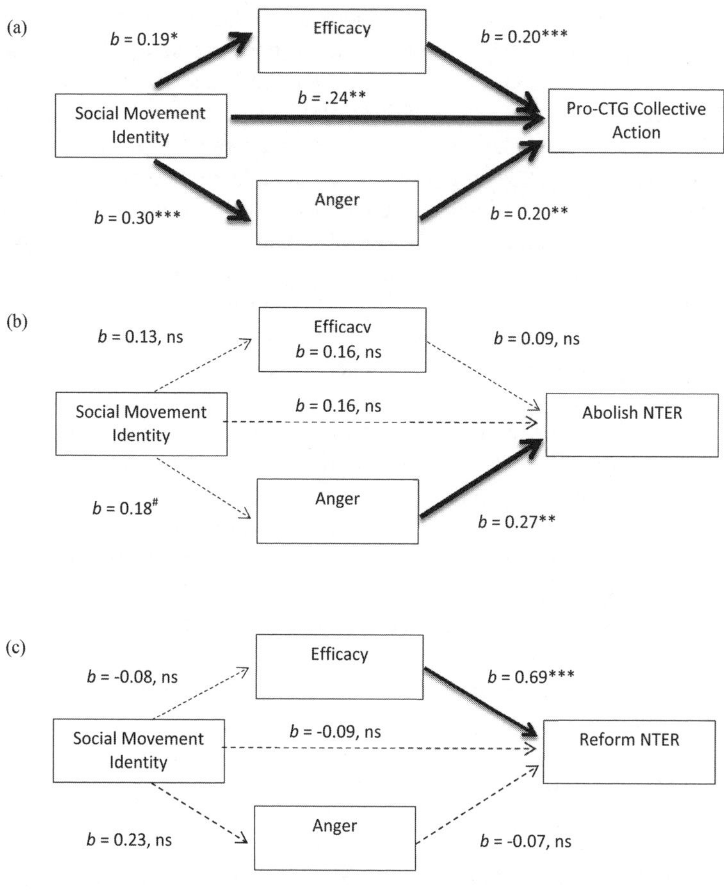

Fig. 1. Models of predictors of collective action for proclose the gap and NTER positions.

model, to unpack the different motivators of action for activists. Building on the work of van Zomeren et al. (2004) and Simon and Klandermans (2001) our results suggest ways to interpret different aspects of social structure. It follows that these findings will have implications for theorizing about identity, group-based emotion, and efficacy. We now address these diverging patterns.

Diverging Patterns of Social Identification

The results for the CTG policy showed that, as predicted, for a unified social movement, identity was a predictor for action. For the NTER policy where the social movement was divided, the role of social identification was not so straight-forward. As expected, SM identification was a poor predictor of action about the NTER initiative. The lack of predictive value of social identification for the NTER issue reflects there has been a failure of development of identities that were compatible with social change. In a recent social psychological model of social change, Thomas et al. (2009) propose that sustainable and ongoing commitment to action often involves crafting a social identity with a relevant pattern of norms for emotion, efficacy, and action. On the other hand, in contexts where there is intense dissensus about a disputed issue, we suggest that identities can become compromised (i.e., disconnected from action) because there has not yet been an effective organization around an identity that has action-orientated norms such as relevant efficacy beliefs and action-orientated emotions.

The idea of compromised social identities maps nicely onto Klandermans' (1998) differentiation between consensus formation and consensus mobilization in the development of social movements. Klandermans argues that consensus formation involves the convergence of opinions about a particular issue without the development of action. In other words, consensus formulation does not guide how people should address their shared grievance. Consensus mobilization, by contrast, involves the deliberate attempt of people joining together to form a common cause and to take action. We suspect that division in the social movement and SMO may have hampered consensus mobilization.

Diverging Patterns of Emotion and Efficacy Beliefs

A key question also raised by the findings is how to make sense of the diverging predictive patterns of emotion and efficacy beliefs for the three activist stances. Anger was a predictor of action for Stop NTER supporters while efficacy was a predictor of action for Pro-CTG and Reform NTER. These findings extend van Zomeren et al.'s (2004) dual model of collective action by suggesting that emotion and efficacy beliefs apply differently for different social contexts.

Although research has begun to unpack the conditions under which anger (e.g., Stürmer & Simon, 2009) and efficacy (e.g., Hornsey et al., 2006) will be more effective motivators of actions (see also van Zomeren, Spears et al., 2008), our findings suggest that perceived consensus is also important to consider. More research examining the differential role of group-based efficacy and emotions in certain social contexts would therefore seem valuable.

Our first study pointed to the role of perceived social structure in shaping action by activists in traditional (face-to-face) settings. We next introduce a study that explored how perceptions of social structure are presented and deployed in online environments.

Study 2

Activism is often seen as being all about taking action but contentions about talking and acting come to the fore in the online environment. For example, online activists are often dismissed as "slacktivists" or "clicktivists" (see Curtin & McGarty, 2016, for an overview). On the other hand, if perceived social structure does play a crucial role in informing and sustaining collective action one way that such perceptions can develop is through interaction with others.

We were able to explore this idea through data collected for a study that investigated the role of online communities in facilitating social action. In that study, we asked activists involved in a range of issues why they regularly participated in their online forums and the value they placed on their participation. Interestingly, while the original focus of our study was on the relationships between collective action and online groups, our results also highlighted the importance of social structure in activists' interactions.

Participants and Method

Participants were members of online activist forums hosted under the "Issues and Causes" subcategory of groups on the Yahoo Web portal. Forty activists (23 male, 16 Female, 1 not specified) from 16 different forums took part. Participants nominated a 10-year age category ranging from 11 to 60-plus with an estimated median age of 35. Participants were recruited from forums that had 30 or more members and in which there had been recent online activity. Sampled forums covered a wide range of issues including, for example, a movement fighting against size discrimination, a forum based in Malaysia advocating rights for Malaysian-Indians, and a community campaigning for an independent Ambazonia Republic (in Southern Cameroon). Participants answered a series of open-ended questions about why they joined and how they used their forums. Here, we describe our analysis of the following key questions: "Why did you first become interested in [your online forum]? Why is [your online forum] worthwhile? When you first started using [your online forum], how much did you think it would be used to plan and take part in action? How much did you think your forum would be a place to discuss and debate relevant issues and ideas? What is it about the forum that makes you committed to it?" Responses to four questions unrelated to social structure have been excluded from this analysis (two questions asked participants about a specific taxonomy proposed by the researcher related to forum use, and two questions asked for participants' ideas about forum development). Questions were administered using dedicated text-based chat software with the data consisting of textual responses recorded on the research server. Responses were typically one to two sentences in length. Nearly half ($n = 18$) of the participants came from a single forum (an antisize discrimination movement), one forum supplied six participants (a group seeking education reform), two forums supplied two participants each ($n = 4$), and the remaining 12 forums each supplied a single participant.

Analysis

The data were collected during a mixed-methods study exploring the relationship between online communities and social action. The original study design was based on Creswell and Plano Clark's (2007) ideas about triangulation for research including both qualitative and quantitative data. Along those lines, the qualitative data were subjected to thematic analysis where an iterative process of review was used to identify similar patterns of content across individual responses. Participant responses were reviewed three times by the second author over a 10-day period (i.e., the same researcher recoded the data at different time intervals). At the first review, content reflecting key ideas was identified and extracted. Subsequent reviews were used to check extracted content for relevance, to produce a core set of categories common across many participants, and to test reliability of the categorization process. As this component of analysis formed part of a wider mixed-methods study, following principles of data triangulation (e.g., Creswell & Plano Clark, 2007) the validity of categorizations was determined through comparison with the broader set of results (for a further discussion of the broader study, see McGarty, Lala, & Douglas, 2011).

Two overarching and intersecting themes were apparent across responses, supporting the idea that participants were genuine and engaged activists. First, participants said they joined their forums because they recognized the importance of achieving positive change in relation to relevant issues and believed the aims of their forums were to accomplish that change. Second, participants generally perceived that discussion could be as effective as action in achieving change. The following section more fully illuminates how those themes intersected with participants' perceptions and presentations of social structure.

Results and Discussion

Participants' forum use fell into three distinct categories—"Information Exchange," "Action Planning," and "Unity and Support." Examples of category content are provided below (see supplementary materials for further excerpts).

Participants commonly mentioned the value of their forums for facilitating the exchange of information. Participant 1 (P1) suggested her forum achieved change "By sending out postings related to positive change – information about issues and causes that would effect change." Similarly, P3 identified the educative value of his forum, "it has contributed enormously towards letting the world and even the UN understand the demise of our masses under the Cameroun's dictatorships!" (P3). These and similar responses suggest that participants used the exchange of information and opinion as a way to influence public opinion about important issues. Moreover, participants explicitly identified consciousness raising as an important mechanism for achieving change. For example, P6 noted that his forum was "achieving its goals by raising consciousness worldwide on important issues" (P6), an idea also raised by P8, "it's just like sending a message that here in this part of the world, someone is taking action and it counts on that kind of light" (P8). Information exchange became a way to seed ideas about relevant sociopolitical relationships—participants were presenting their versions of social reality in the hope that others would believe and adopt (or at least, sympathize with) them.

In addition to championing consciousness raising through the distribution of ideas and opinion, participants also noted the importance of sharing information about actions and events. Along these lines P2 commented, "I wanted to be up to date on plans for protests . . . ," while P6 suggested they obtained "a great deal of useful information about not only local happenings but broader national & international political issues" (P6). Notably, we differentiate between sharing information about events and actually planning actions. In our analysis, information about events serves a similar purpose to sharing ideas and opinions. It builds a version of social reality and encourages and reinforces its robustness and legitimacy.

On the other hand, participants also used their forums for planning and decision-making; so participants explicitly referred to overt action planning. Here, participants noted the role their forums played in facilitating planning and decision-making, and even argued their forums were places where action could itself take place. For example, P1 said her forum was "more for organising and taking part than discussing and debating relevant issues and ideas" (P1), and P4 noted that people used his forum to organize "community services . . . like visits to disabled folks home, bringing orphans for outing, school visits, donation drives etc." (P4).

Even in action planning though there were nuances so that participants linked action to interaction by asserting that intraforum communication is noticed and has consequences outside the forum, including change through growing participation. For example, P14 suggested that their forum was worthwhile " . . . because we are actually being heard by the media and other organizations . . . " (P14). Similarly, P6's forum was encouraging widespread participation: "the most important achievement was that it has helped many Sri Lankan Buddhists scattered all over the globe to share information as well as build up friendships and also attract even non-Sri Lankan Buddhists/Hindus to contribute to the forum" (P6).

Along those lines, participants valued their forums not only as places for information exchange or action planning but also because forums provided a sense that activists and supporters were not alone in confronting issues: they affirmed there were others who shared the same problems and sought similar solutions. Thus, participants described their forums as accomplishing change by fostering unity and support by connecting similar people, increasing awareness of shared goals, and promoting similarity (c.f. ideas about belongingness; Simon & Klandermans, 2001).

P8 addressed this idea directly when he said "... in my mind, people should be brought to a certain level of unity or common desire before we can push for change" (P8). P40 mentioned the sense of "continuity, tolerance, and acceptance" (P40) that they experienced in their forum. Unity and support straddle both action and interaction in that perceptions were driven by interaction demonstrating that problems and concerns were shared by like others.

Related to the idea of fostering unity, a number of participants raised the role of networking. P2 offered a personal example, "I met a Chicano man who liked my anti-racist, feminist writings and asked if I would be on the Pacifica radio station" (P2), while P4 noted the role of his forum in arranging networking activities, "[our forum] has just taken the first few steps of that journey by having games, get-togethers, treasure hunt, charity programs, donation drives etc." (P4).

The potential to connect to others extended to nonparticipating observers (lurkers). For example, P3 suggested that "their perception improves over time and they become educationists on person to person contact, in as much as they also forward the message to show that what we are doing and say[ing] is the truth and important" (P3). P4 addressed the same themes, "they may not reply, but they may forward to others, or take action offline. Worst case, at least information is disseminated" (P4). Finally, P6 seemed more convinced about the power of debate to influence observers, "it influences people since the debates and discussion makes them think about the issues we are dealing with" (P6).

The view that interaction can lead to a realization of shared interest and fate taps into the idea that talk itself can lead to change, if strengthening awareness of a shared grievance is also seen as increasing the potential for others to accept a particular version of social reality, and identify with and join a social movement because of a sense of belongingness. Participants valued interaction as providing information, opinion, and support to existing and potential forum members. They either explicitly or implicitly acknowledged that interaction influenced those engaging in talk and had the potential to affect observers, be they forum lurkers, out-group members, or significant third parties (e.g., the media). Not only did forum members appreciate direct action-related forum interaction (e.g., talk about organizing and planning), they also acknowledged a wider role whereby talk could influence opinions and ideas, build capacity for a cause, and less directly lead to action. That acknowledgement suggests that activists understood the potential for their online interactions to influence others' perceptions of social reality and explicitly used their forums as mechanisms to present and shape social structure, even if they did not expressly define their experiences in those terms.

We suggest that our data provide useful insights into the form and role of online activist interaction; however, it is also important to clarify what we believe the nature of our data to be. We asked activists a series of open-ended questions about their online activities to which they were able to freely respond. We did not take further checks on the veracity of answers or motivations behind these. However, if these responses accurately represent participants' beliefs and perceptions about their online experiences, they allow us to draw conclusions about the wider motivations behind activists' online participation.

These responses do reveal a strategic dimension in activists' interactions. After all, we have framed our participants' online forum use as sites where they seek to influence others' perceptions of social structure. It is certainly likely then that their responses to our questions also had a strategic element. Put another way, we acknowledge that participants were likely to present their online forums in a particular, mainly positive, light. However, we also suggest that does not diminish our broader interpretations of the nature of activists' online forum use.

Those interpretations are supported by two factors. First, our participants were drawn from a wide, varied, and unconnected range of activist communities. The emergence of common themes across that variation suggests similarity on relevant dimensions and lends credence to the idea that participants' responses were genuine. Second, our findings about social structure were serendipitous. Study 2 was originally designed to investigate online social action; that our analysis revealed the role of social structure in activists' interactions was largely unforeseen. As with the emergence of common themes across variation, the unexpected revelation of social structure as a central thread through multiple interactions is suggestive of a legitimate characteristic.

Our analysis illuminates the relationship between social structure and online activism, however, it has some potential limitations. We address questions about the veracity of participants' responses above, as well as the consequences of the potentially tactical focus of activist communities. In addition to these points, the overall number of participants was relatively small. Although low response is not uncommon in online research (Tourangeau, 2004), greater number of participants would clearly increase validity. Similarly, while a range of different activist communities was canvassed, increasing the scope of sampled communities could strengthen the study.

General Discussion and Practical Implications

Our findings highlight the ways in which perceptions of social structure, conceptualized as perceptions of intra- and intergroup relations within the context of (broader) social/sociopolitical categories, impact activists' collective action processes in relation to predicting more traditional forms of offline collective action (Study 1) and for shaping perceptions of shared opinion, structure, and action in online activism (Study 2). In particular, our findings suggest that perceived consensus can capture some of the aspects of social structure in psychological terms and highlight the importance to activists of a consensualized position about social structure, and their efforts to reach that consensus (within their in-group and with third parties, for example). Although we cannot conclude that measures of perceptions of consensus in Study 1 capture "reality," they do suggest that activists face varying social realities and these social realities were associated with different relationships with collective action. An important practical implication is not only that calls for collective action should be framed in different ways to target various groups (a point made elsewhere by Hornsey et al., 2006), but they may need to be specifically crafted for different issues. Our results in Study 1 suggest that this is particularly important for issues that are deeply contested such as the NTER policy initiative.

In this regard, where the opinions of social movement members are not endorsed by their existing organization or the wider movement, or where there is a disconnection between the views of the members and the organization, it makes sense to form groups that are clearly ideological; that is, groups about which there can be little debate about consensual positions. Put another way, where social change campaigners wish to shape productive support for an issue that is highly contentious, calls to action may need to create groups based on shared opinion (opinion-based groups). In this sense, the use of opinion-based groups can deal with issues of subgrouping in a broader supporter population and can deal with the political cleavages at the incipient stages of action formation (Hartley, McGarty, & Donaghue, 2013; McGarty, Bliuc, Thomas, & Bongiorno, 2009). We are not advocating here that this is what social movements should do to become successful but rather, describing what groups that successfully mobilize actually do. While a social movement built around a shared course of action is mobilized to act to create consensus, a lack of consensus across constituent categories is an obstacle for collective action for a superordinate identity but it is a precondition for (consensus seeking) action for an opinion-based group.

Furthermore, this is not to argue that, for politically contentious issues, social identification with a minority opinion group or a counternormative social movement is not useful. In fact, often dissensus is what fuels the formation of such groups (e.g., the fat acceptance movement, lesbian and gay liberation). Rather, it is to suggest that channeling action around groups that have more specific identity content might help in the initial stages of action mobilization, particularly when action has been so clearly compromised at a political level. This is in line with arguments raised by Curtin, Kende, and Kende (2016) and Louis, Amiot, Thomas, and Blackwood (2016) about the challenges of engaging in activism that involves multiple and overlapping identities.

Our findings also yield important implications for models of collective action that emphasize three broad social psychological variables: social identity, the experience of group-based injustice, and group efficacy. In Study 1, we find that no single set of predictors satisfactorily predict collective action intentions for activists confronting different circumstances. We propose one explanation for why this might be the case, by focusing on social structure through perceptions of consensus from within political, public, and social movement spheres. Further research is needed to unpack the psychological mechanisms that help to explain the influence of social context.

We have suggested that the opinions of others are an important consideration when activists negotiate social reality. In Study 1, we showed how perceptions of intramovement social structure relate to support and engagement in collective action. While such perceptions play an important role in determining mobilization strategies, the perceptions of others (e.g., nonactivists, observers) also have consequences for recognition and support of movements (e.g., Simon & Klandermans, 2001). Study 2 further explored that idea and provided insights into how activists use interaction to understand and shape social structure, both for others as well as their in-group.

One key finding from Study 2 was that activists who participated did not appear to use their online forums to work toward consensus in any meaningful form. Instead, they already agreed about key issues and ideas and so used their forums to present a common, consistent face for their goals and ideals, and to define and capture the prevailing mood as they would ideally have it. The overt process of consensus formation was unimportant as these were groups based on an already shared opinion. Forums were used to promote a general movement zeitgeist to observers (e.g., lurkers, the general public) through the overall tone and nature of posts. Accordingly, online forums may be less about identity formation than identity presentation where interaction is used to sharpen and present views of the world, to present an idealized social structure.

The exchange of information through interaction was valued as an end in itself. Activists understood and appreciated their body of interaction as a resource for the provision of information about their movement—information about ideals and goals, support and membership, strategies and arguments, etc. Thus, we contend that online communities are ideology banks for social movements and their participants where individuals use interaction to deposit information that adds value to the bank's holdings. Those holdings remain open and accessible for others to view and absorb. Although anyone can add to the bank (e.g., current supporters, potential members, adversaries, the nonaligned), deposits from in-group members predominate by far in successful online communities and so those communities accurately present a movements' idealized zeitgeist or, in other words, reality, as the movement would have it.

One way to understand this is by reference to the idea of entrepreneurs of identity (e.g., Reicher, Haslam, & Hopkins, 2005). Reicher and colleagues argue that one method movement leaders can use to mobilize action is by shaping and defining the definition of categories around which social action occurs. Category definitions espoused by these entrepreneurs of identity have, in turn, the potential to influence social reality as experienced by movement participants. We contend that online activist communities are forums for participants to shape categories, and so their participants can act as entrepreneurs of identity. More than that, however, online interaction can arm people to be entrepreneurs of identity. In other words, forum interaction itself is not just an instantiation of entrepreneurship, but an ideology bank that participants can draw on to enable them to be entrepreneurs. Simply put, ideology banks are where entrepreneurs of identity raise their capital.

While our analysis supports our views about the way that social structure is perceived and deployed by activists in offline and online settings, we must also consider what effect the rapid spread and evolution of online communications technologies may have for the ways in which activists engage in the future. For example, Study 2 involved activists who took part in text-based interaction in online forums. Although traditional text-based interaction is still a significant component of online interaction, new forms of information exchange are now also pervasive (e.g., video sharing, micromessaging—Twitter, social networking—Facebook). An important avenue for future research is to explore the role that richer and more diverse forms of interaction might play in the formation and presentation of identity and identity-related processes (e.g., McGarty, Thomas, Lala, Smith, & Bliuc, 2014; Thomas et al., 2015) as well how such interaction links with collective action outcomes.

In summary, our article highlights the possibility that the degree of consensus within a given relevant social context (whether it be "real" or perceived) has implications for whether or not someone is likely to engage in group-based actions, both in traditional (face-to-face) and in online environments. Furthermore, our findings point to the importance for activists to have a consensualized position about social structure, and of their activists' efforts to reach that consensus in both online and offline contexts. Social structure is notoriously difficult to incorporate in psychological analyses and our research suggests that perceived consensus is one way to approach this.

Appendix: Study 2 – Category Examples

Information Exchange

"direct action without enough grassroots support might not have the necessary impact and would backfire, as well as fail to move the cause forward" (P3)
"it provides a place to share information and opinions" (P7)
"[the forum keeps me] . . . aware of the meetings and events" (P11)
"this group keeps me updated on issues" (P15)
"it gives me good info. and allow[s] me to express my opinions" (P20)
"we are trying to broaden the number of people who are informed" (P34)

Action Planning

"[the forum involves] … good people cooperating to achieve a better community and world" (P1)

"I am a single mother living very remotely. Not only have I been able to attend one demo in DC due to the monetary assistance I received from other members, but several people have sent me money for my art as well as helping me when my van broke down" (P2)

"[I expect my forum to] … focus and [increase] membership so as to create a following for our cause and eventually be able to cause pressure to bear on the Cameroon government and the international community"(P3)

"It [the forum] provides an important bulletin board regarding organising" (P26)

"It facilitates decision-making, information sharing, and task sharing quickly and efficiently across large distances" (P32)

"[the forum] … helps people in a particular geographical region organise and educate around a broad range of social justice issues, both local and global" (P35)

Unity and Support

"sometimes we had infiltrators who attempted detracting from the main idea and focus … " (P3)

"my groups have influenced me and opened me up to all the possibilities in the world" (P5)

"silence meant three things, they dint (sic) know and would want to learn more on issue given, they dint want to be know or identified with allies or supporters of corrupt and inept government officials and or they are learning from us who usually interact with other members" (P8)

"[my forum] … makes me feel good about myself, knowing that there are women going through the same things that I go through, the same situations and emotions" (P9)

"the web is fantastic at creating a web, connecting people who would not usually connect and I think that is what the discussion group is about" (P9)

"I started reading the boards and now I realize I'm not the only one in the world dealing with issues" (P18)

References

Amnesty International (2009). New poll delivers scathing verdict on Government's handling of Indigenous policy. Retrieved on October 24, 2013 from http://www.amnesty.org.au/news/comments/21626/.

Chandon, J. L., Chtourou, M. S., & Fortin, D. R. (2003). Effects of configuration and exposure levels on responses to web advertisements. *Journal of Advertising Research, 43*, 217–229.

Creswell, J. W., & Plano Clark, V. L. (2007). *Designing and conducting mixed methods research.* Thousand Oaks, CA: Sage.

Curtin, N., & McGarty, C. (2016). Expanding on psychological theories of engagement to understand activism in context(s). *Journal of Social Issues, 72*(2), 227–241.

Curtin, N., Kende, A., & Kende, J. (2016). Navigating multiple identities: The simultaneous influence of advantaged and disadvantaged identities on politicization and activism. *Journal of Social Issues, 72*(2), 264–285.

Giddens, A. (1984). *The constitution of society.* Cambridge, UK: Polity Press.

Hartley, L. K., McGarty, C., & Donaghue, N. (2013). Understanding disagreement within the majority about action to atone for past wrongs. *Journal of Applied Social Psychology, 43*, E246–E261. doi: 10.1111/jasp.12023.

Hayes, A. F., & Preacher, K. J. (2014). Statistical mediation analysis with a multicategorical independent variable, *British Journal of Mathematical and Statistical Psychology, 67*, 451–470. doi:10.1111/bmsp.12028 [online supplement].

Hornsey, M. J., Blackwood, L., Louis, W., Fielding, K., Mavor, K., Morton, T., O'Brien, A., Paasonen, K. E., Smith, J., & White, K. M. (2006). Why do people engage in collective action? Revisiting the role of perceived effectiveness. *Journal of Applied Social Psychology, 36*, 1701–1722. doi: 10.1111/j.0021-9029.2006.00077.x.

Iyer, A., Schmader, T., & Lickel, B. (2007). Why individuals protest the perceived transgressions of their country: The role of anger, shame, and guilt. *Personality and Social Psychology Bulletin, 33*, 587–596. doi: 10.1177/0146167206297402.

Jost, J. T., Pelham, B. W., Sheldon, O., & Sullivan, B. N. (2003). Social inequality and the reduction of ideological dissonance on behalf of the system: Evidence of enhanced system justification among the disadvantaged. *European Journal of Social Psychology, 33*, 13–36. doi: 10.1002/ejsp.127.

Klandermans, B. (1997). *The social psychology of protest.* Cambridge: Blackwell.

Klandermans, B. (1998). The formation and mobilization of consensus. *International Social Movement Research, 1*, 173–196.

Leach, C. W., Iyer, A., & Pedersen, A. (2006). Anger and guilt about in-group advantage explain the willingness for political action. *Personality and Social Psychology Bulletin, 32*, 1232–1245. doi: 10.1177/0146167206289729.

Leach, C. W., van Zomeren, M., Zebel, S., Vliek, M. L. W., Pennekamp, S. F., Doosje, B., Ouwerkerk J.W., & Spears, R. (2008). Group-level self-definition and self-investment: A hierarchical (multicomponent) model of in-group identification. *Journal of Personality & Social Psychology, 95*, 144–165. doi: 10.1037/0022-3514.95.1.144.

Livingstone, A. G. (2013). Why the psychology of collective action requires qualitative transformation as well as quantitative change. *Contemporary Social Science, 9*, 121–134. doi: 10.1080/21582041.2013.851404.

Louis, W. R. (2009). Collective action – and then what? *Journal of Social Issues, 65*, 727–748. doi:10.1111/j.1540-4560.2009.01623.x.

Louis, W. R., Amiot, C. E., Thomas, E. F., & Blackwood, L. (2016). The "Activist Identity" and activism across domains: A multiple identities analysis. *Journal of Social Issues, 72*(2), 242–263.

McGarty, C., Bliuc, A. -M., Thomas, E., & Bongiorno, R. (2009). Collective action as the material expression of opinion-based group membership. *Journal of Social Issues, 65*, 839–857. doi: 10.1111/j.1540-4560.2009.01627.x.

McGarty, C., Lala, G., & Douglas, K. M., (2011). Opinion-based groups: (Racist) talk and (collective) action on the Internet. In Z. Birchmeier, B. Dietz-Uhler, & G. Stasser (Eds.), *Strategic uses of social technology: An interactive perspective of social psychology* (pp. 145–171). Cambridge, UK: Cambridge University Press.

McGarty, C., Thomas, E. F., Lala, G., Smith, L., & Bliuc, A. -M., (2014). New technologies, new identities, and the growth of mass opposition in the 'Arab Spring'. *Political Psychology, 35*, 725–740. doi: 10.1111/pops.12060.

Moscovici, S. (1988). Notes towards a description of social representations. *European Journal of Social Psychology, 18*, 211–250. doi: 10.1002/ejsp.2420180303.

Newspoll and The Australian (2007). Thinking about Prime Minister John Howard's recent intervention in the indigenous communities of the Northern Territory, do communities?

Retrieved on June 15, 2013 from http://www.newspoll.com.au/image_uploads/0703%20NT%20intervention.pdf.

Reicher, S. D. (2004). The context of social identity: Domination, resistance and change. *Political Psychology, 25*, 921–945. doi: 10.1111/j.1467-9221.2004.00403.x.

Reicher, S. D., Haslam, S. A., & Hopkins, N. (2005). Social identity and the dynamics of leadership: Leaders and followers as collaborative agents in the transformation of social reality. *The Leadership Quarterly, 16*, 547–568. doi: 10.1016/j.leaqua.2005.06.007.

Sani, F., & Reicher, S. (1998). When consensus fails: An analysis of the schism within the Italian Communist Party. *European Journal of Social Psychology, 28*, 623–645. doi: 10.1002/(SICI)1099-0992(199807/08)28:4<623::AID-EJSP885>3.0.CO;2-G.

Simon, B., & Klandermans, B. (2001). Politicized collective identity: A social psychological analysis. *American Psychologist, 56*, 319–331. doi: 10.1037/0003-066X.56.4.319.

Stürmer, S., & Simon, B. (2004). The role of collective identification in social movement participation: A panel study in the context of the German gay movement. *Personality and Social Psychological Bulletin, 30*, 263–277. doi: 10.1177/0146167203256690.

Stürmer, S., & Simon, B. (2009). Pathways to collective protest: Calculation, identification, or emotion? A critical analysis of the role of group-based anger in social movement participation. *Journal of Social Issues, 65*, 681–705. doi: 10.1111/j.1540-4560.2009.01620.x.

Stürmer, S., Simon, B., Loewy, M., & Jörger, H. (2003). The dual-pathway model of social movement participation: The case of the fat acceptance movement. *Social Psychology Quarterly, 66*, 71–82. doi: 10.2307/3090142

Tajfel, H. (1982). *Social identity and intergroup relations.* Cambridge, UK: Cambridge University Press.

Tajfel, H., & Turner, J. (1979). An integrative theory of intergroup conflict. In W. Austin & S. Worchel (Eds.), *Psychology of intergroup relations* (pp. 33–48). Monterey, CA: Brooks/Cole.

Thomas, E., McGarty, C., & Mavor, K. (2009). Aligning identities, emotions, and beliefs to create commitment to sustainable social and political action. *Personality and Social Psychology Review, 13*, 194–218. doi: 10.1177/1088868309341563.

Thomas, E., Mavor, K., & McGarty, C., (2012). Social identities facilitate and encapsulate action-relevant constructs: A test of the social identity model of collective action, *Group Processes & Intergroup Relations, 15*, 75–88. doi: 10.1177/1368430211413619.

Thomas, E. F., McGarty, C., Lala, G., Stuart, A., Hall, L. J., & Goddard, A. (2015). Whatever happened to Kony2012? Understanding a global Internet phenomenon as an emergent social identity. *European Journal of Social Psychology, 45*, 356–367. doi: 10.1002/ejsp.2094.

Tourangeau, R. (2004). Survey research and societal change. *Annual Review of Psychology, 55*, 775–801. doi: 10.1146/annurev.psych.55.090902.142040.

Turner, J. C., Hogg, M. J., Oakes, P. J., Reicher, S. D., & Wetherell, M. S. (1987). *Rediscovering the social group: A self-categorization theory.* Oxford, UK: Basil Blackwell.

van Stekelenburg, J., Klandermans, B., & van Dijk, W. W. (2009). Context matters: Explaining how and why mobilizing context influences motivational dynamics. *Journal of Social Issues, 65*, 815–838. doi: 10.1111/j.1540-4560.2009.01626.x.

van Zomeren, M., Spears, R., Fischer, A., & Leach, C. W. (2004). Put your money where your mouth is! Explaining collective action tendencies through group-based anger and group efficacy. *Journal of Personality and Social Psychology, 87*, 649–664. doi: 10.1037/0022-3514.87.5.649.

van Zomeren, M., Postmes, T., & Spears, R. (2008). Toward an integrative social identity model of collective action: A quantitative research synthesis of three socio-psychological perspectives. *Psychological Bulletin, 134*, 504–535. doi: 10.1037/0033-2909.134.4.504.

van Zomeren, M., Spears, R., & Leach, C. W. (2008). Exploring psychological mechanisms of collective action: Does relevance of group identity influence how people cope with collective disadvantage? *British Journal of Social Psychology, 47*, 353–372. doi: 10.1348/014466607×231091.

Wilson, G. (1962). *A theory of public opinion.* Chicago, IL: Henry Regnery.

Wright, S. C. (2009). The next generation of collective action research. *Journal of Social Issues, 65*, 859–879. doi: 10.1111/j.1540-4560.2009.01628.x.

LISA K. HARTLEY is a Senior Lecturer at the Centre for Human Rights Education, Curtin University. Her research focuses on the rights of asylum seekers and refugees; prejudice toward marginalized social groups; and the factors that foster activism and advocacy about social justice issues.

GIRISH LALA is a Research Fellow in the Institute for Culture and Society at Western Sydney University. He was previously at Murdoch University working in the areas of social cohesion and social action. His research interests include online identity and interaction, technological mediation of social change, and facilitating innovative cross-disciplinary methodologies and interventions through new communications technologies.

NGAIRE DONAGHUE is an Associate Professor in the Social and Political Research Unit at Murdoch University. Her work centres around questions concerning the relationships between social ideologies and embodied identities, with a particular focus on how neoliberal discourses of individualism and self-responsibility are manifest in the subjective experiences of citizens in contemporary neoliberal democracies.

CRAIG MCGARTY is Professor of Psychology at Western Sydney University. He was previously the Director of the Centre for Social and Community Research and Director of the Social Research Institute at Murdoch University and the Head of the School of Psychology at The Australian National University. He is an author of *Categorization in Social Psychology and Research Methods and Statistics in Psychology* and an editor of *The Message of Social Psychology and Stereotypes as Explanations*.

Journal of Social Issues, Vol. 72, No. 2, 2016, pp. 399–412
doi: 10.1111/josi.12172

Separating Social Science Research on Activism from Social Science as Activism

Anna Kende[*]
Eötvös Loránd University

This special issue illustrates that for a better understanding of activism, we need to look at activities that differ from one another in their means and goals. As the topic is inherently politically contentious, reflection on what, why, and how we study activism becomes especially important. Drawing on the findings of the studies in this special issue, this concluding article outlines five propositions for areas of self-reflection from scientific and policy perspectives. The propositions touch on (a) broadening the scope of activism research to include movements with politically antagonistic goals, (b) the importance of examining activities that contest the social structure as well as those that work within the system by providing support and services, (c) the necessity of testing traditional theories of activism in a technologically changing context, (d) endorsing methodological plurality in activism research, and finally (e) researchers' responsibilities for the practical implications of their findings.

What is activism? How is it different from collective action? Is understanding activism the same as knowing what sort of people become activists? How does activism contribute to social change? What do activists think they are doing and why do they do it? These are some of the questions that the contributors to this issue have grappled with.

The common grounding for the papers is Curtin and McGarty's (2016) definition of activists "as people who actively work for social or political causes and especially those who work to encourage other people to support those causes" (p. 3), in contrast to van Zomeren's (2015) perfectly serviceable but operationally narrower definition as "members of social movements or action groups" (p. 3).

---

[*]Correspondence concerning this article should be addressed to Anna Kende, Department of Social Psychology, Eötvös Loránd University, Izabella utca 46, 1064 Budapest, Hungary. Tel: +36 1 4614500 [e-mail: kende.anna@ppk.elte.hu].

The author would like to thank the coeditors of this special issue, Craig McGarty and Nicola Curtin for their invaluable feedback on earlier versions of this article.

The wider definition allows us to incorporate a wide range of actions and issues in which activists engage. This richness, however, creates some challenges that social scientists need to address to establish scientific explanations for when and why people engage in activism. In the current article I will present some propositions that emerge from the process of dealing with these challenges.

The thematic focus of research presented in this special issue reflects current trends in collective action and related research, such as the positive and negative consequences of the role of ideology and identity—marginalized, advantaged, multiple, shared or superordinate—in building social movements and achieving social change (Cakal, Eller, Sirlopú, & Pérez, 2016; Curtin, Kende, & Kende, 2016; Hartley, Lala, McGarty, & Donaghue, 2016; Louis, Amiot, Thomas, & Blackwood, 2016); these contributions build on previous research on politicized collective identity (Simon & Klandermans, 2001), the role of privileged identities in social change (Case, 2012; Montgomery & Stewart, 2012), and multiple identities (Phalet, Baysu, & Verkuyten, 2010). The papers also extensively deal with the psychological and societal benefits and pitfalls of engaging in ally activism (Curtin et al., 2016; Droogendyk, Wright, Lubensky, & Louis, 2016; Russell & Bohan, 2016; Wright & Lubensky, 2009), and offer a critical look at intergroup contact and collective action engagement (Cakal et al., 2016), and especially at seeking intergroup harmony for promoting social change for its sedative/demobilizing effect (Droogendyk et al., 2016), recently also discussed in connection with confronting sexism (Becker, Zawadzki, & Shields, 2014) and racism in various societal and cultural contexts (Durrheim, Jacobs, & Dixon, 2014; Saguy, Tausch, Dovidio, & Pratto, 2009).

The papers address the psychological side of broad macro-social concerns such as the relevance of cultural contexts (Cakal et al., 2016), social structure (Hartley et al., 2016), institutional agents or organizations (van Stekelenburg, Klandermans, & Akkerman, 2016; Russell & Bohan, 2016, for similar issues discussed in connection with sexism see Buchanan, Settles, Hall, & O'Connor, 2014), and the microlevel processes of activism as they relate to social relations between individuals, for example, in the studies about ally action and the role of multiple identities (Curtin et al., 2016; Louis et al., 2016; Russell & Bohan, 2016).

Five Propositions

Thematic special issues offer a unique opportunity to reflect on the scientific assumptions of a field. This is important to do when the topic of study is ubiquitously present in the world around us but research on that topic is rarely, if ever, integrated in one place. Moreover, such a reflection is especially relevant as the topic of study is inherently politically contentious. Activism is all about changing or preserving the social order and the work of activists will almost inevitably be contrary to the (perceived) political or economic interests of powerful elements of the society they operate in. Here, I make an attempt to offer a critical reflection on what, why, and how we investigate in connection with activism as psychologists (but clearly working at the boundaries with political science and sociology) when we look at the demand for activism created by the societal context, at the unjust and hierarchical intergroup relations that activists seek to change, at intragroup processes that facilitate group based actions, and at consensus-building. Specifically, I will draw conclusions about the focus on social change (what), the often unacknowledged motivations of social scientists (why), and some of the methodological concerns in the field (how). Based on this overview, I will make five propositions about the implications of activism research for science and society.

Proposition 1. *To adequately reflect on prevalent forms of activism, research should broaden its scope to include movements with politically antagonistic goals.*

Research on activism is especially sensitive to actual societal processes and problems because people engage in activism on real political and societal issues. The focus on real-life movements, as reflected in the current issue, entails that research is less bound to laboratories and student samples, and can therefore claim greater ecological validity. But more importantly the focus on movements with different goals, and different means to achieve these goals, can guarantee that activism research accurately represents the most prevalent and influential forms of activism.

Hartley et al. (2016) for example look at two movements concerning Indigenous and non-Indigenous Australians that chose different courses of action: the first promoting reconciliation between the groups by means of offering economic development for improving the health status of Indigenous Australians and thereby working toward equality between them, and the second one seeking the protection of Indigenous children through more coercive interventions. Louis et al. (2016) examine the concept of activist identity as a generic one, and search for the conditions of cross-domain activism. Finally, the plurality of activist goals appears in the interviews of Curtin et al. (2016), including the narratives of activists across the political spectrum. Their analysis concludes that similar identity processes facilitate activism across domains.

Social psychological analysis should be able to deal with all forms of activism, especially as some of the most understudied issues actually constitute larger and (for the time being) more successful social movements than many of those studied by social psychologists. For example, extreme right wing mobilization may be among the most successful and substantial forms of activism currently in Europe (Klandermans & Mayer, 2005), but appears less frequently in research, as social psychologists still mostly focus on movements promoting egalitarianism and democracy within a social justice framework (for a review see Wright & Lubensky, 2009). We also see a rise in reactionary activism, especially but not exclusively in the United States, that intends to conserve traditional values, opposing multiculturalism and immigration. Reactionary activism falls outside the focus of most social psychologists, with some notable exceptions such as research on transforming intergroup relations between climate change "believers" and "skeptics" (Bliuc et al., 2015). The papers of this special issue point out that we need to broaden the scope of activism research for a better understanding of issues that more accurately reflect prevalent forms of activism. Future research need to systematically test the applicability of theories to politically different issues to fully grasp the social implications of these findings.

Proposition 2. *To adequately reflect on the different actions in which activists engage, research on activism should broaden its scope to include both protest and service-type of actions.*

The papers of this special issue highlight many different aspects of social change activism, and point out the importance of testing our theories in different cultural contexts (Cakal et al., 2016) and across domains (Louis et al., 2016). However, it is clear that most papers are more concerned with social change activism than with activism toward social cohesion. In other words, the papers regard intergroup conflict as the essential basis of reaching social change through collective action as opposed to interventions and services with the aim of working toward the well-being of all members of society by fighting social exclusion and building trust (Wright & Lubensky, 2009). This latter approach fits more closely with the concept of volunteerism (Snyder & Omoto, 2008). However, volunteerism and activism are not always so clearly separable, and volunteerism actually constitutes a substantial part of the activities activists engage in, and fits into the broader category of engaging in social action, that is to "take action for the benefit of other people, their communities, and society at large" (Snyder, 2009, p. 227). Yet, we know very little about the psychological processes distinguishing between political activism and volunteerism; or to put it differently, between engagement in forms of activism that contest the social structure and those that work within the system by providing support and services. This absence is all the more problematic as volunteerism and providing support can fulfill goals similar to those reached by means of protest. For example, a person volunteering to distribute food and arrange shelter for refugees actually takes over state responsibilities by offering these services, and by taking over these tasks, the volunteer may also express political dissent. However, only by addressing the structural causes of inequalities can charity organizations and volunteers offer services that—beyond improving the situation of the individual—can also lead to social change (Penner, 2004).

As all helping relations necessarily entail a power hierarchy between helper and help recipient, engaging in volunteerism can actually maintain rather than challenge existing intergroup hierarchies. Furthermore, people can engage in volunteerism for other, more individualistic reasons than achieving social change, such as personal relationships (Russell, 2011), or the quest for personal growth (Omoto & Snyder, 1990). The theory of intergroup helping as a power relation, and specifically the concept of dependency-oriented helping (Nadler, 2002), as well as the theory of strategic intergroup helping (van Leeuwen & Täuber, 2010) explain that people actually engage in helping relations *in order to* reinforce in-group superiority and maintain intergroup distance.

Therefore, the proposition to extend research on activism to include both protest and service type actions needs to also reflect on the role of these different types of activities in bringing about social change. The understanding that different forms of actions can offer alternative paths to achieving social change is a valuable insight for both organizations mobilizing their supporters for direct political action, and for volunteerism. People may be motivated to engage in social change activism without the willingness to become political activists. Recognizing that service type of actions can also serve this purpose if they take place with hierarchy challenging rather than hierarchy maintaining goals, means that those motivated to help and to change the social structure can be mobilized through volunteerism.

Proposition 3. *Research on activism should empirically test whether current understanding of the psychological mechanisms can adequately grasp activism in a technologically changing online context.*

Related to the previous proposition about the inclusion of volunteerism in activism research, we recognize that in the context of social media, the boundary between offering services and causing disruption is even more blurred. For example, alternative business models, crowdsourcing, sharing of copyrighted materials, and leaking various types of sensitive political or business information can be interpreted both as services and as disruptive processes, that is, as forms of volunteerism and of protest. Therefore, in the study of activism, we need to understand the qualitative change that social media use entails for activism and test whether traditional theories of activism apply to the online context.

There is clearly a growing interest in online activism and online mobilization in recent years. In the current issue, Hartley et al. (2016) elaborate on the influence of developing an opinion based identity through participation in online debates on activist engagement, and demonstrate that apart from the instrumentality of the internet and the use of people's existing social networks for mobilization (Bennett & Segerberg, 2012), identity formation may be particularly important in the context of new technologies and new forms of online and offline behavior.

Social media facilitates the strategic management of identities according to studies conducted in the SIDE model tradition (Social Identity model of Deindividuation Effects; Reicher, Postmes, & Spears, 1995), as participation in online communities leads to higher adherence to group norms and engaging in normative group based behaviors such as collective action (see Douglas & McGarty,

2002; Reicher, Levine, & Gordijn, 1998; Spears, Lea, Postmes, & Wolbert, 2011). Therefore, participating in a protest *only* to post a "protest selfie" online can be understood as a form of political participation that fits with the strategic side of the SIDE model. Although only one article deals explicitly with online activism, some of the studies in this special issue also point to topics that are relevant for keeping up with the changing context of activism. For example, Louis et al. (2016) demonstrate the influence of the size and type of existing social networks for mobilization, a particularly important aspect of activism if we take into account that using social media can affect people's social ties and the size of their social network (Donath & Boyd, 2004). Van Stekelenburg et al. (2016) distinguish between the influence of different types of organizations which has changed rapidly as a consequence of people relying on their existing online social networks for mobilization rather than traditional organizations, such as trade unions (Bennett & Segerberg, 2012).

These studies illustrate that moving away from the comparison of efficacy of online and offline mobilization or the substitution/slacktivism hypothesis (Christensen, 2011; Schumann & Klein, 2015, also discussed by Curtin & McGarty, 2016), social scientists should debate the qualitative change that online activism may entail (McGarty, Thomas, Lala, Smith, & Bliuc, 2014), and test the validity of previous theories for current actions. It is no longer a question whether social scientists should pay attention to online activism, as activism is happening—though not exclusively—online. Even if an action includes offline behavior, such as mass protests, people are simultaneously present in their online and offline social networks; furthermore, organization, recruitment, debates, and broadcasting would certainly take place online. The consequences of the rapidly changing technology influencing people's online and offline behavior is still not well understood, but it becomes increasingly clear that the online–offline distinction, also in the context of activism, is futile (Kende, Ujhelyi, Joinson, & Greitemeyer, 2015; Thomas et al., 2015).

The current issue cannot fill the gap that exists in social psychological theory of online activism, and further research is therefore needed to empirically test the applicability of existing theories to the changing technological context and behavioral forms of activism.

Proposition 4. *Researchers should embrace diverse methods to grasp the various levels of influence and understand both the universal human and contextual aspects of activism.*

Questions of methodology are just as political as research aims are, as choice of method, sample selection, sample size, and statistical analysis all influence the findings and their interpretation, and consequently their practical applications and impact (Massey & Barreras, 2013). Social psychology has faced several waves of criticism for its narrow choice of in-lab studies using student samples (see Henry, 2008; McGuire, 1967). Most research on collective action aims to understand the motivations of nonactivists to engage in collective action (van Zomeren, Postmes, & Spears, 2008), for which the use of nonactivist student sample may be an appropriate choice. If we seek to focus on activists, then as Curtin and McGarty (2016) point out, several ethical and practical constraints guide the methodological decisions, while the choice of method is also influenced by the specific population at hand. However, these constrictions can potentially enrich rather than impair activism research, as is demonstrated in this special issue. Authors used a wide range of quantitative and qualitative, experimental and nonexperimental methods to explore activism.

The diverse methods used in these studies allow us to understand how the interplay between processes at the individual, societal, and cultural level actually operates in and outside organizations, in protest movements, in institutional settings, in volunteer work, and in online social networks. The relevance of social identity theory is reaffirmed by the articles, but its role is refined by the methodological plurality of the studies. People hold multiple social identities, some of which are based on privileged, while others on disadvantaged group membership (Case, 2012; Curtin et al., 2016). Identities develop on the basis of salient opinions (Hartley et al., 2016; McGarty, Bliuc, Thomas, & Bongiorno, 2009) that either reinforce or restrict activist identities and therefore activisms across domains (Louis et al., 2016), and through membership in particular social movements (van Stekelenburg et al., 2016; Stürmer & Simon, 2004). Communities and social networks are more often formulated online than offline as movements begin to show a connective rather than collective character (Bennett & Segerberg, 2012; Hartley et al., 2016). The studies of this special issue pointed out that for (sustained) engagement in activism, social identity should be understood as a process that is as much the source of activism as the result of it (see Curtin et al., 2016; Russell & Bohan, 2016; van Stekelenburg et al., 2016).

The articles highlight practical strategies for mobilization and sustaining activist engagement. However, more importantly, the diversity of the questions and the plurality of the methods suggest that by understanding activism in different political and cultural contexts, on different social issues, we can get a more comprehensive picture of activism, and an overview of the general psychological processes that are potentially applicable across contexts. Methodological plurality is therefore the only guarantee that the challenging political issues can be adequately dealt with, because it serves the analysis of highly different types of actions, and because it offers a chance for self-reflection to the researcher in justifying the selection of the research tools. Methodological plurality also guarantees that the voices of activists in different domains are represented in scientific research and therefore both policy regarding global and local issues, and practice in general can directly benefit from these studies.

Proposition 5. *The direct practical implications and possible applications of research findings should be thoroughly and responsibly taken into account when designing and conducting research.*

Research on activism grew out of both a theoretical interest in tackling intergroup conflicts by means of collective action (Tajfel & Turner, 1979) and an interest in real life cases of activism and protests (e.g., Reicher, 1984). Consequently, the majority of research on activism, including most of the articles in this special issue, deals with movements that promote social change toward more egalitarian, democratic, and environmentally conscious societies. The direct implication of this focus is that research findings can inform organizations with corresponding goals on how to increase their mobilization potential, define the pool of possible recruits, and identify efficient strategies for sustaining action and reaching their goals. After all, the promotion of active citizenship and volunteerism are important pillars of democracy, and research can inform policy to reach these goals. Social scientists can therefore directly serve activists' goals.

The current studies do indeed outline practical implications. For in-group activism, Cakal et al. (2016) identify the positive role of common in-group identity for collective action among disadvantaged group members in the need for more inclusionary policies in both Mexico and Chile. Van Stekelenburg et al. (2016) specify which organizations do and which do not function as stepping stones for political action—the threshold lies between leisure organizations versus interest and activist organizations—and also pinpoint the limits of what civic organizations can offer as a supply for activism.

For ally activism Russell and Bohan (2016) show that for achieving second-order change (following Watzlawick, Weakland, & Fisch, 1974) the myth of the all-positive image of ally activism needs to be dismantled both on the individual and on the institutional level. Their study implies that not all forms of ally activism can achieve fundamental social change, and ally activists need to take into account both the structural aspects of inequalities and their individual responsibilities in it. Droogendyk et al. (2016) outline the pitfalls and dilemmas connected to ally activism, and in line with Russell and Bohan (2016) and others (Case, Hensley, & Anderson, 2014), advise advantaged group allies to reflect on their privileges and support social change by offering autonomy oriented help, and condemning inequality in cross-group contact.

Building on the assumptions of Case (2012) about the role of intersectionality, Curtin et al. (2016) point out that understanding the role of multiple – advantaged and disadvantaged—identities can help movement building among in-group members and allies in much the same way, specifically by strengthening intersectional rather than singular identities. Louis et al. (2016) explain that activism in one domain can be positively correlated with activism in a different domain along opinion based identities, and outline its implications for ally action and forming strategic alliances. However, they also touch upon the problem of normative fit (or ideological alliance) and its constraints on cross-domain activism, and thereby offer a critical reflection on the applicability of findings across ideological boundaries. Hartley et al. (2016) show that mobilization for various causes may actually depend on antagonistic strategies, as successful movements for reconciliation (and achieving a superordinate identity) require a preexisting consensus, while movements that attempt to build a new consensus (i.e., a new opinion-based group) stem from dissent.

A closer look at these studies allows us to conclude that the findings may be applicable to settings other than social change movements, and also have implications for some of the more understudied areas of activism. In other words, some of the findings may be applicable to both social change movements and reactionary ones, to politically left and right wing movements, and to moderate and radical forms of actions.

This brings us to the more general question about the ethos of social science, namely whether it has a descriptive or a prescriptive/normative role, and the societal responsibilities that come with conducting research (see Merton, 1973) that social psychologists are reminded of in times of severe social tensions. Massey and Barreras (2013) introduced the term impact validity to grasp "the extent to which research has the *potential* to play an effective role in some form of social and political change, or is useful as a tool for advocacy and activism" (p. 616, original italics). Recent comments by the presidents of The Society for the Psychological Study of Social Issues (SPPSI) also highlighted the challenges of guiding policy in the context of highly politicized issues (Abrams, 2014; Eagly, 2014). The recent scandal of APA's apparent complicity in torture has forced psychologists to once again review the connection between science and practice, and as Yosef Brody (2015) bluntly raised the question in his APA address, "should psychology serve all human beings or should it serve nations, states, empires?" Avoiding this fundamental question of why we conduct research and specifically research on activism is a strategy that results in a gap in research topics—namely a lack of interest in extreme right wing, populist movements and reactionary activism—and leads to a limited understanding of the implications of research findings. After all, scientists should not just be activists, but people who can critically reflect on the limits of their objectivity, the objectivity that scientific analysis strives for.

Some of the most fruitful periods of social psychology were stimulated by severe societal crises that social psychologists sought to understand and work to solve. Nonetheless, these periods would not have been so fruitful if social psychologists had not reflected on their own political ambitions in tackling these problems. Therefore, we need to answer the question of why we study activism in general, and why we study particular social movements. It is crucial to clarify whether we study social change movements with the same scientific interest as reactionary ones, and whether the questions, methods, and implications of our findings are formulated differently depending on the goals and means of a particular movement. As long as the political outcome of research is not critically reflected upon, many important research implications will remain unacknowledged. For example, a study about the pro-choice movement may offer valuable information about mobilization, but this information could be equally applicable to the pro-life movement. Social psychologists can adequately inform governments, policy institutions and civil organizations about the challenges of the refugee crisis following the war in Syria and how to tackle them. However, this information is also available to those who perceive refugees as positing a physical and cultural threat and therefore seek to protect their country even by inducing conflict. Research may provide tools for better recruitment among groups that do not promote the kind of social changes that social psychologists seek, but rather fight against them, perhaps even by means of violence and terrorism. Finding a tight, but balanced connection between research and policy is an important and complex issue that needs to be repeatedly addressed under the changing social and political climate that social psychologists work in (see Glick, 2014; Riggs, 2013; Rivera, 2014). Activist goals cannot simply be categorized as fulfilling objectively positive or negative purposes, since a specific course of action may be normative to and thus positively evaluated by the in-group, and nonnormative or negative to the out-group (as suggested by the SIDE model, for a meta-analysis see Postmes & Spears, 1998). Therefore, we can raise the question of whether the evaluation of the goal of a protest should influence the research questions and design, and how the findings are interpreted. The answer may not be straightforward, but the question needs to be asked nevertheless, and the potential impact of our research needs to be thought through.

Conclusions

A critical look at what, why, and how we study when it comes to psychological questions of activism, based on both the articles of this special issue and other research, allowed me to make five propositions about broadening the scope of activism research, methodological concerns in research on activism, and questions of responsibility about the wider implications of research findings. These propositions outline future directions for research to fulfill the goals of ecological validity, more objective scientific outcomes, and adequate answers to current societal problems in the forms of policy recommendations or direct recommendations for practice. The articles in this special issue demonstrated that a theoretical interest in activism and the political aim of social change are reconcilable. Consequently, activism research could benefit from broadening its scope to include not only protest movements but also volunteerism, not only social change movements but also reactionary movements, not only supportive but also disruptive actions, and not only left wing movements, but movements across the political spectrum.

In reaching these goals, findings of other disciplinary fields could inform social psychologists in areas that are yet understudied, taking into account that political science and sociology are highly concerned with reactionary activism (e.g., Tope, Pickett, & Chiricos, 2015), communication studies with the role of social media (e.g., Rainie, Smith, Schlozman, Brady, & Verba, 2012), and social work theory looks at the political consequences of volunteerism and service types of actions (e.g., Fischer, 1995; Powell, 2001). Finally, the political self-reflection on social science as a form of activism as it actively work(s) for social or political causes would guarantee the scientific standards of the field.

References

Abrams, D. (2014). Reality check: Rigor, relevance, and the value of social psychological research, *Forward*, *251*, 1–6, Retrieved on August 31, 2015 from http://www.spssi.org/_data/n_0001/resources/live/SPSSI-Forward-Newsletter-Summer-2014-Iss251%20(1).pdf.

Becker, J. C., Zawadzki, M. J., & Shields, S. A. (2014). Confronting and reducing sexism: A call for research on intervention. *Journal of Social Issues*, *70*, 603–614. doi: 10.1111/josi.12085

Bennett, W. L., & Segerberg, A. (2012). The logic of connective action: Digital media and the personalization of contentious politics. *Information, Communication & Society*, *15*, 739–768. doi: 10.1080/1369118X.2012.670661

Bliuc, A.-M., McGarty, C., Thomas, E. F., Lala, G., Berndsen, M., & Misajon, R. (2015). Public division about climate change rooted in conflicting socio-political identities. *Nature Climate Change*, *5*, 226–229. doi: 10.1038/nclimate2507

Brody, Y. (2015). U.S. psychology after Torture: The APA torture scandal, science, ideology, and the future of psychology. *Psychology Today*. Retrieved on August 20, 2015 from https://www.psychologytoday.com/blog/future-directions/201508/us-psychology-after-torture.

Buchanan, N. T., Settles, I. H., Hall, A. T., & O'Connor, R. C. (2014). A review of organizational strategies for reducing sexual harassment: Insights from the US military. *Journal of Social Issues*, *70*, 687–702. doi: 10.1111/josi.12086

Çakal, H., Eller, A., Sirlopú, D., & Pérez, A. (2016). Intergroup relations in Latin America: Intergroup contact, common ingroup identity, and activism among indigenous groups in Mexico and Chile. *Journal of Social Issues*, *72*(2), 355–375.

Case, K. A. (2012). Discovering the privilege of whiteness: White women's reflections on anti-racist identity and ally behavior. *Journal of Social Issues*, *68*, 78–96. doi: 10.1111/j.1540-4560.2011.01737.x

Case, K. A., Hensley, R., & Anderson, A. (2014). Reflecting on heterosexual and male privilege: Interventions to raise awareness. *Journal of Social Issues*, *70*, 722–740. doi: 10.1111/josi.12088

Christensen, H. S. (2011). Political activities on the Internet: Slacktivism or political participation by other means? *First Monday*, *16* (2). Retrieved on August 20, 2015 from http://firstmonday.org/ojs/index.php/fm/article/view/3336/2767"%3B#%3B#p5 doi: http://dx.doi.org/10.5210%2Ffm.v16i2.3336

Curtin, N., Kende, A., & Kende, J. (2016). Navigating multiple identities: The simultaneous influence of advantaged and disadvantaged identities on politicization and activism. *Journal of Social Issues*, *72*(2), 264–285.

Curtin, N. & McGarty, C. (2016). Expanding on psychological theories of engagement to understanding activism in context(s). *Journal of Social Issues*, *72*(2), 227–241.

Donath, H. S., & Boyd, D. (2004). Public displays of connections. *BT Technology Journal*, *22*, 71–82.

Douglas, K. M., & McGarty, C. (2002). Internet identifiability and beyond: A model of the effects of identifiability on communicative behavior. *Group Dynamics: Theory, Research, and Practice*, *6*, 17–26.

Droogendyk, L., Wright, S. C., Lubensky, M. E., & Louis, W. R. (2016). Acting in solidarity: Cross-group contact between disadvantaged group members and advantaged group allies. *Journal of Social Issues, 72*(2), 315–334.

Durrheim, K., Jacobs, N., & Dixon, J. (2014). Explaining the paradoxical effects of intergroup contact: Paternalistic relations and system justification in domestic labour in South Africa. *International Journal of Intercultural Relations, 41*, 150–164. doi: 10.1016/j.ijintrel.2013.11.006

Eagly, A. (2014). Can SPSSI serve as honest broker in a politically polarized environment? *Forward, 252*, 1–4, Retrieved August 31, 2015 from http://www.spssi.org/_data/n_0001/resources/live/Forward-Newsletter-SPSSI-Fall-2014-Issue-252.141031.pdf.

Fisher, R. (1995). Political social work. *Journal of Social Work Education, 31*, 194–203.

Glick, P. (2014). Commentary: Encouraging confrontation. *Journal of Social Issues, 70*, 779–791. doi: 10.1111/josi.12091

Hartley, L. K., Lala, G., Donaghue, N., & McGarty, C. (2016). How activists respond to social structure in offline and online contexts. *Journal of Social Issues, 72*(2), 376–398.

Henry, P. J. (2008). College sophomores in the laboratory redux: Influences of a narrow data base on social psychology's view of the nature of prejudice. *Psychological Inquiry, 19*, 49–71.

Kende, A., Ujhelyi, A., Joinson, A., & Greitemeyer, T. (2015). Putting the social (psychology) into social media. *European Journal of Social Psychology, 45*, 277–278. doi: 10.1002/ejsp.2097

Klandermans, B., & Mayer, N. (2005). *Extreme right activists in Europe: Through the magnifying glass.* New York, NY: Routledge.

Louis, W. R., Amiot, C. E., Thomas, E. F., & Blackwood, L. (2016). The "Activist Identity" and activism across domains: A multiple identities analysis. *Journal of Social Issues, 72*(2), 242–263.

Massey, S. G., & Barreras, R. E. (2013). Introducing "impact validity." *Journal of Social Issues, 69*, 615–632. doi: 10.1111/josi.12032

McGarty, C., Bliuc, A. M., Thomas, E. F., & Bongiorno, R. (2009). Collective action as the material expression of opinion-based group membership. *Journal of Social Issues, 65*, 839–857. doi: 10.1111/j.1540-4560.2009.01627.x

McGarty, C., Thomas, E. F., Lala, G., Smith, L. G., & Bliuc, A. M. (2014). New technologies, new identities and the growth of mass opposition in the 'Arab Spring'. *Political Psychology, 35*, 725–740. doi: 10.1111/pops.12060

McGuire, W. J. (1967). Some impending reorinetations in social psychology. *Journal of Experimental Social Psychology, 3*, 124–139.

Merton, R. K. (1973). The normative structure of science. In N. W. Storer (Ed.), *The sociology of science: Theoretical and empirical investigations* (pp. 267–278). Chicago, IL: The University of Chicago Press.

Montgomery, S. A., & Stewart, A. J. (2012). Privileged allies in lesbian and gay rights activism: Gender, generation, and resistance to heteronormativity. *Journal of Social Issues, 68*, 162–177. doi: 10.1111/j.1540-4560.2012.01742.x

Nadler, A. (2002). Inter–group helping relations as power relations: Maintaining or challenging social dominance between groups through helping. *Journal of Social Issues, 58*, 487–502.

Omoto, A. M., & Snyder, M. (1990). Basic research in action volunteerism and society's response to AIDS. *Personality and Social Psychology Bulletin, 16*, 152–165.

Penner, L. A. (2004). Volunteerism and social problems: Making things better or worse? *Journal of Social Issues, 60*, 645–666.

Phalet, K., Baysu, G., & Verkuyten, M. (2010). Political mobilization of Dutch Muslims: Religious identity salience, goal framing, and normative constraints. *Journal of Social Issues, 66*, 759–779. doi: 10.1111/j.1540-4560.2010.01674.x

Postmes, T., & Spears, R. (1998). Deindividuation and antinormative behavior: A meta-analysis. *Psychological Bulletin, 123*, 238–259.

Powell, F. W. (2001). *The politics of social work.* London, UK: Sage.

Rainie, L., Smith, A., Schlozman, K. L., Brady, H., & Verba, S. (2012). Social media and political engagement. *Pew Research Center's Internet & American Life Project.* Retrieved on August 31, 2015 from http://www.pewinternet.org/files/old-media/Files/Reports/2012/PIP_SocialMediaAndPoliticalEngagement_PDF.pdf.

Reicher, S. D. (1984). The St. Pauls riot: An explanation of the limits of crowd action in terms of a social identity model. *European Journal of Social Psychology, 14*, 1–21.

Reicher, S. D., Spears, R., & Postmes, T. (1995). A social identity model of deindividuation phenomena. *European Review of Social Psychology, 6*, 161–198.

Reicher, S. D., Levine, M., & Gordijn, E. (1998). More on deindividuation, power relations between groups and the expression of social identity: Three studies on the effects of visibility to the in-group. *British Journal of Social Psychology, 37*, 15–40.

Riggs, D. W. (2013). Impact validity: A politics of possibilities. *Journal of Social Issues, 69*, 797–803. doi: 10.1111/josi.12042

Rivera, L. M. (2014). Ethnic-racial stigma and health disparities: From psychological theory and evidence to public policy solutions. *Journal of Social Issues, 70*, 198–205. doi: 10.1111/josi.12055

Russell, G. M. (2011). Motives of heterosexual allies in collective action for equality. *Journal of Social Issues, 67*, 358–375. doi: 10.1111/j.1540-4560.2011.01703.x

Russell, G. M., & Bohan, J. S. (2016). Institutional allyship for LGBT equality: Underlying processes and potentials for change. *Journal of Social Issues, 72*(2), 335–354.

Saguy, T., Tausch, N., Dovidio, J. F., & Pratto, F. (2009). The irony of harmony intergroup contact can produce false expectations for equality. *Psychological Science, 20*, 114–121.

Schumann, S., & Klein, O. (2015). Substitute or stepping stone? Assessing the impact of low-threshold online collective actions on offline participation. *European Journal of Social Psychology, 45*, 308–322. doi: 10.1002/ejsp.2084

Simon, B., & Klandermans, B. (2001). Politicized collective identity: A social psychological analysis. *American Psychologist, 56*, 319–331.

Snyder, M. (2009). In the footsteps of Kurt Lewin: Practical theorizing, action research, and the psychology of social action. *Journal of Social Issues, 65*, 225–245.

Snyder, M., & Omoto, A. M. (2008). Volunteerism: Social issues perspectives and social policy implications. *Social Issues and Policy Review, 2*, 1–36.

Spears, R., Lea, M., Postmes, T., & Wolbert, A. (2011). A SIDE look at computer-mediated interaction. In Z. Birchmeier, B. Dietz-Uhler, & G. Stass (Eds.), *Strategic uses of social technology: An interactive perspective of social psychology* (pp. 16–39). Cambridge: Cambridge University Press.

Stürmer, S., & Simon, B. (2004). The role of collective identification in social movement participation: A panel study in the context of the German gay movement. *Personality and Social Psychology Bulletin, 30*, 263–277.

Tajfel, H., & Turner, J.C. (1979). An integrative theory of inter-group conflict. In W.G. Austin & S. Worchel (Eds.), *The social psychology of inter-group relations* (pp. 33–47). Monterey, CA: Brooks/Cole.

Thomas, E. F., McGarty, C., Lala, G., Stuart, A., Hall, L. J., & Goddard, A. (2015). Whatever happened to Kony2012? Understanding a global Internet phenomenon as an emergent social identity. *European Journal of Social Psychology, 45*, 356–367. doi: 10.1002/ejsp.2094

Tope, D., Pickett, J. T., & Chiricos, T. (2015). Anti-minority attitudes and Tea Party Movement membership. *Social Science Research, 51*, 322–337. doi:10.1016/j.ssresearch.2014.09.006

van Leeuwen, E., & Täuber, S. (2010). The strategic side of out-group helping. In S. Stürmer & M. Snyder (Eds.), *The psychology of prosocial behavior: Group processes, intergroup relations, and helping* (pp. 81–99). London: Blackwell.

van Stekelenburg, J., Klandermans, B., & Akkerman, A. (2016). Does civic participation stimulate political activity? *Journal of Social Issues, 72*(2), 286–314.

van Zomeren, M. (2015). Collective action as relational interaction: A new relational hypothesis on how non-activists become activists. *New Ideas in Psychology, 39*, 1–11. doi:10.1016/j.newideapsych.2015.04.001

van Zomeren, M., Postmes, T., & Spears, R. (2008). Toward an integrative social identity model of collective action: A quantitative research synthesis of three socio-psychological perspectives. *Psychological Bulletin, 134*, 504–535. doi: 10.1037/0033-2909.134.4.504

Watzlawick, P., Weakland, J. H., & Fisch, R. (1974). *Change: Principles of problem formation and problem resolution.* Oxford, UK: W. W. Norton.

Wright, S.C., & Lubensky, M.E. (2009). The struggle for social equality: Collective action versus prejudice reduction. In S. Demoulin, J.P. Leyens, & J.F. Dovidio (Eds.), *Intergroup misunderstandings: Impact of divergent social realities* (pp. 291–310). New York: Psychology Press.

ANNA KENDE is an Associate Professor at Eötvös Loránd University, Budapest. Her research focuses on prejudice, intergroup relations, identity formation and political activism from a social psychological perspective. She has carried out several policy research projects about early selection in schools and worked as a policy advisor on educational integration of Roma people in Hungary.

Journal of Social Issues, Vol. 72, No. 2, 2016, p. 413
doi: 10.1111/josi.12173

Erratum to "When Passionate Advocates Meet Research on Diversity, Does the Honest Broker Stand a Chance?"

Alice H. Eagly
Northwestern University

The content of this article has been changed on 3 June 2016 after the first publication on 9 March 2016. Due to an error during the publication of this article, two reference citations were altered incorrectly.

On p. 212, the reference citation, 'Eagly van Engen & van Knippenberg, 2004' should be replaced with 'Eagly et al., 2004'.

On p. 213, the reference citation, 'Antonakis van Engen & van Knippenberg, 2010' should be replaced with 'Antonakis, Bendaham, Jacquart, & Lalive, 2010'.

The publisher apologizes for this error.

Discover Psychology with Wiley

For Psychology researchers, students, and faculty, Wiley's varied list of distinctive journals, books, and online resources provides the highest level of scholarship that spans the breadth of the discipline.

Applied Psychology

Clinical Psychology

Cognitive Psychology

Developmental Psychology

Educational & School Psychology

Family Therapy

Industrial & Organizational Psychology

Physiological Psychology

Psychotherapy & Counseling

Social Psychology

Discover all that Wiley has to offer in your field
wileyonlinelibrary.com/subject/psychology

2016 Vol. 72, No. 2

Understanding Activism

Issue Editors: Craig McGarty, Anna Kende, and Nicola Curtin